Notable British Trials S

TRIAL OF

FREDERICK BAKER

EDITED BY

David Green

MANGO BOOKS

Notable British Trials imprint ©William Hodge & Company (Holdings) Ltd
Used with kind permission.

General Editors:
David Green - M.W. Oldridge - Adam Wood

Published by Mango Books
www.mangobooks.co.uk
18 Soho Square
London W1D 3QL

Notable British Trials Series No. 91

TRIAL OF

FREDERICK BAKER

EDITED BY

David Green

Frederick Baker.

CONTENTS.

LIST OF ILLUSTRATIONS.

Cover: Frederick Baker. From *The Police News Edition of the Life and Examination of Frederick Baker* (1867) © British Library Board.

FREDERICK BAKER.

INTRODUCTION.

I.

Every year, in the last few days of August, the hop-pickers came to Alton. They arrived on foot, in horse-drawn carts and wagons, and increasingly by train – gypsies and Diddakoi gangs, itinerant workers from Portsmouth, entire families of poor and unemployed people from Birmingham and the East End of London. And for three or fours weeks the Hampshire town came alive with the sounds and smells of the annual harvest.

Hops had been grown in the area for well over 200 years. In the late 1860s nearly 3,000 acres of hops were cultivated in the fields around Alton. The Congregational minister and Plymouth Brethren preacher Samuel Chinn, writing in his memoir *Among the Hop-Pickers*, estimated that as many as ten thousand people annually made the trek to take part in the Hampshire harvest.[1] The hop gardens were laid out in 'hedges' forming alleys or tunnels stretching the entire length of fields. Throughout the early spring the hops with their light green flowers and golden fruit were encouraged to grow up nine or ten feet tall scaffold poles set on small mounds. At harvest time the hops were plucked off the bines into bushel wicker baskets, which were then emptied into huge sacks called pokes before being carted off to the kilns for drying. The bulk of the crop was used by local breweries for beer making, or samples were taken by wagon to Weyhill Fair near Andover to be traded with dealers or hop factors.[2]

From early morning until late afternoon, men, women and children grafted in the hop gardens. For many poor urban families, the hopping season was a welcome break from the depredations of city life. It provided an opportunity to get out into the open and savour the country air.

There was a tendency among some elements of middle-class Victorian society to take a rather romantic view of hop-picking, investing the great country event with an almost Arcadian charm and innocence. Visions of cream-boarded cottages and red brick oast houses merged with sentimental images of young children gambolling naked in the summer fields and Romany families in flamboyant costumes sitting around camp fires in the evening eating kippers and baked potatoes. In fact, hop-picking was arduous and poorly-paid labour, and working conditions were sordid. The migrant pickers were crammed together in

---

1   Samuel Chinn, *Among the Hop-Pickers* (London: Shaw, 1887).
2   'Hop-Picking – Its Impact on Alton and District', *Alton Papers*, Number 3, 1999.

ramshackle huts and sheds, which in winter were inhabited by pigs and cattle. It was not until the 1870s, and then only gradually, that bye-laws seeking to ensure sanitary and hygienic conditions came into force in hopper camps.

Hop-pickers were a motley crew. They brought with them the style and habits of the East End:

> The gardens are not safe patrolling at night, and scarcely safe by day. It is only a wonder we do not hear of murders in the districts... Certain it is that a more hideous conglomerate of scoundrelism could not be made up in the world than that which leaves London annually for the hop-gardens.[3]

Inevitably, there were tensions between the incomers and local farm workers. Violent drink-fuelled affrays may not have been exactly common, but they occurred frequently enough to warrant extra constables being drafted in during the hop-picking season to keep the peace.[4] Irish travellers were considered the worst troublemakers. Alton farmer William Terrell Gunner recorded one such incident in his diary:

> Last night there was a most awful row among our Irish party. They fell out among themselves and fought like bulldogs – men, women and children. They knocked each other down with hop poles and fought as if they would kill one another. The Police took charge and some and all who could left in the morning.[5]

By the late 1860s dark forces were already gathering in the hop gardens of Hampshire. The abolition in 1862 of the import duty on hops permitted competition from overseas, and in the following decade the first hop-picking machines were brought over from America into the Wealden districts of Kent and Sussex, thereby beginning the slow, gradual toll of seasonal hop-picking labour in England.

*

On Saturday, 24 August 1867, just a few days before the start of the picking season, the body of a young girl was discovered in the hop gardens next to Amery Farm in Alton. It had been dismembered and was grotesquely mutilated:

> A more horrible crime than that which has been committed at Alton has never

---

3   'The Custom of Hop-Picking', *Pall Mall Gazette*, 27 August 1869.
4   Ian A Watt, *A History of The Hampshire and Isle of Wight Constabulary 1839–1966* (Hampshire and Isle of Wight Constabulary, 1967), p. 53.
5   Diaries of William Terrell Gunner, 28 September 1850. HRO 284M87/2.

Introduction.

been recorded, and could scarcely be conceived... If a savage wild beast had appeared in the green Hants fields and ravaged the farmer's flocks, it would not be so strange as the sudden apparition of a ferocious human being who could take a girl-child from her companions at play, and, after unspeakably brutish treatment, chop her body into pieces, and scatter them about the soil like the leavings of a tiger in the jungle.[6]

II.

Just after one o'clock on Saturday, 24 August, eight-year-old Fanny Adams, her younger sister Lizzie and their friend Minnie Warner, aged seven, went out to play in the meadows near their home. It was a warm, sunny afternoon, continuing the spell of dry weather that had lasted for several weeks. In the fields, the wheat was already three-quarters under cover, and the hops were progressing satisfactorily – a brief but heavy thunderstorm a few days earlier had provided a welcome watering.

The three girls lived in Tanhouse Lane on the north side of town.[7] Fanny's father, George Adams, was a bricklayer employed by the well-known firm of local builders J.H. and E. Dyer.[8] That afternoon he had gone off to play for the church bell-ringers in the annual cricket match against the 'village band' at The Butts, an area of open land at the western end of Alton. By contrast, Fanny's mother, Harriet, was always busy in the home. She made ends meet by taking in her neighbours' washing. On that fateful day, harassed and preoccupied, she had probably shooed the children out of the house to play.

The girls strolled to the end of Tanhouse Lane where the Jefferis tanyard was situated. Fanny's grandfather, George Adams senior, had worked there for many years. Animals were brought to Alton market for butchering, and their hides ended up in the tannery, where they were dunked into drums of lime solution to loosen the rotting flesh and hair. It was a damp, odorous place, and after heavy rainfall the stench would have been particularly unpleasant. Fanny and her companions made their way through the gate into Flood Meadows, crossing the lower fields to reach the banks of the river Wey.

Flood Meadows lies on the western edge of town in the valley of the Northern River Wey. The river rises a few hundred yards further downstream on the other side of the old road to Odiham, and meanders east into Alton. In

---

6   *Daily Telegraph*, quoted in the *Surrey Advertiser*, 31 August 1867.
7   Fanny's grandparents, George and Ann Adams, lived next door; the Warner family lived next door-but-one. The property boundaries have been re-divided since Fanny's time making it difficult to ascertain the exact curtilage of the dwellings in the 1860s.
8   Dyers made the headstone for Fanny's grave in Alton Cemetery.

places the water is deep and slow enough to become ponded, forming pools (and later watercress beds) where local boys sometimes bathed in the summer. The Meadows has a gentle tilt, south to north, rising to Amery Farm and the hop gardens on the crest of the hill; to the north-west the ground rises more steeply. Today the site is maintained by the town council as an open green space, but in the 1860s the fields and pastures to the north of the Wey belonged to Amery Farm and were used mostly for rough grazing.

An ancient footpath crosses the Flood Meadows, following the course of the Wey until the river swoops south and the path turns north to join the old cartway leading over Southwood Hill towards Applesome Wood and the village of Shalden. Where the lane traverses Chauntry Piece field there was a gate and a stile; here a section of the old road had become sunken or hollow, shielded by thick hedges on both sides. In the autumn and winter, after heavy rain, the Hollow became a thick dark mire. Near the end of the ascent there was another gate and stile leading eastwards to the fifteen-acre hop gardens of Henry and John Chalcraft of Amery Farm.

Just after half-past one, the girls were picking flowers beside the river. There may have been a sense of excitement in the air because the previous week Minnie Warner had made a new friend. A man friend. He had approached Minnie and her playmates Ellen White and Annie Kemp while they frolicked in Flood Meadows, and he had taken them into the Hollow. Although he was a grown-up he seemed to enjoy the company of small girls, and he knew lots of exciting games and magic tricks. Cigarette smoking was becoming popular in the 1860s: the man could hold a lighted cigarette in his closed fist so that smoke leaked out between his fingers – and then he'd open his hand and the cigarette was gone! And right on cue, here he was once more, coming down the hill to meet them.

'Hello my little tulips, here you are again' was his jovial greeting to the girls in the wildflower-strewn meadow. He was dressed like a gentleman in a light waistcoat and trousers, a black frockcoat, and a tall dark hat. His complexion was unnaturally pale, like the macerated skin under a soiled bandage: it was as if he shunned daylight or worked long hours in an office. The man quickly put the girls at ease, feigning interest in their tattle and their collection of flowers. After a short while he suggested a racing game – could Minnie beat Fanny in a sprint up to the Hollow? Off dashed the two older girls, leaving little Lizzie trailing behind. The pallid stranger followed them up the hill at a more leisurely pace, puffing on a cigar. He gave the children some halfpennies for their exertions. Then it was into the Hollow to gather the small red fruit that grew in the hedges there; the children called them 'hedge haws' – they were hawthorn berries, soft

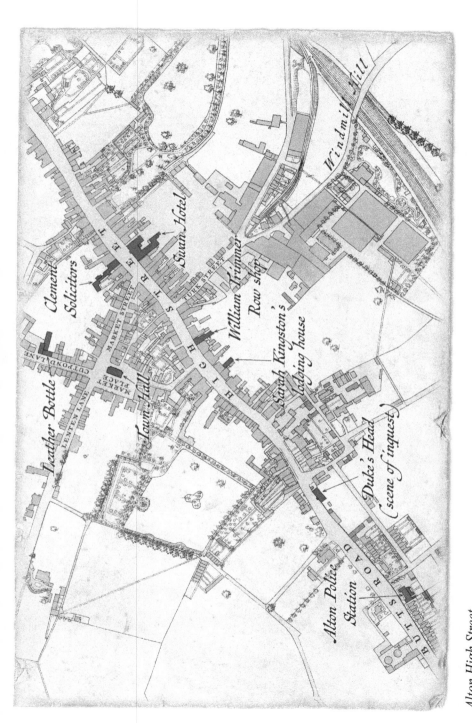

Alton High Street.

Courtesy Bill Citrine.

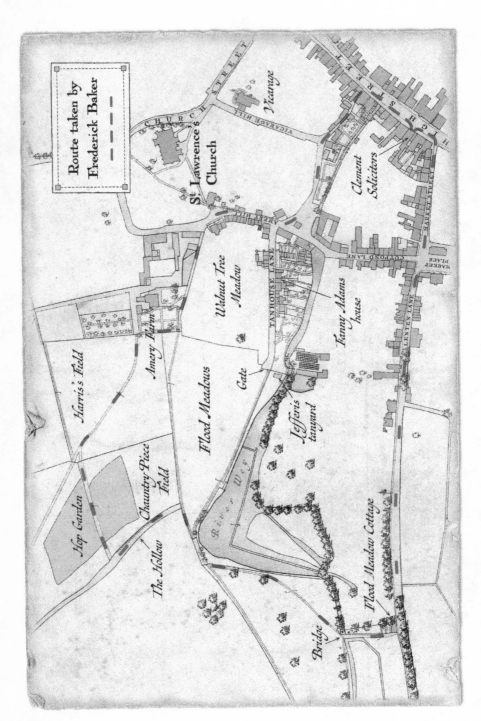

Frederick Baker's route.

Courtesy Bill Citrine.

Introduction.

in the mouth, with little stones in the middle, and they left crimson stains on the tongue and lips, like beads of blood.

All around there was activity in the fields. Hay-making was in progress, peas were being harvested, makeshift shelters were going up at Amery Farm in readiness for the influx of hop-pickers. Solitary farm labourers ambled across the landscape with their scythes and short-handed sickles. For anyone watching, it must have seemed an idyllic rural scene – children at play in the meadow, the white clouds reflected in the river, the chimes of St Lawrence sounding over the summer fields. The *Illustrated Police News* depicted the scene like this:

> Three happy English girls at their small sports among the ripening blackberries and hop-gardens of Alton, their mothers' cottages within hail, the public footpath close by! What harm, in pity's name, could happen to such an innocent triplet – everybody's friends – except perhaps if a bumble bee should sting them, or a great frog frighten them on the way to the water.[9]

The pale stranger had, in fact, already been noticed several times that day.

William James Walker, a whitesmith and bellhanger, saw the man striding across the top of Walnut Tree Meadow, which adjoins Flood Meadows. He guessed it was just after one thirty, although more likely it was a little earlier than that, possibly twenty or twenty-five past one. The two men grunted as they passed within a couple of yards of each other. Walker was struck by how vacant and glazed the other man looked, as if he was 'partly intoxicated'. And he was right – the man had been drinking gin and beer on and off all morning since before ten o'clock.[10]

William Allwork, a cricket bat maker, was also out and about at this time. He was crossing Flood Meadows, heading back into town after visiting Lasham to deliver a telegram. It was a quarter to two, or thereabouts. He saw a man, almost twenty yards away, leaning against the gate leading into Chauntry Piece; he didn't know the man's name but he'd seen him around town several times. Their eyes briefly met. Further down the hill, he could see a group of children at play; their voices carried in the still summer air, and he heard one of them shout out, 'I'll tell your mother, Minnie.'

Shortly afterwards, Eliza White and three other women were returning home after a morning spent cutting wheat at the bottom of White Hill. It was a few minutes before two o'clock. As she was walking along the footpath that

---

9   *Police News Edition of the Life and Examination of Frederick Baker* (1867), p. 15.

10 Walker's testimony comes from the committal hearing on 31 August 1867. He gave evidence at the trial but only in relation to the alleged murder weapon his son found in the hop garden and brought home as a souvenir.

crossed Harris's field, she looked down and noticed the man and the children near the Hollow. She recognized the children perfectly well because they were playmates of her own daughter Ellen – they were Minnie Warner and two of the Adams girls. The man she hadn't seen before. There was nothing alarming about the scene, nothing she could put her finger on particularly, but she was curious enough to study the group intently for perhaps ten or fifteen minutes until they disappeared from view into the Hollow.

William Allwork's testimony is significant because it reveals that the children were squabbling. Minnie and Fanny had had a falling out. Perhaps Minnie was miffed because her man friend seemed to be paying more attention to Fanny than to her. Or perhaps there was a dispute over who should carry the halfpennies. We aren't sure exactly what happened next, but it seems the man and Fanny went together up the Hollow, leaving the other children to return home and spend their windfall at the sweet shop. According to Minnie's evidence at the trial:

> He told Fanny to come along with him and he would give her two pence more. I saw him open the gate. He lifted Fanny up in his arms and carried her away, up the Hollow and into the hop ground. Fanny cried out, saying her mother would be calling her and she wanted to go home. I and Lizzie went straight home and spoke to my mother.

Yet there is good reason to doubt this version of events, or at least part of it. We know that Minnie and Lizzie returned home briefly around two thirty, but they showed no signs of distress and they failed to raise the alarm: instead, they loitered around town for two or three hours seemingly more concerned with buying 'mixed sweets' at Knight's corner shop than they did about the welfare of Fanny. In all likelihood the children hadn't apprehended that Fanny was in any danger from the man in the high hat. Minnie admitted that she was not at all frightened that afternoon. It is true that Lizzie started crying shortly after Fanny went off with the man, but this was because she had something in her eyes. The evidence suggests that Fanny wasn't physically abducted at this point; more likely she was *lured* or decoyed deeper into the hop garden with the promise of an extra tuppence, while her companions were happy to run off into town without a backward glance.

After watching the girls, Mrs White crossed over the stile into Flood Meadows and was making her way down the hill when she heard a child cry out from across the hop garden on the farthest side. 'It did not seem to be a cry of pain,' she recalled, 'but such as children would raise when caught hold of in play.' She thought nothing more of it and went home.

Introduction.

The next sighting of the man in the high hat was at ten or fifteen minutes to three. He was coming out of the hop gardens and heading towards the church when he was spotted by Ann Murrant, the wife of an agricultural labourer. What had the man been doing in the hop fields for thirty or forty minutes? As they approached each other, the man held open the churchyard gate for her. 'Nothing about the man or his appearance struck me as peculiar,' she recounted at the trial, 'save his civility in holding the gate open for me.'

The man continued loitering in the area. Under-shepherd George Noyce, who was carrying a watch and could therefore time the encounter precisely, testified to seeing the man at two minutes past three, walking along the footway running beside Kiln Piece and heading *towards* the hop gardens. He was behaving rather oddly: when the man saw that Noyce had caught sight of him, he attempted to conceal his hands under his coat skirts. Separately, the two men made their way down the hill, their paths diverging as the stranger veered west over Turville's Meadow. He crossed the river by a bridge leading to the old Basingstoke Road (Lenten Street today), pausing briefly to throw something into the water. Then he passed beside Flood Meadow Cottage and turned left towards the town centre. The cottage had formerly acted as the toll-house for the Alton–Basingstoke Turnpike; Mrs Porter lived there now with her husband William, a gardener. On that warm and dusty afternoon she was sitting out in her garden and she watched the pale man amble past her house. He didn't seem in any particular hurry and he made no attempt to conceal his face.

III.

We know hardly anything at all about Fanny Adams, barely the rudiments of her short life. She was born in Alton on 30 April 1859, making her eight years and four months old in August 1867. In July 1859 she was baptised in the old font at St Lawrence Church. If she attended school it would most likely have been the National School next to the church on Amery Hill.[11] The newspapers described her as 'a pretty little girl' or 'an interesting looking child – whose melancholy fate has been deplored by thousands'[12] or as 'a comely and intelligent child of a lively and cheerful disposition'. On the day she died she was attired in a white pinafore, red wool underskirts, and, unusually, a brown velvet hat. She was also wearing stays, which were actually quite common for both boys and girls in the 1860s as a means of improving posture rather than creating a narrow waist. She was a little taller than most girls of eight, and overall she bore the appearance of

---

11   The school admission registers have not survived.
12   *Illustrated Police News*, 14 September 1867.

Baker.

being several years in advance of her age.

There are no photographs of her, no drawings from life. All we have are a few contradictory accounts of her last movements, an autopsy report, and hundreds of prurient newspaper columns devoted to the ravishment of her body before and after death. Her name has been immortalised in the expression 'Sweet Fanny Adams' or 'Sweet FA' meaning not much or nothing at all,[13] but even before this, by the time of the trial, her personhood was becoming erased: in his trial notes, Mr Justice Mellor refers to Fanny Adams as 'it'.[14]

As the afternoon wore on, Fanny's disappearance was gradually noticed. At some point between four thirty and five o'clock, still busy with her housework and her neighbours' laundry and an eleven-month-old baby, Mrs Adams first properly realised that Fanny hadn't returned home with the other children. She made enquiries of her neighbours, but they hadn't seen Fanny either. Half an hour later Mrs Jane Gardener, who lived three doors away, called on Mrs Adams for an update on Fanny's whereabouts. As the two women were conferring on the doorstep, Minnie Warner returned from one of her trips to the sweet shop. Asked directly by Mrs Gardener when she had last seen Fanny, Minnie repeated her account of events earlier that day in Flood Meadows – the flower-picking besides the river, the arrival of the pale stranger in the high hat, the racing game, Fanny going off with the man into the Hollow. This time she had the full undivided attention of adults, and her words must have sent a shiver of dread through Mrs Adams.

Harriet Adams and Jane Gardener set off urgently in search of Fanny. As they were crossing Flood Meadows, they noticed a man emerging from the Hollow and descending the bank towards the Basingstoke Road. He was dressed in light trousers, dark coat and high hat. Minnie Warner, tagging behind, confirmed he was the same man who had gone off with Fanny earlier in the day. Mrs Gardener called out to him twice, and on the second occasion he stopped and came over.

'What have you done with the child you took away?' demanded Mrs Gardener.

'I have not seen a child,' replied the man, flustered by the direct accusation.

'Did you not give some children some half-pence?' she persisted. And he admitted he had.

There then followed a brief and rather petty disagreement over how much money he had given the children: 'Three pennies,' stated Minnie. 'No, it was three half-pence,' corrected the man. It was perhaps easier for him to pettifog

13   See Tony Rice, 'Sweet Fanny Adams revisited: what's in a name?', *Alton Papers*, Number 20, 2016, pp. 3–16. The name 'Fanny Adams' was also used by the Royal Navy to describe the unappealing appearance of a new issue of canned beef made in-house at Deptford Dockyard around the time of the murder.
14   See Appendix D.

and focus on trifling details rather than dwell on the enormity of what had taken place three hours earlier that day.

By now the man had largely regained his composure, and he smoothly consented to accompany the two women to the police station to sort the matter out. His ploy worked, for Mrs Gardener began to backtrack:

> Thinking from his manner that I had done wrong, I said, 'Sir, the reason for my speaking to you in this way is because an old gentleman has been passing this way, giving children half-pence for no good purpose, and if I have ill-judged you, or done wrong in speaking to you, I humbly beg your pardon.'

There was a bow, a curtsy, and the man turned around and began walking away. Despite everything – the little man's half-cut and overheated state, his wet and dusty shoes, his corpse-white face on that beautiful summer's day – he was still, indubitably, a member of the gentleman class, and Mrs Adams and Mrs Gardener were, indubitably, the wives of men of the working or servant class (Mrs Gardener's husband was a general servant). This dynamic will have shaped the confrontation in the meadow and encouraged the women's deference.

When he was a short distance away, Mrs Gardener called out, 'We will have your name.' But he failed to stop, only shouting back, 'Never mind my name, you will find me at Mr Clement's office if you want me.'

It was a strange, unsettling encounter even if there was nothing exactly suspicious or improper about his conduct. Admittedly, the man came straight over when called and he made no attempt to shield his face or run away. And he gave his address readily enough when asked. Only afterwards did the two women realise he had never once taken his hands out of his pockets.

Of course, the man's hands were bloodied. He made his way along the banks of the Wey, where a small boy named Alfred Vince claimed he saw him climb down into the river to rinse his hands: 'I saw his hands were red but they were white afterwards,' he explained at the trial. For the second time that day the man passed Flood Meadow Cottage. It was about a quarter to six o'clock. He was observed once more by Mrs Porter, who was still sitting out in her garden. This time he stared hard at her and looked over his shoulder as he went by to see if she was still watching him.

IV.

Just before sunset, with the Adams child still unaccounted for, bands of men and women began gathering in Tanhouse Lane. They carried wooden hay rakes, billhooks and sickles. Some brought candles and lanterns with them. There was little conversation. They took comfort in small unrealistic hopes: perhaps Fanny was playing hide-and-seek in the woods for a lark; perhaps she'd twisted her ankle and was resting in a nearby outbuilding. They set off across Flood Meadows, sweeping up the darkening hillside towards the hop gardens. From the crest, on a bright day, you could look down and see the whole town, the river and the cricket ground, the chalk pits over at East Worldham, the electric telegraph line winding though Mount Pleasant and Chawton and Ropley.

Agricultural labourer Thomas Gates, who worked at Amery Farm, was the first person to come across the scattered human remains. He spotted a scrap of chemise snagged in a hedge. It was covered in blood. Walking a little further into the plantation, he found the severed head of a child resting on two hop poles lying on the ground. It had been ravaged by scavenging animals and was already infested with vermin. But it also bore the marks of mutilation from a human hand. The right ear was cut off and missing, both eyes had been gouged out, and there was a terrible deep gash running across the face from above the nose to the end of the lower jaw. Gates was only able to tell it was a female child by the long hair.

> I took it up by the long hair, and laid it on my arm. I then went a few yards further and found a leg and thigh separated from the body, which I also picked up and placed on my arm. Coming down towards Flood Meadows I found the trunk of the body about fifteen or sixteen yards from the hedge which separated the hop ground from the meadow. The body had been cut open like a sheep that had been killed; I looked inside and found it was all cleaned out – the bowels were gone. I laid the head, leg, and other part down by the trunk. I was frightened and greatly shocked by what I saw.

Gates was soon joined by Charles White, an engine driver, and Thomas Light, a police constable from Alton station. They found Gates slumped on the ground, utterly distraught. White wrapped the portions of the child in a cloth and apron and carried them down to the Leather Bottle public house on Cutpond Lane (today 16 Amery Street), where he laid them out in an upstairs room.[15] Later that evening, Constable Light moved the remains to the police station in Butts Road; he deposited them in an old sack used for carrying hops, and locked them securely in a cart shed in the stable.

The search continued well into dusk and would resume at first light on

15   Referred to as the 'Leathern Bottle' in many newspaper reports. According to A.H. Gill, the great grandson of the landlord of the Leather Bottle in 1867, 'subsequent landlords claimed that the room was haunted by a chilly atmosphere, and the wife of one of them would never sleep in it'. A.H. Gill, *Hampshire* magazine, April 1963, p. 61. See also Kevin Osmond, *Ghosts and memories: four centuries in the life of a Hampshire market town* (privately published, n.d.), p. 55.

Introduction.

Sunday morning. Piece by bloody piece, the scattered body parts were gradually recovered – part of the left arm below the elbow, some splintered ribs, a pile of intestines concealed under a hop vine. Harry Allen, a coach painter, found the heart and lungs and the upper part of the left arm. With gruesome irony, Thomas Swayne, a shoemaker, came upon the left foot of a child in a clover field; it had been sawn off at the ankle. A brown velvet hat was retrieved from the middle of a hedge.

In total, it took nine men to collect all the remains. The new body parts and the items of clothing were taken to the police station and stored with the other remains in a second sack.

It wasn't until Tuesday afternoon that the eyeballs were located by two police constables trawling the river. Almost miraculously, they spotted the organs staring up at them through ten inches of water on the lower side of the bridge towards Alton where the footpath crosses the Wey to reach the former toll-house on Basingstoke Road.

Struggling to find words to describe the sheer barbarity of the crime, the newspapers fell back on superstitions and notions of blood-sucking creatures drawn from nightmare:

> The act resembled less that of a man than that of a vulture or a hyena; but even those brutes cease to mangle and lacerate their prey after satisfying their hunger. No tiger of the jungle, no jackal roaming famished about a city of the dead, could so fearfully have mutilated its victim. In the middle ages the deed would assuredly have been attributed to a ghoul or vampire, and in earlier times to the ogres of Eastern fable.[16]

V.

At around eight o'clock on Saturday evening, Superintendent William Cheyney, the chief police officer at Alton, received the shocking news that a child had been murdered in Chalcraft's hop garden. He hastened to the scene. On the way he met Charles White coming down the hill with the bundle of remains. The policeman opened the cloth to look inside – a severed head, a right leg, a thigh with the stocking tied above the knee. The unmistakable stench of decaying flesh drifted out into the warm summer air, turning his stomach.[17]

16   *London Evening Standard*, 29 August 1867. Alton farmer William Terrell Gunner also recorded the discovery of the body in his diary: 'A horrible murder took place here today – a clerk of Clements, the lawyer decoyed away a little girl and murdered her in Shalden dale: I sincerely hope the man was insane. Alas, for the poor parents! What must their feelings be; the father's name was Adams, he works for Mr Dyer.' Diaries of William Terrell Gunner, 24 August 1867. HRO 284M87/2.

17   Superintendent Cheyney might have been sharply reminded of one of the first cases he dealt with after

Baker.

Making enquiries, he quickly learnt that Frederick Baker, a solicitor's clerk who worked at the local law firm of W. & J.W. Clement, was suspected.

By the time he reached Clements, a small crowd had already gathered in the street outside. Baker was in the front office, leaning against a desk, still wearing his high hat. He was nonchalantly smoking a cigar. Cheyney went straight up to Baker. 'A child has been murdered in Mr Chalcraft's hop garden,' he said.

'Yes; they say it's me, don't they?' replied Baker. He exhaled a mouthful of cigar smoke, and the smell of alcohol wafted in Cheyney's direction. 'I am innocent, and am willing to go where you like.'

On being asked to turn out his pockets, he produced two knives – a white handled one and another with a buckhorn handle. But they were the implements a scrivener might use for trimming quills or opening business stationery. They were hardly the weapons of choice for a maniac intent on dissecting and eviscerating a child.

Cheyney instructed Constable Watkins to stay with Baker while he went off to make further enquiries. Returning shortly, having secured descriptions of the prisoner from Mrs Gardener and Minnie Warner, he arrested Baker on suspicion of murder. 'I am innocent as the day I was born' was Baker's response. He was smuggled out the back door of the office to avoid the increasingly unruly crowd congregating in the High Street, and quickly escorted to the police station, where he was searched by Superintendent Cheyney before being locked up in one of the station's three cells.

Later that evening he was ordered to undress in the presence of Cheyney and Dr. Louis Leslie, the police surgeon for Alton. The two men noticed he was almost completely hairless, like a small boy. His shoulders and hip bones were sharp as knives. There were tiny bramble scratches on his thighs; an unpleasant smell exuded from his backside, as if he'd soiled himself earlier or rolled in the faeces of another animal. The left leg of his trousers, and his left boot and sock, were still quite damp from their dunking in the river earlier in the day: 'Well, that won't hang me, will it?' commented Baker. The doctor also noticed several faint stains that looked like blood on the wristband of the prisoner's shirt; Baker couldn't account for them, although later, after he'd had time to think, he blamed them on nosebleeds. Cheyney asked whether a telegram communicating the news of his arrest should be sent to the prisoner's father in Guildford – 'No!' Baker replied.

being transferred to Alton earlier in the year. Two tramps had stolen meat from a butcher's shop in Froyle: he had searched the woods at No Man's Land, and had found a leg of pork hidden in a coppice. *Hampshire Advertiser*, 27 April 1867.

Introduction.

*

That night little Minnie Warner was allowed to sleep over at the Adams house with Lizzie. 'I did not go to bed so early that night,' she told the jury at Winchester, 'because I waited up till Fanny was found. I heard Mrs Adams crying at night.'

VI.

By all accounts Frederick Baker was an unusual creature. Even in the middle of summer his face was a pale, ashen colour, like celery blanched in a shed. His dark brown hair and hazel eyes served only to accentuate his sallow complexion. He was a thin, gaunt man under middle height (he was five feet three and weighed under eight and a half stone) who tended to walk with a slouch, shoulders hunched and head down, which made him appear even more diminutive. He seemed harmless enough on first acquaintance, yet anyone who made the effort to get to know him quickly sensed there was something not quite right with him. Most of the time he behaved in a calm and rational manner, but these lucid periods were succeeded by outbursts of wild frenzy in which he seemed to abandon all self-control.

Frederick was born in Guildford in 1838. He was baptised on 15 July, taking the same name as his father. At that time Guildford was a small market town on the North Downs with some 4,000 inhabitants. It had an ancient castle and a Tudor grammar school; the river Wey passed through the town from its source at Alton to join the Thames at Weybridge. The Bakers occupied a terraced house in South Street, near the town centre, and to all intents and purposes they appeared a perfectly ordinary, respectable lower middle-class family. Mr Baker senior was a master tailor, well-known and well-respected in the town, and every Sunday the family dutifully worshipped at the red-brick Anglican church of Holy Trinity at the top of the cobbled High Street.

Yet the Baker household was a gloomy and forbidding environment for a child growing up, and signs of emotional distress and profound psychological trauma are everywhere to be found in Frederick's early years. Much of this troubled backstory would emerge during the trial in a bid by defending counsel to convince the jury that Baker was mentally unbalanced and therefore not responsible for his actions. Dr Henry Taylor, a surgeon living at Guildford, who had been the Bakers' family physician for more than twenty years, spoke in the witness box of watching young Frederick's character change from a weak and sensitive child to a swaggering, intemperate monster.

There was a history of derangement on both sides of the family. Frederick's

Baker.

father suffered from paranoid delusions – he thought his children were trying to poison him – which made him lash out at those who cared for him most. On one occasion he attempted to strike his daughter, Mary Ann, with a poker. The family had to employ a minder to watch over him night and day.

An even more troubled individual was Frederick's cousin, Richard Row, who had been in and out of lunatic asylums for many years on account of his aggressive behaviour. Knives and other sharp objects needed to be kept out of his reach. Doctors considered him a potentially dangerous offender capable even of murder, and he was currently confined in the County Lunatic Asylum at Fareham diagnosed with homicidal mania.

Frederick's mother, Elizabeth (*née* Trimmer), was also plagued with psychological torments: a frail woman troubled by unspecified nervous ailments, she spent her days sunk in sorrow on the edge of a mental breakdown, endlessly fretting over real or imagined conflicts and exaggerating even the slightest discomfort into a major crisis. She would die of consumption when her son was twenty-one.

Given this fractured domestic environment, it is hardly surprising that young Frederick absorbed these Gothic taints and turned out a rather strange adult.

Frederick's early years were spent as a semi-invalid. He was a weak and sickly boy, prone to frequent nosebleeds and vomiting, and he complained constantly of terrible headaches. His neurotic mother insisted he be kept at home, away from the perceived dangers of the outside world. As a result, Frederick missed out on schooling for the first twelve years of his life and developed into an isolated, socially-backward youth. Dr Taylor related how, if anyone spoke to him, the boy would blush and quiver anxiously, as if scared or upset.

No doubt Frederick's father expected his son to follow him into the tailoring business (his daughter Mary Ann was already working from home as a seamstress and dressmaker), but young Frederick showed no interest at all. He continued to mope around the house, morose and impenetrable. In what may have been a final, desperate bid to make something of his son and to improve his employment prospects, Frederick was enrolled by his father at the Stoke House Academy in Guildford in the autumn of 1851. This was a boys' boarding school that aimed to prepare pupils for university, professional or commercial life, although they also took in a small number of day pupils at eight guineas per annum.

Nothing is known of Frederick's schooldays beyond a single newspaper item reporting that in 1853 a Frederick Baker was awarded second prize in Latin at the annual prize-giving.[18] Although clearly an intelligent child, Frederick was

14

Introduction.

an indifferent scholar. It seems he took no part in sports or other social activities, and was glad to escape home at the end of lessons. Perhaps he only became truly animated when the sergeant major of the 2nd Surrey Militia came over from Aldershot to give the boys instruction in Sword Exercise.

A severe attack of typhoid fever when Frederick was sixteen ended all ambitions for a university education. He was ill for almost a year with lingering complications, falling back all too easily into his previous semi-invalid state.

Gradually, though, against all expectations, he began to emerge from the shadows of South Street and take his place in adult society. While he never developed any serious outside interests or hobbies, and seemed incapable of forming meaningful relationships with either men or women, his parents nonetheless encouraged him to help out as a Sunday school teacher at Trinity and St Mary's National School. This gave him an excuse to get out of the house and moreover provided him with access to a steady supply of small children, especially girls, for whose company he had a predilection. A little later, he also started attending meetings at the Guildford Mechanics' Institute, eventually becoming secretary of the newly-formed Young Men's Debating and Elocution Society, and acting as a working director of the Guildford Penny Savings Bank. The Mechanics' Institute offered a laboratory, a library, a regular programme of public lectures and evening classes, and other useful resources for the technical education of working men, as well as numerous amenities for social, cultural and sporting development. Mr and Mrs Baker will have welcomed their son's involvement, however nominal, in these wholesome pursuits.

It was perhaps through connections made at the institute that Frederick found work as a junior clerk at the offices of Messrs. W.H. and M. Smallpiece, solicitors, at 138 Guildford High Street, although Frederick's father testified at the trial that 'We put him into the office of Mr Smallpiece', suggesting that family influence rather than any initiative from the son had been instrumental in bringing about this employment.[19] While it was dry, unexciting work, involving preparing abstracts of wills and proofreading deeds and other legal documents, it suited Frederick's pedantic and fastidious temperament and gave him a measure of financial independence from his coddling family.

For some reason though, after five-and-a-half years working at Smallpieces, he handed in his notice and moved a few buildings down the High Street to join the rival law firm of Philip W. Lovett, at No. 53. His duties were more onerous at this new place of work, and without any commensurate increase in salary to offset the additional responsibilities, Frederick quickly came to regret his hasty decision to change jobs. During lunch breaks, he crawled home and repeatedly

18   *Sussex Advertiser*, 20 December 1853.
19   *Police News Edition of the Trial and Condemnation of Frederick Baker* (1867), p. 11.

burst out crying in front of his father, sobbing over the injustice of his tragic situation.

The beginning of Baker's decline – some say the beginning of his descent into madness – is a matter of dispute among alienists, although it is around the time of his ill-judged move to Lovett's, and the death of his mother in 1860, that the first signs of gross eccentricity became apparent. He started binge-eating with the relish of an ogre, scoffing king-sized portions of raw or half-cooked meat and washing them down with beer. And yet, by some quirk of metabolism, he failed to put on weight:

> At the Cannon Inn in the Portsmouth Road, after playing at bagatelle, he sent out for three pounds of pork sausages, and ate every particle of them in a ravenous fashion before they were half-cooked. At another time, at the Angel Hotel, he ordered three bottles of stout and three large pork pies. He ate the pies, knocked the heads off the bottles and drank the frothing stout out of the jagged necks. He did all these things in the coolest possible manner, and always appeared rather gratified than otherwise if his gluttony excited astonishment or remark... It is reported that he could at any time dispose of 3lb of beef steak without the slightest assistance.[20]

Frederick may have been suffering from bulimia nervosa (unrecognized as an eating disorder and mental health condition in the nineteenth century), although lurid accounts in the *Illustrated Police News* would later interpret this bestial craving for raw meat and cold fat as evidence of human cannibalism, foreshadowing the ideas of the Viennese psychiatrist Richard von Krafft-Ebing who wrote of the 'appetite (*Gelüste*) for the flesh of the murdered victim' among sexual murderers.[21]

Baker's boozing and late-night boorishness would have been frowned upon not only by his pious, teetotal family (and by officials at the Sunday school), but by his colleagues in the Mechanics' Institute, who allied themselves closely to the temperance movement and regarded sobriety as one of the prerequisites for individual self-improvement. It was certainly a strange double-life Baker was leading: in the early evening he might chair a dignified debate on 'Which is the Greater Genius – Milton or Shakespeare?' while a few hours later he'd be drunk in the Angel Hotel with his face in a pork pie.[22]

During his final years in Guildford, there were rumours that Frederick was 'intimately connected' with the Guildford Guys, and 'shared in their most

---

20   *Morning Advertiser*, 9 September 1867.
21   Richard von Krafft-Ebing, *Psychopathia Sexualis: A Medico-Legal Study*, 7th ed, trans. Charles G. Chaddock (London: F.J. Rebman, 1894), p. 63.
22   *West Surrey Times*, 1 March 1862.

Introduction.

dangerous proceedings'.[23] The Guys were a semi-organised band of high-spirited rioters who donned weird animal masks to avoid recognition and terrorized the town on Bonfire Night and at other times.[24] Communicating with hunting horns, they ran amok though the streets defying the police and officials of the town, and causing widespread damage to property.[25] Their affrays were becoming increasingly lawless, and in 1864 four youths were charged with the attempted murder of a police constable. Such a group, operating illicitly on the margins of society, may well have appealed to a misfit and loner like Baker, trapped as he was at home and bored and dissatisfied at work. While there is no firm evidence linking Baker to these mobs, we can readily picture him drunkenly cheering them on to commit further acts of vandalism and arson.

More worrying was Frederick's presumed paedophilia.[26] Of course, the Victorians knew all about adults who were sexually interested in children, even if the clinical and medico-legal language with which to discuss the phenomenon did not exist till much later. When Mrs Gardener encountered Frederick Baker in Flood Meadows on the afternoon of the murder and told him about 'an old gentleman giving children half-pence for no good purpose', it is clear what she meant; and when the *Illustrated Police News* described Baker as a 'prowler among children' it is clear they meant the same thing.

Like Lewis Carroll[27] and Francis Kilvert, Baker's life history reveals an intense and possibly erotic attraction to a succession of small girl children and, like his illustrious near contemporaries, his sexual urges were sluggish and usually operated on a fantasy level. He made friends with children while strolling in the fields and highways around Guildford, giving them small amounts of money to spend time in his company. We must take care not to read too much into this (i.e. inferring 'sublimated' or 'repressed' paedophilic inclinations where none existed), yet at the same time contemporary newspaper reports did not hold back from accusing Baker of child violation crimes:

> There is no doubt that Baker was under suspicion whilst in Guildford of having decoyed a little girl into an old chalk pit known as the 'Echo pit' for felonious purposes; and one of the borough constables had a warrant for some time for his

---

23   *Wrexham Advertiser*, 7 September 1867.
24   For a discussion of Baker's possible association with the Guys, see Keith McCloskey, *Killed a Young Girl. It was Fine and Hot* (Independently published, 2016), pp. 37–55.
25   See Eric Russell Chamberlin, *Guildford: A Biography* (Macmillan, 1970), pp. 177–179.
26   The term *paedophilia erotica* was first coined in 1896 by Krafft-Ebing to describe 'psychopathological cases of immorality with children'. See Morton L. Kurland, 'Paedophilia erotica', *Journal of Nervous and Mental Disease*, Vol. 131, 1960, pp. 394.
27   In 1868 Lewis Carroll took occupancy of The Chestnuts, a town house close to South Street in Guildford where the Bakers lived.

apprehension. The matter, however, was hushed up through the intervention of friends, and the little girl and her parents soon after quitted the town.[28]

Whatever the precise nature and scope of Baker's sexual identity, his interests were apparently not exclusively directed towards children. For almost a year it seems he paid his addresses to a 'highly respectable young person' – her name has not come down to us – who was in service as a lady's maid to Mrs Elizabeth Haydon of Guildford.[29]

The Haydons were an important banking family in Guildford. Samuel Haydon was a former mayor of the town and now a justice of the peace. He was involved in the Penny Savings Bank where Frederick held a directorship,[30] and he was also related to the Smallpiece family, for whom Frederick had worked as a clerk. Samuel and Elizabeth lived at 29 High Street, together with their son George and five servants.[31] Mr Haydon may have vaguely known who Baker was, but it is unlikely he will have paid much attention to the gawky young man hanging around the servants' quarters.

One wonders what Baker and his fiancée saw in each other. Perhaps Baker was looking for a cook and a housekeeper to help him escape his family's domination; perhaps he was trying to scheme his way into Haydon's home in an effort to improve his prospects as a solicitor's clerk. What is clear, though, is that Baker must have been a plodding and unimpressive suitor. On top of everything else, in addition to his drinking and gluttony, his lust for children and his general lack of social skills and adult functioning, he had recently acquired several odd behavioural tics – he pulled faces involuntarily like a gurner at a country fair, he growled and repeatedly cleared his throat, and he succumbed to sudden outbursts of laughter in public for no apparent reason.[32]

What is also clear is that the 'romance', if we can call it that, was brought to a quick and decisive end. Someone tipped off the girl's parents, and her brother stepped in to warn Baker off. While Baker's sweetheart didn't seem too upset at the broken match – she was soon seen walking out with a different young gentleman – Baker himself was completely distraught. Lacking the emotional maturity to deal with being jilted, he fell to pieces. His precarious mental and

28   *Morning Advertiser*, 9 September 1867.

29   The 1861 Census lists Ellen Stanton, 23, a housemaid, as a member of the Haydon household. She was the same age as Baker, and in the intervening six years it is possible she may have graduated from general housemaid duties to lady's maid. She was born in Marylebone, the daughter of a gardener, and she had an older brother, Frederick.

30   This job title gives an inflated impression of Baker's responsibilities at the bank: his role was more that of a bookkeeper or ledger clerk, keeping records of incoming and outgoing payments.

31   The Haydons had an older daughter, Fanny Margaretta (1840–1927), who married Lt Gen Sir Charles Warren, the Metropolitan Police Commissioner at the time of the Jack the Ripper murders.

32   These are all characteristics of what today we know as Tourette's syndrome.

Introduction.

physical health rapidly deteriorated, and he 'gave way to drunkenness and other vices'. He was sacked from his position as secretary of the Debating Society. Most nights he cried himself to sleep. He began exhibiting signs of severe depression, carrying a pistol and a dagger around with him and speaking constantly of suicide.

VII.

In April 1865, Baker suddenly vanished from Guildford. If anyone imagined he had run away to nurse a broken heart, they were mistaken; the evidence suggests he left town in a hurry to avoid criminal charges of child molestation. We know he spent at least one night (7/8 January 1866) in the casual ward of Lambeth Workhouse,[33] but apart from this his whereabouts for the fifteen months he was away are a complete mystery. Almost certainly he will have lived as a tramp and itinerant beggar for some of this time, sleeping in barns and ditches, and wandering at large among the lunatics who roamed the Victorian countryside at all hours of the day and night. Speculations in some newspapers that during this period Baker acted as a friar or 'travelling mendicant' can only have originated from Baker's defence team keen to portray their client in as positive a light as possible. Other wild rumours, quite unverifiable, have Baker spending time at sea.

Frederick's father was cross-examined during the trial about his son's disappearance. Didn't Frederick abscond from Guildford because of allegations of misconduct, the prosecution wanted to know. Mr Baker cannot have been under any illusions about the sexual antics of his son, but he denied the imputations, and the spectre of child sexual abuse never really reared its head in court. Besides, there were other 'allegations of misconduct' hanging over Frederick: it was averred by some local newspapers that he had embezzled money from his employers P. W. Lovett, and that it was only thanks to his father reimbursing the defalcations that he had managed to evade prosecution.[34]

Whatever the reason for Frederick leaving Guildford, we know that when he returned home in July 1866 he was in a dreadful state: dirty, malnourished, and possibly close to death. It says much for the love and practical resourcefulness of Frederick's father, still battling his own demons, that the errant son was patched up and restored to some semblance of health.

---

33   *Portsmouth Times*, 4 January 1868. See Keith McCloskey, *Killed a Young Girl. It was Fine and Hot*, pp. 58–76 for a discussion of this period in Baker's life. Lambeth Parish Creed Registers for January 1866 give no record of a Frederick Baker staying at the Workhouse on 7/8 January, but he could have used a false name.

34   See for example *Hereford Times*, 31 August 1867.

Baker.

Guildford was still a little too 'hot' for Frederick, so the family decided to send him to Alton, twenty miles away. It was a sedate place without many of the distractions of Guildford, and it was a place Frederick knew reasonably well.[35] He may have spent boyhood holidays there with his mother's family in Froyle.[36] His uncle, William Trimmer Row, lived and worked in Alton, where he ran a clock and watchmaking business at 61 High Street with his wife Mary Ann Baker, so if Frederick relocated there he could perhaps keep an eye on the lad. Admittedly, Frederick had disgraced himself on his last visit to Alton in December 1864 – during a psychotic episode he had marched up and down in the middle of the High Street as if trying to get himself run over – but on the whole nobody knew him there, and in theory at least he would be able to make a fresh start and put all his troubles behind him. Moreover, the railway line had recently been extended from Guildford to Alton (via Farnham), making it easy for the Baker family to keep in touch.

Lodgings were found for Frederick at Sarah Kingston's boarding house at 69 High Street (conveniently just four doors up from the Row family), and in early August he crossed the county border into Hampshire and took up employment as an engrossing clerk at Clements solicitors at 42 High Street.[37]

At first, things seemed to be going splendidly. He was a model lodger – quiet, tidy, respectful. He came home at a sensible hour. Often, in the summer months, he would recline on the bench in the back garden while smoking his pipe and reading a good book. There were no complaints either about his conduct or the standard of his work at the solicitors' office: his fellow clerks thought him a decent enough chap, if a little despondent and remote at times. And most significantly, it seems he was abstaining totally from alcohol and refrained from entering a public house under any circumstances.

Around July 1887 he wrote a series of letters to friends and former colleagues at the Guildford Mechanics' Institute, telling them how much he had changed the course of his life:

> My quiet life here at Alton has enabled me to reflect upon the errors of my past

---

35   Alton had a population of 4092 in 1871. See G.S. Minchin, 'Table of population', in W. Page (ed.), *Victorian history of Hampshire and the Isle of Wight* (London, 1912), vol. 5, p. 437.

36   Elizabeth Trimmer was likely related to the family of Thomas and Ann Trimmer from Froyle. The suggestion by Kathryn Hughes that Frederick enjoyed childhood holidays with his maternal grandmother in Amery Hill and played in Flood Meadows as a boy seems to be part of the mythology surrounding Baker (see Kathryn Hughes, *Victorians Undone* (London: 4th Estate, 2017), p. 347).

37   The law firm of W. & J.W. Clement and Son was established in the 1820s by brothers William and James White Clement. The Clements had a connection with the Austen family in nearby Chawton – a third brother, Henry, had once been in partnership with Jane's banker brother Henry, who acted as Jane's literary agent. In 1867, the senior partner, William Clement (76), was semi-retired and living at 6 High Street, Alton; James White (70) lived further down the hill above the offices at 42 High Street.

Introduction.

life. I have quite reformed. I drink little, go to bed early, and do not neglect my Sabbath duties. I often think of my foolish conduct at Guildford, but I have prayed to God for His grace, and I now feel a better course is open to me. I am very happy here, and my employers are exceedingly kind to me. Remember me to all old friends, and tell them that Fred Baker is not now a drunken sot, but, by God's grace, a steady, respectable man.

The clue here is the giveaway phrase 'I drink little'. A few months earlier he hadn't been drinking at all. Gradually, the old temptations came back – the warm smell of hops and the reek of beer from the Swan Tap, the sounds of children at play in the barley fields, pork chops and trays of mince in the butcher's shop window and the slaughteryard round the back. Gradually, the familiar urges and the intemperate habits began to reassert themselves.

He boasted of his new outdoor activities which included boating and country walking. He kept a diary, too, in which he recorded the everyday mundane happenings of life in a small rural town – births and marriages, the July lamb show on The Butts, a march by the Alton Foresters headed by a stirring brass band. Curiously, though, he always kept the diary under lock and key in his office desk, and this was because an increasing number of entries betrayed his fascination with morbid subjects: the diary was full of obituaries, death notices, reports of agricultural injuries and fatalities. In May 1867, when a little boy called Arthur Fowler drowned while playing near King's Pond, Baker scribbled the details in his diary and popped over after work to survey the scene.

By the summer of 1867, Baker was well and truly back to his old ways. He was even drinking during the day, nipping out from the office at all hours for beer and glasses of gin and milk. He resumed his predatory child-watching activities:

> The human beast prowled about rural coppices and leafy glades to steal upon the children at their play, to give them half-pence, to decoy them to lonesome spots, to wreak on them, God knows what nameless horrors.[38]

His father came over on a visit in late May and was shocked by his son's appearance and manner. When Frederick's sister called round in mid August, she too found her brother in a terrible state, wild and restless, and with an expression in his eyes so fierce and unnatural she feared for his sanity. Even Sarah Kingston, his landlady, noticed the wildness in his eyes: 'On the Friday and Saturday previous to the murder,' she would later tell the court at Winchester, 'I commented to my husband on how bad he looked.'

38   *Hampshire Chronicle*, 14 December 1896.

Baker.

In Guildford, while drunk and raving, he had once threatened 'to do something that would be talked about'. This kind of boastfulness suggests that Baker may have suffered from a narcissistic personality disorder causing him to seek attention and infamy to an unnatural degree. Certainly, events were coming to a head in Alton; he was planning on leaving his job to go 'up north', and Sarah Kingston and others had serious misgivings about Baker's current behaviour and what the future held in store for him.

VIII.

A post mortem on the body of Fanny Adams was conducted on Sunday afternoon the 25th of August by Dr Louis Leslie, the Divisional Police Surgeon for Alton. He had been called to the police station the night before to view the remains of a child, but had waited until the following day to make his full examination. By then, additional body parts had been recovered from the hop garden and brought to the makeshift autopsy room in readiness for the examination.

It was Dr Leslie's twentieth year as a physician in Alton. Mortuary provision was almost non-existent in the town, and that weekend he will have laboured under very rudimentary conditions indeed. The examination took him a gruelling two-and-a-half hours. The fact that the body had lain in the fields for many hours before discovery will have considerably complicated the autopsy: some of the mutilating injuries may have been aggravated by postmortem animal scavenging.

In total, the body had been cut into twenty pieces. Methodically, Dr Leslie reassembled them as best he could. A number of body parts remained unrecovered – both eyes (although they would later be found in the Wey), the sternum, and the vagina. In his view all the dismemberments were effected after death; he estimated the killer could have been occupied for upwards of an hour in his grisly work. The cause of death was a fracture to the skull by a blow from a heavy object, possibly the slab of stone found at the scene. In Dr Leslie's opinion, Fanny would have died instantaneously and she suffered no torture.

*

Shortly after Dr Leslie had completed his examination, George Adams was ushered into the room by Superintendent Cheyney and allowed to view the remains. A sheet will have covered most of the child's body, hiding the worst of the injuries. There was just enough left for him to identify his daughter.

Earlier that day, in his cell at the back of the station, Frederick Baker had enjoyed a sumptuous breakfast. Prisoners were usually served dry bread or oatmeal gruel with salt, but Baker, it seems, had his meals sent in by a friend – three eggs, rashers of bacon, a large quantity of bread and butter, and a mug of tea.[39] He wolfed it all down, and slept soundly, like a wintering animal, despite the yells and hoots of the mostly female crowd gathered outside the station.

*

Even before the weekend was over, ghoulish sightseers and souvenir-hunters were starting to flock into Alton. According to the *Chichester Express*,

> Thousands of persons visited the site of the harrowing tragedy, where pools of the life-blood of the innocent child were painfully visible. The morbid feeling animating the public was conspicuously developed by the denudation of the hops and the cutting off of pieces of the plants and hedges growing in the immediate vicinity.[40]

IX.

Early on Monday morning, Baker was taken under police escort to Chawton House, the Elizabethan manor house just outside Alton, home to Edward Knight, a former High Sheriff of Hampshire, and a long-serving magistrate.[41] As the cart swept up the long rising driveway through the meadows and landscaped gardens of the fourteen acre estate, Baker may have felt like a prince or an important visiting dignitary. But the fantasy was short-lived: he was curtly remanded on a charge of wilful murder and bundled back into the cart for the return journey to Alton police station.

Later that afternoon, Superintendent Cheyney made a significant discovery which seemed to settle the question of Baker's guilt beyond all dispute. Searching Baker's desk at his office, he found a diary tucked away behind some law papers, and turning to the entry for Saturday, 24 August, he read:— 'Killed a young girl. It was fine and hot'. It was in the prisoner's handwriting. Making enquiries among the other clerks in the office, the policeman determined that Baker must have made the entry before knowledge of the murder of Fanny Adams became generally known around eight o'clock on Saturday evening.

The *Illustrated Police News* reflected on this diary entry:

39   *Hampshire Chronicle*, 31 August 1867.
40   *Chichester Express and West Sussex Journal*, 3 September 1867.
41   Knight was the nephew of Jane Austen.

Baker.

'Killed a young girl—it was fine and hot.' These words will henceforth be as memorable in the chronicles of crimes as the 'I never liked him, and so I finished him off with a ripping chisel' of George Frederick Manning.[42] 'Killed a young girl—it was fine and hot'—the cool confession and the commonplace remark appended to the admission form one of the most remarkable and one of the most appalling examples ever known of deep-dyed, ingrained, insatiate, unrepenting wickedness... So calmly does the murderous clerk of Alton register his atrocity that one might be almost led to think that the murdering of children, and the tearing of them asunder, were quite as much a matter of form and business as making out bills of cost or engrossing deeds. To a wretch whose mind must be in a thoroughly non-natural condition, it may have seemed quite a natural thing to associate God's sunshine and the genial warmth of summer with the satisfaction of unutterable lusts and the indulgence of a taste for blood.

If a tiger could write, the beast might scrawl with ensanguined claw, 'Killed an antelope—it was fine and hot.'[43]

*

Baker's first public appearance after his arrest was at the inquest. It was held on Tuesday afternoon, 27 August, at the Duke's Head (now The George) on Butts Road in Alton. Mr Robert Harfield, the deputy coroner for Hampshire, presided.[44] In a sense, the Duke's Head was home turf for Baker. He drank there from time to time, and was on first name terms with the licensee and the bar staff: the smells of beer, tobacco smoke and sawdust would have drifted over him throughout the inquest proceedings like odours from a comfort blanket.

Inquests were always convened in the parish where death had occurred, and public houses or vestry rooms in churches were the usual venues because they offered rooms big enough to accommodate the court. Even so, the Duke's Head was a rather cramped space. Every effort had been made by the police to afford accommodation for as many as possible: as a result, the room was 'crowded to suffocation, and the windows were completely besieged'.[45] The coroner, the prisoner, the witnesses and the various spectators, were forced into an uncomfortable intimacy. It was stifling and unbearably hot.

A jury of twelve men were sworn. To serve on an inquest, jurors needed to be householders; they will have been tradesmen, artisans and shopkeepers

---

42   See *Trial of The Mannings* [NBT 90].

43   *Police News Edition of the Trial and Condemnation of Frederick Baker* (1867), p. 14.

44   But for the illness of the coroner, Mr John Todd, the inquest would have taken place the day before, on Monday.

45   *Chichester Express and West Sussex Journal*, 3 September 1867.

Introduction.

drawn from the regular working folk of Alton. Their first duty was to view the body. Accompanied by the deputy coroner and his assistant, they walked the 150 yards or so down the road to the police station. The remains were kept in two sacks in a cart shed in the stable at the back of the station. The sacks were opened, and the sickly sweet smell of decay poured out. The jurymen then walked back to the Duke's Head. It must have been a revolting experience, and one of dubious evidential value.[46]

Amid jeers from the crowd outside, the accused man was brought handcuffed into the inquest room. Police officers were stationed near the door and windows to keep the peace. The prisoner appeared pale and a little ill-kempt. During the proceedings he sat on a sofa behind the coroner looking unconcerned and for the most part indifferent. Only once, when Thomas Gates gave his evidence, detailing his discovery of portions of the body scattered around the hop garden, did Baker waver. His hands came up and he covered his face in shame.

It was the role of the coroner's court to enquire into the cause of accidental, suspicious, violent or otherwise 'unnatural' deaths. Its purpose was therefore investigative rather than adversarial; in theory, it gathered information rather than apportioned blame on a named individual. The Alton jury listened to testimony from a range of witnesses, including relatives of the deceased, Baker's colleagues at Clements solicitors, medical experts, and the police. In truth, it was a rather 'rough and ready' sort of tribunal in which a deputy coroner with no legal or medical training and a lay jury plucked from the High Street were being asked to decide on matters of life and death. Minnie Warner, the first witness, was not able even to identify Baker as the man who had carried Fanny away – the clamour from outside and the leering faces pressed against the pub windows had understandably unnerved her.

As the evidence seemed to implicate the prisoner, the deputy coroner invited Baker to ask questions of any of the witnesses. 'I have no questions to ask at present, thank you' was Baker's languid reply from the settee. When all the evidence had been heard, Mr Harfield again asked Baker if he had anything to say. 'No, Sir. All that I can say is I am totally innocent.'

The deputy coroner then summed up the evidence. The jury retired upstairs, and after deliberating for quarter of an hour, they returned with a verdict of wilful murder against Frederick Baker. A warrant was made out committing him for trial at the next Hampshire Assize, and the inquest terminated.

As news of the verdict spread among the crowd outside, Baker became visibly alarmed. The inquest had dragged on into the early evening so that groups of farm labourers, returning from the fields at the end of the day, had

---

46   The 1926 Coroners' (Amendment) Act restricted the view's role at inquests.

been able to join the infuriated throng surrounding the Duke's Head. Shouts of 'lynch the villain' echoed forth from every quarter. For two hours, Baker and his police minders were trapped inside. It was only as darkness began to fall, and the size of the mob reduced slightly, that the police made their move. Out they ran through a back door – Baker in the middle, Superintendent Cheyney on one side and Superintendent Samuel Everitt[47] on the other, two officers in front and two behind – out they ran, crashing through the stable yard and over a gate before emerging thirty yards away on the main road. But they were spotted, and the crowd gave chase, 'uttering the fiercest threats and the most hideous yells', hurling missiles at the retreating policemen and prisoner. Finally, though, after a smart run, they reached the safety of the station yard and the prisoner was once more locked in his cell.[48]

*

The following afternoon, on Wednesday 28 August, the funeral of Fanny Adams took place:

> Shortly after the jury had viewed the remains of the unfortunate child, they were placed in a coffin and conveyed to the cottage in which she had resided with her parents in Tanhouse Lane. They were interred at the Alton Cemetery on Wednesday afternoon, and a large number of persons assembled to witness the funeral. The burial service was impressively read by the Rev. W. Wilkins, curate of Thedden. Wreaths of flowers were placed upon the coffin, and subsequently upon the grave. The parents of the unhappy victim followed, and their grief appeared to be almost inexpressible.[49]

<h2 style="text-align:center">X.</h2>

Baker's next public appearance was before the magistrates on Thursday, 29 August. Huge crowds were again out in force, but this time the police were better prepared. They had cleared a space in front of the Town Hall, and erected makeshift barriers to keep the onlookers at bay. Baker was driven up in a cab and then hustled by Cheyney and Everitt through the entranceway into the justice room. His hands were tied behind his back. It was shortly after 11 o'clock. When the vestibule door was finally opened to allow admission of the

---

47 He was actually Acting Chief Constable at the time of the Fanny Adams murder.

48 Reports of the coroner's inquest and the near-lynching are taken from the *Hampshire Advertiser*, 31 August 1867, the *Hampshire Telegraph*, 31 August 1867 and the *Hampshire Chronicle*, 31 August 1867. See also Ian A. Burney, *Bodies of Evidence: Medicine and the Politics of the English Inquest 1830–1926* (Baltimore: Johns Hopkins University Press, 2000).

49 *Chichester Express and West Sussex Journal*, 3 September 1867.

Introduction.

public, there was an almighty scramble for seats. Within a minute or two, the court chamber was packed to capacity, with women making up the majority of the spectators. Hundreds of people milled around outside in the Market Square, disappointed at being denied a ringside seat at the 'Alton Tragedy'.

Baker was appearing once more before Mr Edward Knight, the county magistrate for Alton division. The charge was read over and it was ascertained that the prisoner had no legal representation. Baker seemed unruffled and in a relatively relaxed mood – 'self-possessed, cool and collected' is how one journalist described him, although the newspapers couldn't agree: 'agitated' and 'bathed in a clammy perspiration' was the opinion of a second pressman.

Most of the evidence given in court that day recapitulated the testimony heard two days earlier at the inquest, and it would be repeated again when the case came before the assize court at Winchester in December. This was how the criminal justice system worked in cases of alleged homicide; witnesses might sometimes give their evidence three times – at the inquest, at the committal hearing, and at the trial. To a degree, witnesses were thus able to 'rehearse' or 'practise' their evidence in lower courts before it was presented in its final (clearest and most coherent) form at the trial. However, this occasionally meant that witness evidence 'evolved' on its way to the Crown Court, presenting attorneys with opportunities to challenge witnesses on discrepancies and inconsistencies in their various statements. For example, at the inquest Minnie Warner stated that Frederick Baker approached her in Flood Meadows with the greeting 'Hello' or 'Holloa', but three months later, when she gave evidence at Winchester, this had matured into the sinister line, 'Hello my little tulips, here you are again'.

Baker might have expected the committal hearing to extend over two days – which would have meant another full English breakfast and another mug of sweet tea at Alton police station – but it was all over before the end of the afternoon on the first day. He remained unmoved throughout the entire proceedings, his eyes cast down and seemingly oblivious to what was happening around him. He showed no visible emotion – not even when Fanny's torn and blood-drenched clothing was brought into court and laid out on the chamber floor for the magistrates to see, reducing courtroom spectators and even hardened police officers to tears.[50] Not even when Mr Adams, shaking and sobbing, shouted across the courtroom at Baker, 'You're a villain, ain't you'.

There was no surprise when the county magistrate, after conferring briefly with his colleagues on the bench, committed Baker for trial at the Hampshire Assizes. The prisoner was unceremoniously removed from court and bustled

50   *Hampshire Chronicle*, 31 August 1867.

Baker.

into a waiting cab. The crowd surged, booing and yelling its hatred, but the police lines held. One woman got trampled on. For most people, this would be their final sighting of Baker – a white-faced attorney's clerk staring blankly from the window of a carriage as the horses reared up in the din from the crowd. A last-ditch effort to upset the post-chaise was thwarted, and off it sped down Market Street, the driver vigorously plying his whip.

The crowds were slow to disperse. They filled the streets and pavements, unsure what to do now that the source of their anger had been taken from them. Four years earlier, infant school children from all over Alton (almost certainly including Fanny) had marched down the High Street to the town hall to celebrate the wedding of the Prince of Wales. Church bells rang out from St Lawrence. Inside the hall they were regaled with oranges and plum cake, and each toddler was given a new tin cup to mark the merry day. And later that evening, when the children were asleep, or pretending to be asleep, fireworks were let off from Windmill Hill, and a bonfire, saturated with tar, burned for several hours.[51]

XI.

Fanny Adams was murdered on Saturday 24 August, and by the following Tuesday Frederick Baker was committed on a coroner's warrant to stand trial at the Hampshire Assizes. By any reckoning this was speedy justice, but not uncommonly so: inquests were often convened at short notice if only because there was a putrefying corpse that needed to be interred sooner rather than later.

The Hampshire Assizes were held twice a year, once in Lent and once in the summer, although an extra assize might be squeezed in during the winter if there was demand for it. This meant there would often be a delay between the preliminary hearing and the trial simply because the defendant had to wait for the next assizes. Baker seems to have had a fairly clear-headed notion of what the criminal law held in store for him. He must have known in advance what the outcome would be at the magistrates' court, and he was resigned to a lengthy remand at Winchester Gaol. 'Well, I shall have three months indoors at any rate,' he told the police custody officer at Alton, 'but the cold nights are coming on. That will not be so comfortable.'[52]

On Thursday evening he was transferred to the county gaol at Winchester by Superintendent Everitt. Usually prisoners were moved from town to town by train. In Baker's case, though, owing to hostile crowds at the railway station, they travelled by road, a distance of just over 18 miles. Even then, the horse-

51 *Hampshire Chronicle*, 14 March 1863.
52 *Hampshire Chronicle*, 31 August 1867.

drawn carriage was chased out of Alton by a raucous mob throwing stones. Baker and his police escort arrived at Winchester just before 9 o'clock in the bright evening twilight.

*

Life moved on. The hop-pickers came and went, and winter drew in.

In the second half of the nineteenth century, newspaper readership expanded dramatically following the abolition of newspaper tax in 1855 and the removal of paper duty in 1861.[53] The *Daily Telegraph*, for example, boasted a circulation of 150,000 in 1868 rising to 217,000 in 1881, while a weekly paper like *Lloyd's Weekly*, catering more to readers from a lower to lower middle-class background, claimed circulation of 500,000 in 1865 rising to 612,000 in 1881.[54] According to the paper itself, the *Illustrated Police News* achieved a weekly circulation similar to the daily rate of the *Telegraph*, although they quoted sales of 600,000 copies a week if an exceptionally notorious story was being covered. Competition among newspaper proprietors was fierce and canny editors were attuned to the reading public's thirst for stories of crime and scandal. They understood perfectly the appeal and commercial leverage of a murdered child.

Yet even sensational news stories like the Alton murder, widely regarded as a case 'without parallel'[55] and one which threw 'all recent murders into the shade',[56] did not stay in the public view for long. Most murder cases commanded pre-trial coverage for only a few days.[57]

One way the press sought to extend the currency of notorious murder cases was by fleshing out the life stories of felons. These background pieces, which might be published in instalments over several weeks, served to keep the criminal in the public eye; they added context as news events unfolded, and they provided a source of continuing news when there was nothing to report from the police or coroner's courts. In this way, nineteenth century newspapers helped fashion what today we might call 'celebrity criminals'.[58]

---

53   See Martin Hewittt, *The Dawn of the Cheap Press in Victorian Britain: the End of the 'Taxes on Knowledge'*, *1849–1869* (Bloomsbury, 2013).

54   Alvar Ellegård, 'The Readership of the Periodical Press in Mid-Victorian Britain', *Victorian Periodicals Newsletter*, No. 13, September 1971, pp. 3–22.

55   *Sheffield and Rotherham Independent*, 28 August 1867.

56   *Essex Standard*, 28 August 1867.

57   See Judith Rowbotham, Kim Stevenson, Samantha Pegg. *Crime News in Modern Britain: Press Reporting and Responsibility, 1820–2010* (Basingstoke: Palgrave Macmillan, 2013), p. 71.

58   Alice Smalley has examined in detail the way the *Illustrated Police News* covered the Frederick Baker case, elevating him into a criminal celebrity. See Alice Smalley, 'Representations of Crime, Justice, and Punishment in the Popular Press: A Study of the *Illustrated Police News*, 1864–1938'. PhD thesis. The Open University (2017).

Baker.

The newspaper that took the most interest in Baker, and covered the Alton murder with the greatest relish, was the weekly *Illustrated Police News* (*IPN*). It began publication in the 1860s offering a thrilling mix of lurid front-page illustrations and what Judith Knelman has described as a 'typically English, hushed, reverent attitude towards death'.[59]

The *IPN* worked hard to maintain reader interest in the Baker case. Its coverage began on 31 August with a short article describing the discovery of the body, the arrest of Baker, and the coroner's inquest.[60] Over the following weeks and months, as Baker languished in Winchester Gaol, it issued regular news roundups sourced from the London and provincial papers – reports of ghoulish sightseers in Alton, information on the analytical tests being conducted on Baker's clothes and knives, speculation about a possible new trial witness (Alfred Vince), and snippets on the behaviour of the accused in Winchester prison ('He frequently refers to the murder, and says that he wonders who could commit such a crime'). In addition, they harvested and re-used all the gossip and 'human interest' stories circulating about Baker – his gluttony and werewolf appetites, his child molesting, and his heavy drinking and ruffianism.[61]

The *IPN*'s innovative use of front-page woodcut engravings (pictorial blocks) laid out in storyboard format brought a lively tabloid quality to its reporting of the Alton Murder case. Illustrations were central to the process of manufacturing celebrity criminals, and readers were now regaled with portraits of murderers and realistic visual images of violence and death to accompany the court reports and the verbatim testimony of witnesses. To a large extent, our perception and understanding of the Frederick Baker and Fanny Adams drama has been shaped by the pictorial images that were used to illustrate the crime reports in the *IPN*.

While casual readers of the *IPN* might have deplored the vulgarity of its methods, on the whole the Victorian press had few qualms about serving up vivid gory images of dead bodies to the reading public, even if the victim was a child. Inevitably, though, like the earlier penny dreadful comics, the *IPN* was regularly blamed for increases in violent crime and for encouraging anti-social behaviour more generally among lower-middle and working-class juvenile readers. Indeed, in March 1870, Williams Mobbs claimed he had been inspired to murder a little boy after viewing one of the *IPN*'s illustrations of Frederick Baker decapitating Fanny Adams. This case is examined in Appendix G.

---

59   Judith Knelman, 'Transatlantic Influences On the Reporting of Crime: English vs. American. vs. Canadian', *American Periodicals*, Vol. 3 (1993), p. 3.

60   *Illustrated Police News*, 31 August 1867, p. 2.

61   *Illustrated Police News*, 7 September 1867, p. 2.

Introduction.

*

The *IPN* prided itself on the accuracy of its illustrations. In an interview with the *Pall Mall Gazette*, the editor, George Purkess, explained the trouble they went to to secure faithful depictions:

> I know there exists a popular impression that our illustrations are largely imaginative, but as a matter of fact we are continually striving after accuracy of delineation. If a tragedy were to occur in London to-day, we would send an artist straight away to the scene; should a terrible murder or extraordinary incident be reported from the country we would at once despatch a telegram to an artist.[62]

Purkess employed between 70 and 100 freelance artists spread out across the country. As soon as news reached him of the terrible murder at Alton he despatched one of his local artists to the crime scene. Sadly, his name has not come down to us.

The 31 August edition of the newspaper carried two wood engravings depicting the abduction and beheading of Fanny Adams: the artist has not shied away from adding the gory details of a severed arm lying besides the slumped body and splashes of blood on Baker's trousers. The overall effect is powerful and upsetting.

The 7 September edition presents the first full-length portrait of the accused man posing against a plain background and leaning on a table for support; it is a rather poor likeness of Baker, presumably based on sketchy verbal descriptions supplied by colleagues at Clements. Another image shows Baker being mobbed at Winchester police station with a little girl fleeing in terror in the foreground, while a third illustration depicts Thomas Gates in the hop garden grasping hold of the child's severed head in horror.[63]

The reading public had to wait until 14 September for a portrait of Fanny Adams. She is depicted wearing her flat-crowned, narrow-brimmed velvet hat. It is the only image we have of Fanny that may remotely resemble how she actually looked. It was accompanied by a view of her parents' cottage and a drawing of Tanhouse Lane taken from Flood Meadows: 'We can vouch for the correctness of these two illustrations as they are engraved from sketches taken on the spot by a gentleman sent specially down to Alton for the purpose.'[64]

What has become known as the 'corrected portrait' of Baker first appeared

---

62 *Pall Mall Gazette*, 23 November 1886, pp. 1–2.
63 The image of Thomas Gates discovering the remains was reprised by a different artist nearly forty years later when the *IPN* ran its retrospective 'Murders and Mysteries' series. See the *Illustrated Police News*, 30 January 1904. Note: the head was inaccurately depicted as being impaled on a hop pole.
64 *Illustrated Police News*, 14 September 1867, p. 2.

in the supplementary chapbook *The Life and Examination of Frederick Baker*. It was a woodblock engraving produced from a commercial photograph of Baker taken by the Guildford photographer W.H. Steere.[65] The photograph, which has not survived, was possibly taken in Guildford in 1860 or 1861 when Baker was in his early twenties and still working at Smallpieces the solicitors. He is a gloomy figure, standing three-quarter face, with his left arm resting on a cabinet and his right hand in his pocket under his coat tails. In view of what we know about him now, his right arm looks almost as if it is positioned behind his back, holding a penknife.

*

Frederick Baker had been in Winchester Gaol for just over a fortnight when newspaper reports began to surface suggesting that Fanny Adams may not have been his first victim.

In the summer of 1866, a seven-year-old girl called Jane Sax was sexually assaulted just outside Guildford in the fields close to her home in Gomshall. To stop her screaming, her assailant stabbed her in the mouth and throat with a clasp-knife. The neck wound was so deep it penetrated the gullet to reach the spine. Alerted by her cry of distress, a passerby rushed to the girl's aid. She was taken first to a local doctor's surgery and then to the county hospital in Guildford, where she died of her injuries several weeks later.

Labourer James Longhurst, twenty-one, was spotted creeping around the hedgerows close to the scene. He was arrested and taken to Guildford police station. While in custody, a constable observed him coolly licking traces of blood off his hands like a butcher's dog. From her hospital bed, Jane gave a deposition identifying Longhurst as 'the boy' who had attacked her in the wheat field.[66] Described in the papers as a 'notoriously bad character' and a 'sullen, stupid-looking country lad', he was initially charged with attempted murder, but because the child had died within a year and a day of sustaining the fatal injury, the charge was amended to a capital one.[67] He was called up before the Surrey Assizes.

65 William Henry Steere was a commercial photographer with premises at 93 High Street Guildford. He registered as the copyright owner of a photograph of Baker on 29 August 1867. There is a catalogue entry for it at the National Archives, Kew (COPY 1/13/686).

66 There was a delay in submitting the deposition transcript to the inquest jury: the deposition had been notarized by Haydon Smallpiece (senior partner at the law firm in Guildford where Frederick Baker had worked for five and a half years) but for some reason he declined to hand it over to the coroner's court: the deputy coroner therefore had to serve a summons against Smallpiece. When returning their verdict, the inquest jury added a rider castigating Smallpiece for 'not treating the coroner's court with the courtesy which he ought.' *Surrey Advertiser*, 4 August 1866.

67 The year and a day rule was abolished by the Law Reform Act 1996.

Introduction.

Despite attempts by the defence lawyer to argue that children of Jane's age lacked sufficient moral or intellectual understanding of right and wrong to tell the truth, the evidence against Longhurst was overwhelming. Any lingering doubts were firmly put to rest on the day of the execution, when Longhurst effectively confessed to the prison chaplain that he had killed the child. He was hanged outside Horsemonger Lane Gaol by William Calcraft on 16 April 1867.[68]

Yet there were dissenting voices. In September 1867 a solicitor by the name of George John Shaw wrote to the *Law Times* claiming that Longhurst had been wrongfully convicted: the prosecution case had not been satisfactorily established, he argued; the man had gone to the gallows strenuously protesting his innocence, and only half-hearted attempts had been made to induce the authorities to spare his life. Sensationally, he insisted that Frederick Baker, presently lying in Winchester Gaol, was the real murderer of Jane Sax.[69]

Shaw's 'horrible suspicion' proved to be utterly groundless.[70] Admittedly, there were similarities between the two murders – a lone male assailant, a young girl violated in the fields, the use of a knife – and it was true that Baker had returned to Guildford from his mysterious wanderings in the same month that Jane Sax was attacked; but beyond these superficial parallels there was nothing connecting the crimes. Several newspapers, among them the *Illustrated Police News*, denounced the *Law Times* for running such an ill-judged story.[71]

Did Baker delight in being falsely accused of this earlier murder? Did he secretly revel in the burgeoning of his macabre celebrity status? The Jane Sax murder case was reported in all the Surrey and Hampshire newspapers, and it will have been a topic of conversation in many of the offices and public houses around Guildford. Almost certainly Baker followed the drama with keen interest, in addition to which we know he mentioned the Guildford killing when he accompanied Maurice Biddle to the Swan Tap after the disappearance of Fanny Adams. It is going too far, perhaps, to suggest that Longhurst's murder inspired Baker to kill Fanny Adams, but it may have planted the first seed of an idea in his mind.[72]

XII.

68 *Surrey Advertiser*, 4 & 6 August 1866; *Surrey Comet*, 30 March 1867.
69 The *Law Times* described Shaw as a 'highly respectable and responsible solicitor, residing at Alton', but there are no records of a solicitor with this name living in Alton at the time of the Jane Sax murder. In 1871 George John Shaw was living at Frensham in Surrey.
70 Shaw's correspondence with the *Law Times* is reproduced in Appendix H. See also *Kendall Mercury*, 14 September 1866.
71 *Illustrated Police News*, 5 October 1867, p. 1; *Herts Guardian*, 28 September 1867.
72 See *Police News Edition of the Trial and Condemnation of Frederick Baker*, p. 4.

Baker.

For centuries the Hampshire Assizes were held in the Great Hall at Winchester Castle. Sir Walter Raleigh was tried there for treason in 1603, and it was the scene of the 'Bloody Assizes' of 1685 at which 'Hanging' Judge Jeffreys presided.[73]

In the early 1870s the Great Hall underwent extensive renovation. A new roof was added, and some of the stonework was replaced. Spacious new law courts and offices were built adjoining the eastern wall on the site of the old castle ditch.[74] But the 'ugly and ill-arranged' old courts would have to do for the trial of Frederick Baker.[75]

'A more inconvenient court than the Crown Court at Winchester is probably not to be found in any county in England,' complained the *Hampshire Telegraph*, and with good reason. The courts were draughty, poorly ventilated, inadequately lit, and lacking in proper facilities for jurors, members of the Bar, and the press:

> At Winchester there is not even a waiting-room for jurors in attendance; and after travelling from all parts of the country at their own expense, but in the public service, they are compelled to wander about the open hall (certainly not the most agreeable of places during this time of the year) when not serving in the box. The Bar complain that they have no robing-room; while the accommodation (in the shape of seats) for the Press is most unsatisfactory.[76]

The walls were covered in dust and cobwebs.[77] There were sound problems, too. Background noise from adjoining rooms and public corridors impaired the acoustics in the courtroom; jury members strained to hear witnesses, witnesses strained to hear barristers, and Mr Justice Mellor, who was likely already showing signs of the deafness that would bring his legal career to a premature end thirteen years hence, often couldn't hear anyone. On several occasions he threatened to 'disallow witnesses their expenses if they persisted in mumbling'. Two days before the Baker trial, the creaking of a rusty door hinge echoed through the Winchester Hall like the wail of a child from the Alton hop grounds; his lordship was so disturbed by the sound, he ordered a policeman to go into the body of the hall and tell the mother to take the child away. When the deception was explained to him, he laughed heartily – perhaps too heartily.[78]

*

73   See *The Bloody Assizes* [NBT 48].
74   Melville Portal, *The Great Hall of Winchester*, (London: Simpkin & Co, 1899), pp. 69–74.
75   *Hampshire Telegraph*, 18 October 1873.
76   *Hampshire Telegraph*, 7 December 1867.
77   *Bell's Weekly Messenger*, 9 December 1867.
78   *Hampshire Telegraph*, 7 December 1867.

Introduction.

Extra police had been drafted in from all over the county to control the crowds that had been gathering in Winchester since dawn. Winchester was considerably less than a day's walk from Alton, and many of the spectators clamouring for admission outside the Great Hall had made the journey from Alton on foot overnight. When the court finally opened at half-past nine, there was the usual mighty surge and ungodly jostle for seats: the entrances quickly became blocked and constables were sent in to calm the situation. The parts of the court open to the public held no more than 50 or 60 persons, but somehow nearly double than number had been admitted. Additional benches had been set aside near the front of the court for the benefit of journalists, but the seats were quickly filled, not always with reporters, and many pressmen found there was nowhere for them to sit. A couple of reporters found seats in a dark corner near the jury box where there was neither desk nor ink. The majority of the spectators seemed to be women. A sort of indecent excitement floated in the air. It was Thursday morning, 5 December 1867.

The case was heard by Sir John Mellor, a High Court judge of six years' experience. His qualities of fairness and impartiality had made him a perfect choice for the judge's bench. He was gentlemanly in manner, and unfailingly courteous in his dealings with witnesses and jurors, although he lost his temper on several occasions during the Baker trial.[79] His infinite patience served him well when he took part in the longest courtroom battle of the nineteenth century – the trial of Arthur Orton, the Tichborne Claimant, lasting 180 days between 1873 and 1874.

The prosecution was in the capable hands of Montague Bere. Educated at Cheam School and Balliol College, Oxford, Bere was called to the Bar at the Inner Temple in 1850. In the nineteen years before he took silk, he built up an extensive practice mostly in the Nisi Prius courts on the Western Circuit. A genial figure with a keen sense of humour, he was recognised as an eloquent court performer and a 'sound rather than a brilliant lawyer'.[80] In 1866, at the Exeter Lent Assizes, he had defended the soldier John Grant, who was indicted (and later executed) for the wilful murder of a little boy of seven years of age.

The person originally hired to conduct Frederick Baker's defence was John Duke Coleridge, one of the leading barristers of his generation. How exactly Baker's solicitor, J. Rand Capron, had managed to secure such a high-flyer to represent his client is not clear. For one thing, Coleridge's fees were eye-watering: if there was one principle that guided Coleridge's work at the

---

79   *Vanity Fair*, 24 May 1873; J.A. Hamilton, 'Mellor, Sir John (1809–1887)'; rev. Sinéad Agnew, *Oxford Dictionary of National Biography* (2004).

80   *Western Morning News*, 21 October 1887.

English Bar it was the desire to make large amounts of money for himself. Unfortunately, Baker's finances were limited to a paltry fighting fund organised by his supporters in Guildford, supplemented by whatever money his father had left after reimbursing the funds that had gone missing at the solicitor's office and possibly paying out hush money to the family of the little girl molested in the chalk pit. Perhaps Sir William Bovill, the Member of Parliament for Guildford and a barrister himself, was able to exert some influence in this regard.[81] But it was all in vain because at the last moment Coleridge found he was double booked at the Court of Arches. He was forced to resign the brief with only days to go before the trial began.[82]

Another possibility is that Coleridge, on reflection, simply declined the brief and returned the fee because he found the case so unpalatable and the defendant so obnoxious.[83] The 'cab-rank rule' whereby a barrister with time on his hands is obliged to accept any case offered him so long as it falls within his area of expertise and the fee is not unreasonable, seems not to have been observed to any great extent in the mid-nineteenth century. Barristers, or more exactly their clerks, were able to pick and choose among the cases offered them. This practice, of course, worked to the detriment of outcasts like Frederick Baker.

Brought in at incredibly short notice, Coleridge's replacement was the Devonshire lawyer Samuel Carter. Coleridge disliked Carter, and Carter disliked Coleridge, and the pair clashed frequently at the Exeter Assizes. 'The man with the silk gown' was how Carter, in his best West Country accent, sneeringly referred to Coleridge. If Coleridge exemplified the continuity of the traditional route into the Bar – Eton and Oxbridge – Carter came to it from quite a different background. Born in Tavistock in 1814, he began his working life as a tanner and maker of saddles. Described as a 'thin, dark, and gloomy figure', he briefly entered Parliament in 1852 as a Radical candidate advocating votes for women and parliamentary reform. While a member of the House he had the courage to vote against the expenditure of public money (£80,000) on the funeral of the Duke of Wellington.

Carter was admitted to the Bar in 1847 and joined the Western Circuit. In 1865 he led for the prosecution in the Torquay Infanticide case which captured unprecedented national headlines,[84] but mostly he was retained as defence

81 Baker had written to Bovill in August 1867 seeking preferment. His letter, which was never actually posted, was read out during the trial.
82 Coleridge was giving evidence to the Royal Commission at the Court of Arches in the City of London in the St Alban's Ritual Case.
83 Although no such qualms prevented him defending Constance Kent in 1865 on a charge of murdering her three-year-old half-brother.
84 Charlotte Winsor was charged with the murder of a child in her care. It was the first case to bring to wide public attention the issue of 'baby-farming'. See Nicola Goc, *Women, Infanticide and the Press, 1822–*

counsel. While he would eventually become a successful Quarter Sessions pleader, he was too rude, too quarrelsome, and far too uncultured ever to achieve prominence in a profession like lawyering ('He does so overflow with kindness and courtesy' was Coleridge's snide assessment).[85] But he nonetheless gained a formidable reputation as an advocate of the poor and the reviled. His political disposition led him always to range himself on the weaker side. He was hard-working and utterly fearless and pertinacious almost to a fault: he once took nearly five hours to defend a man charged with stealing potatoes.[86] Undoubtedly he was a skilful and effective public speaker, a quality he put down partly to his mastery of language acquired while studying and composing poetry.[87] As one courtroom reporter noted, Carter's 'influence with juries was such that he often succeeded in securing the acquittal of a prisoner whose case seemed absolutely hopeless.'[88] Frederick Baker must have been overjoyed to learn that Samuel Carter had agreed to take the brief for his case: if there was anyone who could save his life, it was the lawyer from Tavistock.[89]

*

Baker was brought into court and placed in the dock. The press had made him out to be a monster, a were-creature from the coombs and dark woods – but the truth was, he looked rather plain and dull:

> He is a young man of middle height, and was moderately well dressed in clothes that have seen some wear. His head, borne erectly and with a certain show of defiance, is not of an ordinary type. His features are distinguished by a prominent nose and somewhat receding chin and forehead, characteristics that are rendered the more observable by the fact that the prisoner's long black hair was carefully brushed back. His face was pale and beardless; but there was no particular expression of care or anxiety on his countenance. Neither did he show anything to denote insanity.[90]

1922: News Narratives in England and Australia (Ashgate Publishing, 2013), pp. 80–82.

85   *Life and Correspondence of John Duke Lord Coleridge: Lord Chief Justice of England* (Heinemann 1904), Vol. 1, p. 197.

86   Ibid.

87   Samuel Carter, *Midnight Effusions* (London: Saunders and Otley, 1848), pp. xii–xiii.

88   *Torquay Times and South Devon Advertiser*, 8 January 1904.

89   For a good summary of Carter's life see David Pugsley, 'Samuel Carter, a maverick on the Western Circuit' [online]. Available from westerncircuit.co.uk/history/samuel-carter-a-maverick-on-the-western-circuit [Accessed 15 May 2020].

90   *Glasgow Evening Post*, 7 December 1867. The *Coventry Herald*, 27 December 1867, noted that 'Phrenologically considered, it is reported by those who had means of knowing, that his head was not a bad one: it was deficient in veneration, but not large in animal passion.'

Baker.

The only sign of turmoil was the occasional twitching of his face and hands. Other newspapers remarked on how stout Baker had become. He was podgy around the cheeks and belly but skinny elsewhere. During his three months at Winchester, he had gained nearly four stone. He was allowed a chair during the proceedings.

Montague Bere rose to his feet. He began with some preliminary opening remarks to the jury about trying the case only on the evidence put before them and not on what they may have read in the newspapers. It was an important instruction because all the jurors would have followed the press coverage of the case over the preceding three months, and many of them will have formed preconceived ideas. Baker was entitled to be tried by an impartial jury, but was that even possible in the circumstances?

Mr Bere then outlined in a general way the facts of the case and the evidence he intended to present to them, reminding the jury that the accused party had in fact already 'confessed' to the killing in his diary.

He conceded that much of the evidence he would place before them was not evidence directly of murder – murder was nearly always an act done in secrecy and in darkness with no eye to see the fatal blow. Many a case of murder would go unpunished if a defendant's guilt could only be proved by direct evidence. Rather, he would place before them circumstantial evidence. He explained to the jury that a case based on circumstantial evidence could be just as convincing and reliable as a case based on direct evidence. Moreover, in some respects, circumstantial evidence was even more reliable than direct testimony: taken individually, circumstantial facts were inconclusive, but a chain of circumstantial facts might, by their number and joint operation, be sufficient to constitute conclusive proof. After all, a chain of circumstantial facts coming from several independent witnesses and different sources was less likely to be manufactured. In this way he would show that Baker was

> the last person seen with the child alive, he should show him as having been in the field where the child was killed, he should show him near every place in which parts of the body were found, he should show him to have had blood upon his clothes, he should show that he had been possessed of instruments with which he might have dismembered the body, he should show him to have made such remarks as might indicate his guilt, and then produce the extraordinary entry in the diary, which, if they believed it, was an absolute confession of his guilt.

The prosecution barrister turned next to the question of motive. There is no requirement in English law to determine a defendant's motive, but if the prosecution is able to do so then a jury may be more readily persuaded of the

Introduction.

defendant's guilt. Baker's motive or lack of motive for murdering Fanny Adams would assume immense significance during the trial despite it being technically irrelevant to his guilt.

Mr Bere asserted that Fanny Adams had been abducted for lustful reasons ('for a certain purpose' is how he delicately phrased it). When she resisted and started screaming, Baker murdered her and subsequently destroyed the lower part of her body in order to conceal the sexual offence. It was part of the prosecution's submission that the accused returned to the scene of the crime several hours after the murder specifically to commit acts of mutilation and excision that would hinder discovery of the sexual assault.

The claim that Fanny had been violated before the murder was highly dubious. It must have been Mr Bere's personal view; it certainly wasn't a position supported by any forensic evidence. In his petition to the Home Office, Dr Henry Taylor would later argue that 'The supposition that the body was mutilated in order to conceal the evidence of a minor offence, while no attempt was made to conceal the evidence of the capital crime, is absurd.' As Samuel Carter pointed out in his opening speech for the defence, if the accused sought only to conceal evidence of a sexual assault, why would he cut out the eyes and dismember the entire body and broadcast the deed by scattering the limbs across the hop fields? To put it bluntly, why didn't he simply dig a hole and bury the body?[91]

The sexual assault theory could not be proved one way or the other because the vagina was missing or had not been found, and no semen was found on the prisoner's linen.

Inevitably, the attempt by Mr Bere to adduce a sexual motive for Baker's crime must be seen as prejudicial, tending to inflame adverse jury feelings. In the end, his sexual assault theory obfuscated rather than illuminated the crime. Perhaps, after all, the *Illustrated Police News* was right when it suggested that Baker's appetites were fundamentally those of a beast or a savage wild animal, and that there was no need to search for a more refined explanation. Or perhaps, as Krafft-Ebing would later theorise, there really was a distinctive type of crime known as *lustmord* driven by a morbid erotic interest in the body's interior:

> The presumption of a murder out of lust is always given when injuries of the genitals are found, the character and extent of which are such as could not be explained by merely a brutal attempt at coitus; and, still more, when the body has

---

91   Of course, it was necessary for the defence to refute these claims of sexual assault because their plea of insanity hinged on the motiveless character of the crime.

been opened, or parts (intestines, genitals) torn out and are wanting.[92]

*

Throughout the day a steady stream of witnesses – twenty-five in all – filed into the courtroom at the castle: farm workers and agricultural labourers, solicitors' clerks, police officers, Fanny's parents, and several children. There were few surprises on that first day – mostly it was testimony that had been heard before in the coroner's court or at the committal hearing. But there was one big difference. For the first time since his arrest in August Baker had recourse to a professional defence counsel who could argue points of law in his favour, examine and cross-examine witnesses, call evidence, and make a speech in his defence. These 'rights' were among the most significant reforms in criminal trial procedure during the nineteenth century, and they helped pave the way for the development of adversarial advocacy.[93] To the dismay of many spectators watching the trial on that first day, the balance of advantage would begin to shift ever so slightly towards the defendant.

No one was suggesting that the prosecution witnesses were lying or that they were hostile or unintelligent or lacked credence. Mr Carter's cross-examination method was far subtler than that: he adopted a courteous, almost a conversational tone of voice, probing gently at inconsistencies and contradictions and improbabilities and uncertainties. It happened often that witnesses took to the stand to relate a certain version of events, only for them to concede under cross-examination that they might have been mistaken or that their memory may have been at fault or that they were confusing one incident with another.

Eliza White, for example, testified that she had seen the three girls playing with Baker in Flood Meadows on the day of the murder, but Carter wanted to know if she might be mixing up her days. Hadn't she seen Baker and the children exactly one week earlier on 17 August? She thought Baker had been puffing away on a pipe or a cigar – she couldn't say which – but no other witness saw him smoking that afternoon. She said she first saw Baker around two o'clock and she watched him for nearly a quarter of an hour; but a different witness, William Allwork, testified to seeing Baker at two o'clock exactly in a different place. She admitted that the child's cry she heard coming from the hop

---

92   Richard von Krafft-Ebing, *Psychopathia Sexualis: A Medico-Legal Study*, 7th ed, trans. Charles G. Chaddock (London: F.J. Rebman, 1894, p. 398). Anil Aggrawal classifies both Baker and Jack the Ripper as class IXa necrophiles who kill and then mutilate the body to have sexual orgasm. *Necrophilia: Forensic and Medico-Legal Aspects* (CRC Press, 2011), pp. 73–74.

93   See David J.A. Cairns, *Advocacy and the Making of the Adversarial Criminal Trial 1800–1865* (Oxford: Clarendon Press, 1999).

garden wasn't the fearful scream of a child in peril – it was a cry made in play and so innocuous she thought nothing more of it and made her way home. Yet according to Mr Bere, Fanny's scream was so loud and so obviously the sound of a child in distress that it panicked Baker into murdering his victim.

And so it continued. George Noyce, the under-shepherd, was the proud owner of a watch, so he could specify the time exactly as two minutes past three when he met the prisoner on the footway heading towards the hop garden; yet Maurice Biddle, the junior clerk at Clements, remembered Baker being in the office at around twenty-five past three. They couldn't both be right; one of them must be mistaken, and if they were mistaken about this particular point in their evidence, they could be mistaken about other things as well.

But naturally it was the child witnesses who fared least well under Mr Carter's cross-examination. Seven-year-old Alfred Vince was a brand new witness. He hadn't appeared at the inquest or the committal, and he had a ghoulish, bloodcurdling tale to tell. He told the court how he had seen the defendant washing his blood-stained hands in the river Wey. 'I saw his hands were red but they were white afterwards.' The man shook his fist at Alfred and ran towards him, presumably intent on killing him. Alfred scarpered, and it was only because he bumped into Mrs Gardener and Emma Smith walking towards Flood Meadows along Tanhouse Lane that he was alive to tell the tale.[94]

Mr Carter suspected that Alfred's testimony had been learnt by heart and that most of it was a fiction. No one else remembered a little boy running for his life, not even Mrs Gardener and Emma Smith. And besides, he seemed an odious child: despite his traumatic experience on the riverbank, he'd hadn't been swayed from venturing up to the hop grounds that evening while the search was underway for Fanny. 'I saw the head and leg part of a child,' he crowed to the jury.

But Mr Carter had the last word. In November, Alfred had been taken to Winchester Gaol to identify the prisoner in a line-up. Although Baker was standing a little way apart from the others, and was the only person wearing a high hat, Alfred failed to identify him. However, at a second line-up his mother was there to lend a hand; Mr Carter elicited from Alfred that 'when my mother gave me a nudge, I said that was the man'. Mr Carter sat down, purring with delight.

Frederick Baker, too, was starting to enjoy himself. Being on trial for murder wasn't quite as bad as people made out. He was seen smiling on several

---

94   A scrambled version of this dubious story had already been reported in the *Chichester Express*: 'It is related that a fortnight ago [August 20] the prisoner accosted a lady in a secluded pathway in Alton, and made improper overtures to her. These she resisted, and ran away. The prisoner, not succeeding in overtaking her, pelted her with stones.' (*Chichester Express and West Sussex Journal*, 3 September 1867.)

Baker.

occasions, and during the cross-examination of Mrs Gardener he actually laughed out loud in mockery at her histrionic performance in the witness box. But he was devious enough to assume a 'concerned and careworn' demeanour when witnesses spoke of the terrible state of Fanny's body. Remarkably, his facial tics and the twitching of his hands had all but disappeared.[95]

As the day wore on, the case for the prosecution looked increasingly shaky. Mrs Adams conceded there were discrepancies between her inquest testimony and her evidence at the trial; Superintendent Cheyney was chastised by the judge for unlawfully attempting to entrap Baker into incriminating himself; Constable Watkins was shown to be a remarkably unobservant police officer – on the day of the arrest he hadn't noticed if Baker's boots were dirty or clean, or even if his clothes were dry or soaking wet or splattered in blood.

The only witness placing the prisoner in the neighbourhood of the hop garden at the time of the murder was Fanny's playmate, Minnie Warner. But Minnie's evidence was flawed in so many respects – even Mr Bere in his opening address had cautioned the jury about accepting her testimony in full. When she volunteered to Mr Bere that she had played with the prisoner from two till four o'clock, and that the church clock struck four when Fanny was being carried away by Baker – two hours, that is, *after* the murder took place – the prosecution case looked almost lost.

The prospect of giving evidence at the old stone castle must have been daunting to a small girl. Did she think if she gave the wrong answers she might be locked up in the dungeons without food? Did she imagine there might be dark spiral staircases and windy battlements off which people were thrown to their deaths? One report suggests Minnie was given a doll to comfort her while giving evidence at Winchester.[96] It may have been a gift from one of the women at the London Missionary Society who travelled around the Hampshire hop gardens tending to the spiritual wellbeing of the pickers. But working-class Victorian girls rarely spent time playing with dolls – there were plenty of real-life babies that needed looking after if they wanted to practice their childcare skills. Toying with the doll, Minnie may have discovered it only needed a couple of twists to remove the head completely from its socket.

*

By six o'clock in the evening Mr Justice Mellor was flagging. He felt 'quite

95   *Hampshire Independent*, 7 December 1867.
96   See Peter Cansfield, *Sweet FA: The Story of Fanny Adams* (Alton: Peter Cansfield Associates, 2nd edn, 2000), p. 52. The doll was described by Minnie Warner's great granddaughter as 'very grand and more expensive than the family could afford'.

exhausted' and complained that his arm was aching from taking down all the evidence. He therefore adjourned the court till the next day. Addressing the jury, he told them everything would be done to ensure their comfort overnight, and he issued the usual cautions to them about refraining from discussing the case.

While the jury may have been well cared for under the sheriff's watch, ensconced as they were at the George Hotel on Jewry Street and feasting on a substantial breakfast of eggs and roasted mushrooms, complaints were brewing among the trial witnesses. Minnie Warner and her father had to travel by rail to Winchester on Monday morning; they then had to sit around for three days in the freezing cold Great Hall until Minnie was called to give evidence. Finally, they weren't allowed to return home till the Saturday. And Mr Warner subsequently discovered that only Minnie's expenses were allowed, and none for himself.[97]

XIII.

The trial went into a second day. A few minutes before half-past nine, the doors were thrown open and again there was a mad dash. Women were by far the most unruly, elbowing each other in the ribs and sending hats flying. Within minutes the courtroom was densely packed. Two or three extra chairs for reporters had been positioned next to the jury enclosure at the front of the court, but still there was not enough seating to go round. Some members of the press were consequently allotted to the dock where they sat alongside the accused; the representative of the Southampton-based *Hampshire Independent* covered the second day of the trial from inside the witness box, having initially been ordered to sit in the second row of the spectators.[98] At the back of the room, and in the gangways, spectators were crammed into every conceivable space. Outside, a large crowd surrounded the hall and lined the road for some distance down Castle Hill. Captain John Forrest, the long-serving chief constable of Hampshire, had turned up in person to supervise the police arrangements.

Baker was brought up from the holding cells, flanked by two warders. The cuffs were removed. He opened and shut his hands rapidly to restore the circulation. When he raised his face to look around the court, he was like some wild creature lifting its head from a meadow stream, nostrils upturned as if scenting children at play.

One of the first witnesses to be summoned that day, at the request of the defence although appearing as a witness for the Crown, was attorney's clerk Frederick French. He had been employed at Clements for nearly thirty years

---

97   *The Times*, 9 January 1868.
98   *Southern Evening Echo*, 22 April 1987.

since leaving school at fourteen.[99] While he didn't have much to say that was material to the murder charge, his evidence was revealing for its depiction of life in a small town solicitor's office in the 1860s. Most solicitors' offices, even those outside London, were open from 9am to 8pm on Monday to Friday, and from 10am to 9pm on Saturday. At Clements at least one clerk needed to be present in the office at all times during the working day; apart from this, staff appeared to have the freedom to come and go pretty much as they liked. Presumably so long as they completed their allotted work in a timely fashion, there was flexibility over the hours they spent in the office. Yet there were clearly discipline problems at Clements solicitors, and a lack of proper supervision of staff. A timetable of Baker's last working day can be pieced together from the trial statements and other sources:

10.00	Baker arrives at the office already partly intoxicated
11.00–11.15	in the Swan/flirting with barmaid
12.15–12.45	in the Swan
13.10–15.15	at lunch/murders Fanny Adams
15.15–16.30	does some work
16.30–17.50	returns to crime scene to mutilate body
17.50–18.45	in the office/cleans penknife/makes diary entry
18.45–19.55	in the Swan
19.55–20.00	at grocery/chemist shop
20.00–21.00	arrested in office

Baker's last action at W. & J.W. Clement and Son was to falsify a daily timesheet claiming eleven hours' work.

It wasn't immediately apparent why Samuel Carter had called French as a witness. His testimony was guarded and prevaricating at times: he couldn't remember this and he had no recollection of that, and he couldn't say one way or the other if something had happened or not – 'I cannot recollect that he was there, but I would not swear that he was not.' But he did recall that Baker had once suffered a nosebleed in the office. The significance of this incident would become clear during the cross-examination of the next witness.

Professor Alfred Swaine Taylor (1806–1880) was perhaps the foremost medical jurist of his day. He was professor of medical jurisprudence, toxicology and chemistry at Guy's Hospital in London. His *Manual of Medical Jurisprudence*, first published in 1844, was a landmark work, and in 1865 he published the first edition of his monumental *Principles and Practice of Medical*

---

99 French lived on Alton High Street. In the 1871 census his immediate neighbour is listed as William Allwork, the cricket bat maker, who also gave evidence at the trial.

Introduction.

Jurisprudence, widely considered the most comprehensive and authoritative reference manual on the subject in its day. Toxicology was his specialism, and he had appeared for the prosecution at the trials of many high-profile celebrity poisoners such as Dr William Palmer (1856)[100] and Dr Thomas Smethurst (1859).[101]

A week after Fanny's murder, on 31 August, Superintendent Cheyney had taken some items of clothing to Guy's Hospital for forensic examination by Professor Taylor. One bundle contained the garments worn by Baker – a black cloth coat, a pair of woollen trousers, a waistcoat, a cotton shirt, and a pair of socks; a second bundle contained shreds of the dress, petticoats and stockings worn by Fanny. In a third parcel was a rock believed to be the murder weapon, and the two pocket knives found on Baker's person when he was searched at the office.

For an expert witness hired by the prosecution, Professor Taylor's evidence was considerably less compelling in places than Mr Bere might have wished. The quantities of blood on the outer surface of Baker's clothing were almost unnoticeable, the professor said, although that was to be expected if Fanny's body had been cut up an hour or so after death – at the instant of death blood ceases to circulate in the arteries, so there would be no spurting from cutting. Under cross-examination he agreed with Mr Carter that a nosebleed might very well account for the marks of blood found on the wristbands of the prisoner's shirt, but he dismissed out of hand the notion that the stains were caused by red office ink. It was even possible, he added, that the blood stains actually pre-dated the murder. Where the prisoner had attempted to soak out blood from the front of his trousers by wading in the river, there was a large area of reddish staining that had diffused into the calico lining.[102]

Taylor had also tested the trousers for the presence of 'marks of intercourse' (i.e. semen) but he found nothing conclusive. Equally, his examination of the two knives detected only a slight smear of blood on one of the blades which might easily have been caused by 'cutting up a beef-steak or mutton-chop'. Images of Baker's ogre-like carnivorous appetites in the Angel Hotel may well have flashed through the minds of the jurymen at this point. Taylor concluded that neither weapon could possibly have been used in the dismemberment and evisceration of the child's body. Replying to a question from Carter, he estimated that even with a proper sharp implement like a kitchen knife it would still have taken an inexperienced person around thirty minutes to cut up the body.[103] Of

---

100   See *Trial of William Palmer* [NBT 15].
101   See *Trial of Thomas Smethurst* [NBT 53].
102   See Appendix A.9.
103   One report suggests that Baker had an interest in comparative anatomy, and had made 'terrible use' of his

course, the point being made here by the defence was that Baker lacked the opportunity to dismember the body: according to one witness Baker left the office at half-past four in the afternoon while a second witness reported him taking a gentle country walk through the churchyard shortly after five o'clock – that didn't leave much time for butchering.

Turning next to Fanny's garments, the professor had little to report – yes, there was evidence of recent blood staining on them, but he could not state categorically that the blood was human in origin, only that it was mammalian.

It was in his capacity as an analytical chemist that Professor Taylor was primarily called to give evidence at the trial. He proved a very convincing witness in the sense that he delivered his testimony in a clear, audible voice free from technical jargon and exaggerated language. Although he had visited the psychiatric wards at La Salpêtrière hospital during his medical training in Paris in the 1830s and had written about the legal and forensic aspects of insanity and homicide in his *Principles and Practice of Medical Jurisprudence*, he was not himself an alienist or a 'psychiatrist' or an asylum physician. Therefore, he may have been slightly surprised when Mr Carter shifted direction and began cross-examining him on Baker's mental health.

Samuel Carter wanted to know if the heinous nature of the murder (by which he meant its singular and elaborate cruelty) might not in itself be proof of the perpetrator's insanity. Instantly, Mr Bere jumped to his feet, unhappy with this line of questioning, and the Judge agreed with him. In Mr Justice Mellor's view – and that's all it was, the personal view of the Judge – the magnitude of a crime should never be taken as evidence of the perpetrator's insanity; terrible, heinous acts could be committed by people who were completely sane. The objection was sustained.[104]

The cross-examination continued. Taylor described to the court a disorder called 'homicidal mania'. First identified earlier in the century by the French psychiatrist Jean-Etienne Esquirol, it was a diagnosis that came up frequently in the courtrooms of Victorian England. In their textbook *A Manual of Psychological Medicine* (1858), John Bucknill and Daniel Tuke cited over forty cases of 'this most remarkable disorder'. Taylor gave a brief summary of the disorder's chief characteristics:

---

knowledge while disarticulating his victim. *Police News Edition of the Life and Examination of Frederick Baker* (1867), p. 3.

104 Had Professor Taylor been allowed to answer the question, he will likely have concurred with Mr Justice Mellor: in *Principles and Practice of Medical Jurisprudence*, he stated 'I agree with a medico-legal writer on this subject [Jamieson], that "no hideousness of depravity can amount to proof of insanity, unsupported by some evidence of a judgment incapacitated, or of a will fettered by disease".' (Vol 2, 2nd edition), p. 570.

Introduction.

The symptoms are that violence is committed by a person on a sudden impulse, and very often on persons to whom the perpetrator is devotedly attached, typically the mother or some near relative. In these cases there is generally no premeditation and no attempt to deny the crime or conceal the deed – rather, there is an attempt by the perpetrator to justify or glorify their act under some delusion, or to ascribe it to God. As a rule, persons suffering from this disease are perfectly indifferent to punishment or consequences, and never deny the act. Sometimes they display no incapacity of intellect. There are cases on record in which such mania is exhibited with no previous indication of insanity.

What this meant was that rational and responsible persons with no intellectual defects might nonetheless be suffering from a form of insanity that caused them to behave violently. However, in conclusion, Professor Taylor expressed the opinion that many of the leading symptoms observable in cases of homicidal mania were absent in Baker's case. Persons suffering from this disorder generally made no attempt to conceal the crime, he said. 'I should look with suspicion on any case where this was not a symptom.'

The final witness for the prosecution was Dr Louis Leslie, who gave details of the results of the post mortem examination. His image of Frederick Baker with his shirt sleeves rolled up, kneeling over the still-warm body and scooping out the contents of the chest and pelvis with his bare hands, was unforgettably gruesome. He flatly refuted any suggestion that the dismemberments were the work of a man with anatomical knowledge – the perpetrator had abandoned an attempt at disarticulation around the joint of the right leg and had literally torn the limb from the body, he said. The young doctor (he was in his mid forties) had grown up in the Scottish Highlands and was familiar with the operation of gralloching or removing the entrails of hunted game: he felt confident enough to contradict the evidence of Professor Taylor as to the time needed to cut up the body – ten minutes to remove the head, he declared with grim precision, and fifty minutes to complete the dismemberment and evisceration. Furthermore, he was convinced that some of the mutilations had taken place within half an hour of death, not sixty minutes afterwards as Mr Bere had posited in his opening address. If correct, then whoever had murdered Fanny had apparently returned to the scene of the crime to commit a second round of mutilations on a corpse that was already horribly ravaged and disfigured.

Baker's 'second round of mutilations', including the excision of the genitalia, may have been motivated by lust/sexual desire. In contrast, the removal of the eyes may have been prompted in part by a superstitious fear of being caught. In the 1860s it was believed by some people that photographing the eyes of a murdered person would reveal the image of the killer imprinted on the retina (in the same way that the eye of a slaughtered calf supposedly retained an image of the tiles of the abattoir floor). According to this theory, as put forward in *The Life and Examination of Frederick Baker*, the eyes were removed to impede identification of the perpetrator:

> There can be little doubt about his having the eyes of his poor innocent little victim in his pocket at the time of his leaving the hop-field as they were afterwards picked up in an adjoining field. Doubtless he had taken them out in consequence of the statement which has been made on more than one occasion that the face of the murderer of any one may be found reflected in the eyes of the murdered person.[105]

Whatever the motive behind these mutilations, they were committed in a cold, dispassionate manner without hesitation, revulsion, or remorse.

XIV.

Samuel Carter came to Winchester with a reputation as a firebrand and a maverick, unafraid to confront judges and eager to pick fights with opposing counsel, yet his conduct during the Baker trial was decorous at all times. With a man's life at stake, he must have known it wasn't the time or the place for courtroom antics. He seemed well prepared and in command of his brief, despite having taken on the case just hours before trial commenced.

The case for the defence opened after lunch on the second day. Mr Carter began by telling the jury that the evidence against his client was contradictory and unsatisfactory. Here was a man who was supposed to have committed one of the most depraved and gruesome murders in living memory, yet not a single witness could honestly say that Baker had behaved oddly or out of character that afternoon. 'The blood of this tragedy must have gushed out in streams from the child's body,' exclaimed Mr Carter (conveniently disregarding Professor's Taylor caveat about spurting arterial blood), but there were no witnesses who could say they had seen bloodstains on the prisoner's clothing. Witnesses had him here, there, and everywhere at the same time, or nearly so. Or they were mistaken as to the date and time of the defendant's movements. Or they had been coached by their mother. The meadows and hop gardens were swarming with labourers that Saturday afternoon, yet none of them had seen or heard anything suspicious.

---

105 *Police News Edition of the Life and Examination of Frederick Baker* (1867), p. 3. The eyes were afterwards found in the river Wey, not in an adjoining field.

Introduction.

The offence was also unaccountable and inexplicable, he said. There was no adequate motive for it. The supposed tools of butchery were knives more commonly used to sharpen quills and slice open envelopes! The prisoner scarcely had the opportunity to commit such a monstrous crime, and he had always indefatigably denied the charge.

Carter had been speaking to the court for an hour and a half. Possibly he had already sown 'reasonable doubt' in the minds of the jurors. Perhaps, if he had concluded his defence at this point, he may have sensationally secured an acquittal. But he pressed on, catastrophically, with a second line of defence. He was like one of those black shire horses trudging across a ploughed field in rural Hampshire, unable to stop. Even if he came close to securing Baker's acquittal, the truth is that his actions inadvertently helped send his client to the gallows.

Thus far his defence relied wholly on the lack of evidence connecting Baker to the murder charge. His client should be acquitted because there was no evidence to convict him. But now he put forward a second defence. If, after hearing all his arguments, the jury still believed that Baker was guilty of murder, then he contended his client was insane and should be consigned to a lunatic asylum. He was at pains to point out to the jury that incarceration in a lunatic asylum was definitely not an escape from justice. 'No,' he emphasised, 'it was placing a person in a living tomb. It was a shutting out from all hopes and pleasures. No more pleasant walks in the countryside. He hardly knew whether death was not preferable.' It seems Baker broke down at this point, and sobbed into his hands. He did not cry out of remorse or from regret at the heartbreak he had caused the Adams family. He wept only for himself at the thought of being shut up in a lunatic asylum for the rest of his life.

As a criminal defence strategy it was high-risk. The jury must have wondered what on earth was going on: was counsel for the defence saying Baker was innocent and sane, or was he arguing that Baker was guilty and mad? In fact, the form of Carter's second defence was that Baker was 'not guilty by reason of insanity'. This special verdict had been available since 1800 following James Hadfield's attempted assassination of King George III at the Drury Lane Theatre. It was always accompanied by the stipulation that the accused party be detained 'at Her Majesty's pleasure' in a lunatic asylum.[106] Carter himself admitted to the jury that the case for the defence was 'unfavourably affected' by this twofold aspect; it would be 'less difficult and embarrassing to him,' he told them, '[if he] could confine himself to one line of defence.' Presumably, Carter must have felt he had sufficient proof of Baker's madness to also raise a plea of insanity. Therefore, even though he risked confusing the jury, he opted

---

106   The Trial of Lunatics Act 1883 would later allow juries to return a verdict of guilty but insane.

to double his client's chances of acquittal by presenting two defences in court.

It would probably have made a safer defence if Carter had admitted guilt at the outset and then pleaded lunacy, or simply stuck to his original defence that Baker was innocent. But the attempt to run both defences side by side at one and the same time was fatal: to argue that Baker was insane, Carter needed to cast doubt on the arguments he had already put forward to support the contention that Baker was innocent; to argue that Baker was innocent, he needed to convince the jury that the plea of insanity was unfounded. You couldn't have it both ways.

As it was, Carter effectively sabotaged his own defence argument, which he had plausibly and competently placed before the jury during the first part of the trial. But more damagingly, the plea for insanity was rushed through at the end in a superficial manner. It was neither sufficiently urged by Carter, nor sufficiently supported by skilled and expert witnesses, and for this reason we can reasonably presume it was insufficiently considered by the jury when the time came for them to deliberate on their verdict.

In the end it all came down to finances. Baker's defence fund was exhausted, and his father's savings were all gone. There was no money left to cover the expenses of partisan expert witnesses who might have testified with authority to Baker's insanity. So, instead of experts on mental illness and professional men familiar with the dark terrain of lunacy and homicide, Carter had to make do with Baker's relatives and other lay persons. He called several witnesses – the prisoner's father and sister, two bricklayers from Guildford, and Baker's landlady in Alton – and they all duly testified that Baker had been despondent, suicidal, disappointed in love, and 'out of his mind' in the weeks and days leading up to the murder. The jury were taken on a bleak journey into Baker's past – his childhood illnesses, his troubled adolescence, the poor judgments and strange behaviours that characterised his adult years. But was it enough to justify acquitting Baker on the grounds of insanity? Could it truly be said he was not legally responsible for his actions at the time of the murder? Was there really any evidence of homicidal mania?

The legal burden of proof rested with Mr Carter; it was for the defence to prove that Baker was insane, rather than for the prosecution to prove that he was not. The insanity defence was essentially a legal concept, not a medical one. In order to establish a defence on the ground of insanity, Carter needed to prove that, at the time of murdering Fanny Adams, Frederick Baker was suffering from a 'defect of reason', caused by a 'disease of the mind', that rendered him incapable of understanding the nature and quality of his act, or, if he did understand it, that he was incapable of distinguishing right from wrong.[107] Crucially, the case was not proved if the prosecution could show that

Introduction.

Baker knew what he was doing at the time of the offence and that he knew it was wrong. Up until the 1880s, physicians and family GPs were still viewed as the *de facto* experts on mental illness even if they lacked formal training or clinical experience. For this reason, the final two witnesses brought forward by Mr Carter, both medical men, offered perhaps his best hope of proving the insanity defence.

Dr William Curtis was a surgeon living in Alton. His father, another William Curtis, had been Jane Austen's medical attendant – her 'Alton Apothecary' – when she lived in Chawton. For many years William Jnr had been physician to William Trimmer Row, Frederick's uncle. Based on his close and continuous knowledge of that family's history he was able to describe to the jury the mental and nervous infirmities of Baker's cousin. A shiver went round the courtroom when Curtis revealed that Baker had a near relative who was currently confined in a lunatic asylum suffering from homicidal mania.

The afternoon was drawing on. Clerks went round the courtroom igniting the gas lights. In their sickly glow Frederick Baker looked even more corpse-like than usual. It was entirely fitting that the globes should come on just then, at the end of William Curtis's testimony, for there had been a gothic intensity to his account of family madness and homicidal mania. He had touched on Victorian fears of hereditary degeneracy and of derangement and criminality passed on down the line, from parents to son, from uncle to nephew, between cousins. Perhaps for the first time during the two-day trial, the jury sensed the darkness edging in from the borderlands of insanity.

Samuel Carter also called surgeon Dr Henry Sharp Taylor to the stand. Henry Taylor had attended the Baker family since Frederick was a boy, and with the exception of his father there was probably no one alive with greater knowledge of the prisoner's mental history and constitution than the Guildford physician. As Quakers, both Dr Taylor and Dr Curtis took the option of affirming rather than swearing an oath. Dr Taylor spoke in detail of Frederick's unhappy upbringing, his mother's nervous frailties, and his father's paranoia and manic episodes. His concluding assessment was that the prisoner was weak-minded, and that this affliction would be exacerbated by the family taint of insanity.

And on that note, Baker's defence came to a close. It was only with the passing of the Criminal Evidence Act in 1898 that defendants at trial were allowed to give evidence on their own behalf. Until then, they had to remain mute in court. One imagines, though, that even if Samuel Carter had been given

---

107 This is the celebrated McNaghten formulation, which provided the legal test for insanity from 1843 onwards.

the option of calling Baker into the witness box, the instructing solicitor, J. Rand Capron, will have advised Carter against that course of action. Their client's callous demeanour, his chilling lack of affect, and his array of facial tics and werewolf growlings will surely have alienated the jury, and an experienced barrister like Mr Bere would pick him apart under cross-examination.

Given the limited resources at his disposal and the lack of time available for him to prepare the case, Mr Carter had done the best he could in the circumstances. Even Mr Justice Mellor would compliment him on 'discharging his duty with great zeal and with very considerable skill'. He had uncovered many weaknesses in the prosecution case, and he had demonstrated insanity in Baker's lineal and collateral relatives. He had shown the jury a man disappointed in love, a man on the verge of suicide, in despair, prone to crying fits. He had shown them an innocent man and a guilty man, a man who was sane and not sane. A man who was part human and part beast.

That his twofold defence strategy was a serious error of judgment cannot be doubted, yet who can blame him for trying absolutely everything in his power to secure the best outcome for his client.

*

Mr Bere rose briefly to make a few closing remarks for the prosecution. He conceded that the timings he had suggested for the crime may have been slightly out, but that on all other matters the case had been substantially proved. He brought up the diary again, reminding the jury that the entry confessing to murder, in Baker's handwriting, had been made *before* the body of Fanny Adams was discovered. And then there were Baker's comments to Biddle in the Swan Tap (again made *before* the body was found) when the accused had said it would be 'awkward' for him if anything had happened to the missing child.

He dismissed outright the second line of Carter's defence, namely that Baker was insane and therefore not legally responsible for his actions. There was absolutely no evidence to support such a claim, he said. The prisoner had been continuously observed for three months while on remand at Winchester Gaol without giving any indication of insanity,[108] and his actions on the day of the murder and afterwards were inconsistent with many of the chief symptoms of homicidal mania as described by Professor Taylor.

*

108 Although this evidence had not been adduced in the record of the trial.

Introduction.

It was getting on for six o'clock when Mr Justice Mellor finally began his summing up. Late-night sittings were still quite common at the assizes right up to the end of the nineteenth century, but the Judge will have been keen to bring the trial to a close that second evening.

He began by declaring that this was one of the most 'remarkable cases' he had ever had to try. So much depended, he said, on what was termed 'presumptive evidence', that is to say on the conduct and statements supposedly made by the prisoner. He told the jury they should not be influenced by Mr Carter's observations on the rights or wrongs of capital punishment – the penalty assigned for the offence of murder was laid down in law, and it was not a matter that need concern them. They must discharge their duty 'within the bounds of the law and the limits of the evidence'.

The judge then turned to the question of insanity, explaining to the jury that an acquittal on the ground of insanity did not mean the prisoner was evading justice. It was not a loophole. It meant being detained in a criminal lunatic asylum during Her Majesty's pleasure. It was therefore a serious matter, and he warned the jury that the plea of insanity needed to be 'clearly proved' before they returned such a verdict.

But what did 'clearly proved' mean? The jury will have looked to Mr Justice Mellor to clarify the nature and scope of the insanity defence and to provide guidance on the criteria for determining criminal and legal responsibility. The Judge was meticulous in explaining to the jury that they needed to frame their deliberations within the legal test for insanity as set down in the McNaghten rules. Beyond that, all he could tell them was that disappointment in love did not create homicidal maniacs. Getting excited by drink wasn't lunacy. An act of atrocity was not, by itself, in his opinion, an indication of madness. The most he could say was that he felt the jury needed to have evidence of 'diseased intellect' or 'hereditary disease of the brain' before they could bring in a verdict of not guilty on the ground of insanity.[109]

The narrow legal test for insanity prescribed by the McNaghten rules, which focused on intellectual impairment and reaffirmed the primacy of reason, effectively doomed Baker to the gallows. Professor Alfred Swaine Taylor was the only witness in court who had spoken with authority on mental disorder, and he had expressed the view that people suffering from 'homicidal mania' did not always exhibit cognitive impairment nor did they necessarily show any signs of hereditary disease of the brain. Homicidal mania was very much a form of 'moral insanity' that might leave the intellectual faculties untouched. But

---

109 The standard medical authority for the view that insanity was brain disease was John Bucknill and Daniel Tuke, *A Manual of Psychological Medicine* (London: John Churchill, 1858).

individuals like Baker who were competently running the affairs of their life (paying rent, working in an office) and who generally exhibited a rational and organized mind, were always going to struggle to convince a McNaghten jury they suffered from emotional lesions and temporary loss of reason.

The judge did direct the jury to treat the two lines of defence as essentially separate and not allow one to reinforce the other. If the jury felt there was insufficient evidence to convict the prisoner, Baker should be acquitted at once without reference to the 'homicidal mania' presumption; if the jury felt Baker was the murderer of Fanny Adams and responsible for his actions, they should find him guilty; if the jury felt Baker was the murderer of Fanny Adams but not responsible for his actions, then he should be found not guilty but insane. What couldn't be allowed was a compromise between the two defences whereby Baker was pronounced insane but innocent.

*

At five minutes past seven, the jurors retired to consider their verdict. They took Baker's diary with them. Twenty minutes later they were back with a unanimous verdict: guilty.

Asked by the Clerk of Arraigns if he had anything to say, the prisoner remained silent. He stood calmly in the dock, clutching his hands in front of him. One of his eyelids was twitching, and the corner of the lip on the same side lifted up and down in time with it, pulling away from the rotten teeth. Mr Justice Mellor put on the black cap and began intoning the sentence of death. Baker 'heard his doom without any signs of emotion, and walked from the dock quite unconcernedly.'[110] The gas lights were turned down and the hall fell empty.

XV.

Baker was taken back to Winchester. He was divested of all his civilian clothes, scrubbed naked in front of the reception officers, given a rough convict uniform, and incarcerated in one of the condemned cells.

Winchester Gaol was opened in 1849 to replace the old county gaol on Jewry Street. There were 400 cells in total, arranged in five wings radiating from a central ventilation tower. In December 1867 it held a daily average of 289 inmates.[111] Debtors were housed in a separate outbuilding. Two or three

110   *Western Daily Mail*, 9 December 1867.
111   *Hampshire Telegraph*, 28 December 1867.

Introduction.

cells at any one time were reserved for prisoners awaiting execution.

In the early 1860s Winchester had gained the reputation as a lax and rather undisciplined place. Convicts were being molly-coddled, it was alleged; they slept for ten hours a days in comfortably warm and well-ventilated cells, they were overfed, they took open-air exercise, and they enjoyed luxuries like footstools, armchairs, cigars and waistcoats.[112] Penal reformers like Henry Herbert, the 4th Earl of Carnarvon, campaigned ferociously for harsher conditions in English prisons, and a return to a more punitive, repressive regime.[113] His ideas were partly implemented with the passing of the Prisons Act 1865. By the time Baker arrived at Winchester, prisoners condemned to hard-labour worked eight hours a day on the treadwheel and two at picking oakum (separating tangled strands of tarred rope). Sleeping arrangements were a plank on the floor with some bedding, upgraded to a hammock for well-behaved and diligent convicts. Each cell had its own dim shaded gas burner high up on the wall; there was an earthenware water-closet, a water-tank and a wash-basin, a stool and a small table.

Prisoners awaiting execution were exempt from working. Their time was spent in solitary confinement reflecting on their moral wretchedness, contemplating their imminent fate, and making peace with God. In the cell door there was an eyelet-hole through which the prisoner could be continually observed from without.

On Saturday morning, 7 December, Baker was visited in his cell by Mr W.H. Sloane-Stanley, the High Sheriff of Hampshire, and the Rev. Christopher Bowen, rector of St Thomas's Church, Winchester. He was told that the date of his execution had been fixed for Tuesday, 24 December, at eight o'clock in the morning.

*

The trial and conviction of Frederick Baker was reported in great detail in the national and provincial newspapers. The *Illustrated Police News* rushed out a special 16-page commemorative edition of *The Trial and Condemnation of Frederick Baker*, which went on sale on 14 December. Local journals such as the *Hampshire Telegraph* and the *Hampshire Chronicle* devoted many densely packed columns to proceedings at the Winchester trial.

While Baker was adjusting to life in the condemned cell, the press reflected on

---

112   Seán McConville, *English Local Prisons, 1860–1900: Next Only to Death* (London: Routledge, 1995), p. 69.

113   At school Henry Herbert was known as 'Twitters' on account of his facial tics, which appear to have been significantly more pronounced than those of Frederick Baker.

his crime and punishment. As a rule, the newspapers steered clear of discussing wider social issues such as child safety and the sexual abuse of children; instead, they focused on Baker's personality and on his supposed motivations. Typical of the media reaction was this piece from the *Western Times*:

> One of the most atrocious murderers the world ever heard of was tried last week at the Winchester Winter Assizes... The perpetrator of such an unnatural crime should have been born and bred in central Fiji, among the savages who the other week killed and ate seven missionaries—naked of body, dark of mind, with the heart of a fiend. He should have worn the most hideous form that ever lodged a human soul; he should have been one who had grown grey in the practice of brutal butcheries of his species. Instead, however, of being a monster of such hideous mien, there stood before the court a young man of pale and beardless face, of middle height, his long black hair brushed smoothly back, his pale features prominent, head and chin receding... He inspires no terror, he excites no disgust. You find he is no ignorant country boor, no rough out of some city slums, no hardened digger from the entrails of the earth, no swearing blustering son of the sea, but a well-conducted member of that respectably educated class of the community, the attorney's clerk.[114]

A favourite theme was the notion of Baker as a brute or a wild beast seized with ferocious, uncontrollable and savage animal passions. Such explanations drew on Cesare Lombroso's theories of atavism and constitutional criminality that depicted offenders as evolutionarily backward individuals closer to primitive animals than normal citizens.[115] The wild beast notion often shaded into ideas about vampires and werewolves:

> The motives which could have impelled him to imbrue his hands in the blood of this innocent child we can but dimly guess at. For the sake of her relatives, we would fain hope with the learned judge who tried the case, that the theory of the prosecution is unfounded, though in that case we must fall back on the supposition that he allowed himself to cherish a sort of rabies, such as an old German legend says at times enters into depraved and cruel souls, by a species of lupine metempsychosis.[116]

*

114 *Western Times*, 10 December 1867. The cannibal incident refers to the supposed massacre in November 1867 of the Rev. Thomas Baker, the Wesleyan missionary, and six native teachers, by a tribe of 'the vilest cannibals' in the mountainous Korobluvu region of Fiji.

115 Anthony M. Platt, 'The Origins and Development of the "Wild Beast" Concept of Mental Illness and Its Relation to Theories of Criminal Responsibility', *Issues in Criminology* Vol. 1 No. 1, 1965, pp. 14–15.

116 *London Evening Standard*, 9 December 1867.

Introduction.

Quick off the mark as always, on 11 December Madame Tussaud's announced that a full-length portrait model of Frederick Baker, taken from life, had been added to the Chamber of Horrors. Children under ten were admitted for 6d.[117]

XVI.

Opposition to capital punishment had been steadily growing in Britain since the 1840s. Between 1840 and 1866 there were nine Parliamentary debates on measures to abolish the death penalty. Reform of a kind came in 1868 with the passing of the Capital Punishment Amendment Act, which put an end to executions in public.[118] But with executions retreating behind prison walls to become private events witnessed only by a few select representatives of the State, the abolitionist cause lost some of its momentum. Another century would pass before the death penalty was finally ended.

Throughout the 1860s there was a hardening of public attitude toward crime, and a reaction against what was viewed in some quarters as morbid sentimentality and sympathy for murderers. Nevertheless, it was inevitable that advocates for the abolition of capital punishment and Quaker philanthropists would latch on to the Baker case and seek to overthrow the verdict. After all, more than a thousand memorials were presented to the Home Office each year for the commutation of sentences of penal servitude and capital punishment.[119] Within days of Frederick Baker being sentenced to death, a campaign to save him from the gallows was underway on several fronts.

Understandably, the people of Alton showed no interest in respiting Baker from the hangman's noose. A petition in the town calling on the Home Secretary to delay Baker's execution until proper medical inquiries had been made into his mental condition was an 'utter failure'. It was reported to have collected one signature only.[120] Accusations that the vicar of Alton, Octavius Hodgson, had pressured Fanny's parents to sign the memorial proved to be false. Dr William

---

117   Item 9 from their 1868 exhibition catalogue contains this description: 'FREDERICK BAKER, formerly a clerk in an attorney's office, murdered Fanny Adams, a little girl at Alton, Hants, and mutilated the body in a most revolting manner. Early in the afternoon of August 4th, 1867, (sic) his victim was playing with several children in a meadow, near Alton Church, near which spot, after enticing her from her companions, he committed the fearful crime for which he was convicted, on the most conclusive evidence, and executed at Winchester Castle, December 24, 1867.'

118   Frederick Baker was the last person to be hanged outside Winchester Gaol. The last man to be publicly executed in the United Kingdom was Michael Barrett on 26 May 1868. He was hanged outside Newgate prison for his part in the Clerkenwell bombing of 1867. The first private execution was on 14 August 1868, when Thomas Wells was hanged behind prison walls in Maidstone.

119   HC Deb 03 December 1867 vol 190 cc551-72.

120   *Hampshire Chronicle*, 28 December 1867.

Baker.

Curtis wrote a paper setting forth his conviction that Baker was 'a man of a very ill-balanced mind' possessing 'very feeble moral control over his actions'; he felt Baker was insane at the time of the murder, or if not insane in the ordinary sense of the term then certainly 'temporarily irresponsible' for his actions.[121] He sent a copy of his thoughts to Mr William Tallack, secretary of the newly-formed Howard Association. But Curtis found himself in an awkward position. While his Quaker beliefs impelled him to oppose the death penalty in all circumstances, even for child murderers, he will have been fully aware of the strength of public feeling against Baker in the town, and he must have known it would have been a deeply unpopular course of action, and potentially damaging on a personal and professional level, for him to openly campaign for commutation of the death penalty on Baker's behalf. In the end he slightly lost his nerve, and indicated to Mr Tallack that he did not wish his comments to 'appear in any shape in public journals in my name'. He was happy for his views on Baker's insanity to be forwarded to the Home Secretary, but that was as far as he felt able to go.

Much less concerned by public opinion was the Liberal Member of Parliament for Oxford, Charles Neate. A well known abolitionist, he wrote an open letter to the *Morning Star* (published on 13 December) in which he powerfully argued that the defence of homicidal mania had been insufficiently and inadequately urged by Baker's counsel. He also launched a withering attack on Professor Taylor, challenging his authority to pronounce on homicidal mania and drawing attention to where the professor's statements of opinion on insanity were at variance with the facts. In Neate's view Baker was a 'wretched maniac' who ought to be condemned to perpetual imprisonment in an asylum rather than brought to the scaffold as a guilty man.[122] Neate sent a copy of his open letter to the Home Secretary, Gathorne Hardy, along with a covering letter stating that in his view Baker had not received a fair trial because he lacked the funds to pay for expert medical witnesses who might have testified for the defence.[123]

Neate's concerns were echoed in part by *The Lancet*, which ran a series of articles entreating the Home Secretary to postpone the execution of Frederick Baker until the Government had carefully enquired into the prisoner's present and past mental condition.[124]

Compared with efforts in Alton, a far more spirited and effective campaign was pressed in Baker's home town of Guildford. A consortium of Quaker philanthropists headed by Edmund Wright Brooks, the anti-slavery campaigner, together with the vicar of St Mary's Church, Robert Trimmer, distributed a

---

121 See Appendix C.2.
122 Neate's open letter to the *Morning Star* is reproduced in Appendix B.
123 Charles Neate to Gathorne Hardy, 13 December 1867, TNA HO 12/176/79865.
124 See Appendices A.1, A.2 and A.3 for *The Lancet* articles.

Introduction.

circular to all householders in Guildford calling for a 'delay in the execution of the sentence as may enable further enquiry to be made by qualified practitioners as to the sanity, or otherwise, of the prisoner.' It contained a letter specially written by Dr Henry Taylor outlining his opinion that Baker was insane at the time of the murder.[125]

The task of preparing the petition, lobbying local politicians, and mobilising resources to collect signatures fell to Baker's solicitor, John Rand Capron. The firm of Capron and Sparkes[126] had offices at 57 Quarry Street in Guildford, opposite St Mary's Church where the Baker family worshipped every Sunday. Understandably, Frederick's father approached his neighbour when seeking a solicitor to represent his son.

Capron was a prominent local philanthropist ever willing to help the poor and distressed. He had been a practising solicitor since 1850 and Borough Coroner since 1854. As a child, just like Frederick Baker, he had suffered a severe attack of typhoid fever: Dr Henry Taylor had lent him a compound microscope which helped ignite the boy's life-long interest in science. Capron later turned to spectroscopy and meteorology, becoming a gentleman astronomer of considerable note and publishing important work on spectra and aurorae.[127]

On 12 December Capron petitioned the Home Secretary for a meeting to discuss deferring Baker's execution. The request was turned down.[128]

Undeterred, on 17 December Capron submitted a memorial to Gathorne Hardy from the inhabitants of Guildford, urging the Government to conduct a full inquiry into Baker's mental state before the sentence of death was imposed. There were 330 petitioners in total, mostly residents from Quarry Hill and Quarry Street and the lanes around St Mary's Church. Among the signatories were gardeners, blacksmiths and solicitor's clerks, drapers, schoolmasters and grocers, a surgeon, and two innkeepers who may have remembered Frederick with affection from his pork pie and raw sausage days. They were all people who knew the Baker family well. Neighbours who had watched Frederick grow up.

Members of the public also wrote directly to Hardy expressing views on the Baker case. There were letters sent to him from people in favour of Baker suffering capital punishment, and letters protesting against the sentence.[129]

---

125 The circular was also printed in several local newspapers. See, for example, the *Hampshire Chronicle*, 14 December 1867. The circular is reproduced in Appendix C.1.
126 The firm survives today as Moore Barlow.
127 P. Fuller, 'The Life and Times of John Rand Capron (1829–1888)', *Antiquarian Astronomer* Issue 8 April 2014. pp. 21–45.
128 See Appendix C.4.
129 See Appendices C.3 and E.1

Baker.

Gathorne Hardy had succeeded Spencer Horatio Walpole as Home Secretary in May 1867, and he had already wrestled with questions of justice and capital punishment in the aftermath of the Fenian Rising when the 'Manchester Martyrs' were executed outside Salford Gaol in November 1867 for the murder of a police officer. It now fell to Hardy to ratify the verdict of the jury in the Frederick Baker trial or to revise the sentence passed by Mr Justice Mellor. The question of criminal appeal was keenly debated in the 1860s: there were those who felt an appeal to the Home Office in capital cases was as an entirely adequate process, but there were contrary voices arguing that a Court of Criminal Appeal was the best place for these kinds of issues to be heard. The debate would rumble on for at least another forty years. In 1867 all Hardy had to go on was a petition from Rand Capron, the trial notes from Mr Justice Mellor stating that 'the defence of insanity wholly failed' (see Appendix D), an article from *The Lancet*, and his own Conservative and Anglican beliefs impelling him to impose the death penalty.[130]

*

The question of Frederick Baker's sanity was also taken up by the press. The *Saturday Review* summed up one side of the debate in a short article entitled 'Is Baker A Lunatic?'

> If Baker was a madman, he somehow seems to have concealed his tendencies with remarkable skill; and certainly he was treated by the world of Alton with extreme confidence in his perfect sanity. Indeed, for his station in life, Baker seems to have filled many and difficult positions, to discharge which a madman is not very likely to be entrusted. He was a lawyer's clerk, a savings' bank manager, member of several literary clubs, secretary to a discussion society, and a Sunday school teacher of twelve years' experience. To say that a man may discharge all these duties, and discharge them well, and be a lunatic, is only to play the fool with language. Baker may be a lunatic for aught we care, if anybody likes the use of that word; but to say that a man living such a life, and discharging all these social functions with punctuality, dutifulness, and the respect and confidence of his fellows, is not responsible for his actions, is not so much silly as mischievous language, which, if it means anything, means that all social responsibility is nugatory, or, indeed, non-existent.[131]

The *Dundee Courier* cautiously presented the opposing view:

---

130 See *Gathorne Hardy, First Earl of Cranbrook: A Memoir* (London: Longman's Green & Co, 1910), Vol 1, pp. 102–3.

131 *Saturday Review*, 15 December 1867.

Introduction.

We are fully sensible of the danger of listening too readily to the plea of insanity when urged on behalf of murderers, and there can be no question that it is a defence which has been much abused; but, at the same time, the facts seem entitled to consideration before an irrevocable sentence is carried out. If it is wrong to allow an atrocious murderer to escape just punishment, it is still a greater wrong to execute a man who is not accountable for his actions. In the present case, it is to be observed that, although Baker's incipient madness was not suspected by his fellow clerks, and, although it may be quite true that he discharged all the duties of his station in a rational manner, yet it is not the less true, we believe, that homicidal mania is in its nature sudden in its development, and it does not seem to be [im]possible, when we know that the disease was in Baker's family, that he himself, when he killed the young child, may have been its victim.[132]

The *Dundee Courier* then turned to the thorny question of motive:

The supposition [that Baker was suffering from homicidal mania] is further borne out by the apparent absence of any motive for the murder. The only explainable theory... is that he had abused the person of the girl, and had afterwards cut up the body with the object of destroying the evidence of his crime. But that is only a supposition, and it will be remembered that it was the opinion of those whose duty it was to investigate all the circumstances of the murder, that no rape had been committed. If so, the murder was utterly without motive; and in that case, it is more explainable in theory that it was the deed of a lunatic than of a sane man.[133]

The *Courier* was mistaken to say that experts believed no rape had been committed. The lower sections of Fanny's body had been completely destroyed and the vagina was missing or had not been found, making it impossible to determine one way or the other if a sexual assault had taken place. But the newspaper was probably correct in its opinion that a motiveless murder was more likely to be the work of a madman.

Did Baker lure Fanny into the hop gardens intending to sexually assault her? Did he then murder her, as the prosecution alleged, and cut up her body in order to destroy the evidence of having raped her? If he did, then it provides a motive of sorts for his actions that day, and it implies that Baker was fully aware of the nature and illegality of his crime. It suggests also that the murder of Fanny Adams was not the result of a sudden and uncontrollable paroxysm of frenzy but an act of calculated barbarity.

---

132 *Dundee Courier*, 19 December 1867.
133 *Ibid.*

Baker.

XVII.

There were reports in the newspapers suggesting that the Government was ready to postpone the execution in order to conduct an inquiry into Baker's mental health. But these reports proved false: the Governor of Winchester Gaol received no such intimation from the Home Department, and Rand Capron failed even to receive a reply from Hardy acknowledging receipt of the petition from the inhabitants of Guildford. There is no evidence in the Home Office correspondence to suggest that the Home Secretary was in any sense moved by Baker's predicament, or that he gave anything other than the most cursory attention to the weight of public opinion urging a review of Baker's mental health. There is an annotation in Hardy's handwriting dismissing *The Lancet* article forwarded by Henry Taylor: 'The article is based on [an] instance of doubtful grounds all of which were before the Jury – no new evidence is suggested but I am called upon to take the chance of some medical man's opinion which will be founded on preconceived theories.'

There were few reserves of public and press sympathy for Baker, and there was almost no clamour for the execution to be halted. The Home Secretary had the power to order that Baker be examined by the local Lunacy Commissioners[134] or that he be sent to an asylum for examination, but he probably felt under no great pressure to interfere with the course of justice and in the end he did nothing.

*

On 7 December, the day when Baker learnt the date of his execution, a great change came over him. For the first time since his arrest more than three months earlier, an element of dejection entered his bearing. He was quiet and subdued. At last he seemed to apprehend the dreadful situation he was in. But it was only a fleeting loss of bravado: he quickly regained his carefree demeanour and retained it to the end. While detained at Alton police station, he had kept his spirits up by chatting with the custody officers and singing verses from an American music hall song, *Cheer Up, Sam!* Now, at Winchester, awaiting execution, he whistled to himself once more and again sang songs, conversing jovially with the attendants employed to watch over him. He placidly counted upon his fingers the days and hours by which his life was numbered. He was frequently visited in his cell by the prison chaplain, the Reverend Foster Rogers, under whose ungrudging ministrations Baker seemed to find some comfort.

---

134   The Lunacy Commission was a government department established by the Lunacy Act 1845 to superintend asylums and oversee the treatment and welfare of insane people in England and Wales.

Introduction.

He immersed himself in studying the scriptures and other religious books and pamphlets, regaining some of the fervour that had marked his early days as a Sunday school teacher in Guildford. He was allowed to attend chapel on Sunday afternoons, although he was kept apart from the other prisoners. There was an expectation among the prison authorities that he might soon make a full confession.

At his own request no one called on Baker as he languished in the condemned cell, not even friends and family. He declined to be visited by his father because he knew it would 'kill the old man'. Several times he enquired about his former fiancée – possibly Ellen Stanton, the lady's maid in Guildford – and asked if she might visit him, but the governor discouraged the idea. He acknowledged the pain he had caused his father, sister, and uncle's family, and in letters to former friends and colleagues he expressed contrition about his wasted and sinful life. But there was no remorse as such. There were no feelings of regret:

> It might have been supposed that haunted by the ghost of little Fanny Adams, aged nine, he would have been worn to a shadow: but no ghost seems to have visited him in his prison cell; no tormenting demon of remorse—no bitter, wasting regret that he had purpled his hands with the innocent blood of childhood and begrimed his soul with stains so deep and foul that they can only be wiped out by the hands of the Infinite Himself.[135]

*

On the eve of his execution, Baker wrote a final letter. It says:

> My dear Friend
> It is with a trembling hand and a heart over-charged with grief that I take up my pen to address you by the endearing name of friend for the last time in this world. What am I now? A wretched culprit condemned to a death of shame with tomorrow's sun by the hands of the common hangman for a crime which renders me an outcast both from God and man – for murder, for sending a poor defenceless little girl before her Creator.
> I have prayed to God for pardon, and I trust I shall be forgiven. Thanks to the worthy authorities of the gaol for their kind attention to me. Dear friend, I wish this letter to be made public.
> From a guilty but repentant culprit,
> Fred Baker.[136]

---

135   *Western Daily Express*, 9 December 1867.
136   Recipient unknown. *Southern Evening Echo*, 22 April 1987.

Baker.

That evening Baker retired at eleven o'clock. He slept serenely for six hours. In the morning he spent considerable time dressing himself in his freshly-laundered office garb, becoming a solicitor's clerk once again. Ridiculously, he donned his tall black hat before tucking in to a hearty breakfast of bread, butter and tea at half-past six. Afterwards he conversed one final time with Reverend Rogers. At 8.00am the prison bell rang, announcing that Baker's doom had arrived.

At Winchester the scaffold – the 'hideous machine' – for public hangings was located on the roof over the main gateway to the prison. In the damp grey dawn thousands of spectators had taken up position in front of the gaol to watch Baker die; others had congregated on Romsey Road or were closely packed in Barnes Road where the 'best' views of the gallows were to be had. People had started arriving the evening before: Mr Gawin Kirkham, the open-air evangelist, had booked a room at the St John's Assembly Hall, and preached to a large crowd on the evils of liquor, spicing up his talk with entertaining anecdotes about the various criminals whose executions he had attended.[137] The London and South Western Railway thoughtfully laid on a special excursion service, bringing hundreds of passengers from Southampton into Winchester for the execution. The carriages pulled into the station shortly after seven o'clock in the morning on Christmas Eve and the new arrivals clambered out and made their way up West Hill to join the throng. There was an almost holiday atmosphere among the waiting crowds; one party had brought their musical instruments; others broke into song. Estimates put the attendance at 'not less than 5,000 or 6,000': mostly they were women and shopkeepers, and 'a sprinkling of nondescripts'. Many of them had walked overnight from Dorking, Alton, and Guildford to get into the city well before first light. Press passes had been issued to two metropolitan and four provincial newspapers; their representatives were admitted to the prison at seven o'clock, and they sat around in a plush reception room for an hour or so waiting for the execution to begin.

The distance from the condemned cell to the scaffold was nearly 200 yards. Accompanied by the chaplain, the under-sheriff Mr T.B. Woodham, the governor Captain Henry Baynes and his deputy Mr Gregg, the prison surgeon Dr Butler, and several warders, Baker was ushered under the chapel, along several corridors, and then outside into the yard. Apparently he was light on his feet, 'tripping down the steps to the courtyard' as if alighting from a train at the start of a brisk country walk. The procession climbed the long and winding stone staircase leading up to the gloomy pinioning room. There was a solitary candle burning in one of the windows. The hangman William Calcraft and his

137 *Hampshire Independent*, 28 December 1867.

Introduction.

assistant were waiting for Baker there. There was a nod of the head, a shake of the hand. Calcraft reached into a black handbag and pulled out the pinioning straps. Baker was seated on a four-legged stool while his arms were restrained behind him. His tall black hat was removed. Then, unassisted and with an unfaltering step, he ascended the final flight of stairs to the scaffold on the roof and took his place under the beam. It was drizzling. A subdued hum of voices came up from the crowd below:

> What followed was the work of a few seconds only, for the executioner, notwithstanding his silvery locks and 40 years' experience, retains much of his juvenile agility and resolution. A long, closely-fitting black cap was drawn over the convict's head and face, reaching the chin; the rope was placed over his head and secured at the neck, the end being thrown over the beam; the legs of the miserable man were secured by leathern straps at the knees and ankles; and a momentary delay, to enable the chaplain to complete a prayer (during which the convict's knees trembled so violently that a fall was apprehended), having occurred, the bolt was withdrawn, the treacherous floor on which Baker was standing gave way with the noise well known to those who have seen an execution, but indescribable to those who have not, and the convict was senseless in a moment. The convulsions with which the body and limbs were shaken gradually subsided to gentle nervous twitchings, and Baker was with the dead.[138]

After hanging for an hour, the body was cut down, and Dr Butler pronounced Frederick Baker dead. A brief inquest was held on the body before it was interred in the chalk grounds of the prison amongst the bones of eight or nine other culprits. The crowd, which had been orderly throughout, rapidly dispersed, to be met at the foot of West Hill by hawkers selling murder and execution ballads.

XVIII.

The *Illustrated Police News* covered the execution of Frederick Baker in its edition of 28 December. The whole of the front page was devoted to a montage of images – the prisoner in his cell, the condemned man ascending the flight of steps to the rooftop gallows, the murderer standing beneath the beam with a panoramic view across the crowds gathered outside the prison. There was even a drawing of the hangman William Calcraft, his portrait tastefully framed in a loop of rope like a noose.

News that Baker had made a full and complete confession began to surface after the execution. On Sunday 22 December he had written to Mr and Mrs Adams admitting his guilt. He told them he had murdered Fanny 'in an

138 *Hampshire Telegraph*, 24 December 1867.

Baker.

unguarded hour, and not with malice aforethought'. He had been 'enraged at her crying', he said, but she had died 'without pain or struggle'. He absolutely denied violating the child or attempting to do so. He hoped the parents would forgive him. Baker handed the letter to the prison chaplain who forwarded it to the vicar of Alton, Octavius Hodgson, who in turn delivered it to the murdered girl's parents.

While it seems that Mr and Mrs Adams were willing to forgive Baker, they begged him 'to divulge the place in which he had concealed the only missing portion of the body.' But Baker ignored them: it was a nasty little secret he kept to himself and took to the grave.

Baker also made a confession to the prison chaplain on the strict understanding it would not be made public until after his execution. This confession, pieced together from various newspaper reports, is reproduced in Appendix F. It was a carefully constructed, boastful statement that differed in several key respects from the 'authorised' version of events presented at the trial, but there is no reason to doubt that fundamentally it is a true account of what happened that day. It was not a premeditated crime, he insisted. He indecently assaulted Fanny while he was carrying her away into the hop field, but there was no rape or attempted rape. He couldn't say, or he chose not to say, why he mutilated and dismembered the body, or why he returned to the murder scene later in the day to inflict yet more damage on the corpse. As for motive, he had been drinking heavily that day, that's all he could say. He admitted he made efforts to avoid detection. He did not think he was mad.

XIV.

The Alton murderer continued to perplex medical science. Henry Maudsley discussed the case in his textbook *Responsibility in Mental Disease* (1874), raising the spectre of 'homicidal mania' as a possible explanation for Baker's crime:

> ...the impulsive character of the crime, the quiet and determined ferocity of it, the savage mutilation, his equanimity immediately afterwards, and his complete indifference to his fate – all these indicated an insane organisation.[139]

Krafft-Ebing included Baker in his classic work on sexual pathology, *Psychopathia Sexualis*, although he misnames Baker as 'Alton' throughout:

---

139   Henry Maudsley, *Responsibility in Mental Disease* (New York: Appleton and Company, 1874), p. 163. See also Appendix A.7

Introduction.

Case 18. Alton, a clerk in England, goes out of town for a walk. He lures a child into a thicket, and returns after a time to his office, where he makes this entry in his note-book: 'Killed today a young girl; it was fine and hot.' The child was missed, searched for, and found cut into pieces. Many parts, and among them the genitals, could not be found. Alton did not show the slightest trace of emotion, and gave no explanation of the motive or circumstances of his horrible deed. He was a psychopathic individual, and occasionally subject to states of depression and tædium vitæ [boredom]. His father had had one attack of acute mania. A near relative suffered from mania with homicidal impulses. Alton was executed.[140]

Opinions varied, but the consensus among psychiatrists in the first few decades after Baker's execution was that, even if there was insufficient evidence to justify an acquittal on the ground of insanity, there ought to have been, at the very least, further inquiry into Baker's mental condition before he was put to death. Baker's crime was terrible, but then so too (Charles Neate will have argued) were the actions of a man like the Home Secretary who sat behind his Whitehall desk and did nothing to prevent legal murder.

*

If Baker had been examined by the Commissioners in Lunacy, or interviewed by an asylum physician, we would be in a better position today to understand his mental state and perhaps comprehend what drove him to murder Fanny Adams.

Baker was small and puny. 'Stunted' is the word that comes most readily to mind. It seems he was unable to grow facial hair, and his body, too, was almost completely hairless, like a schoolboy's. A mouthful of decayed teeth gave his breath a sick, rotten smell. When out and about in town, or walking in the countryside, he customarily wore his black top hat to make himself appear taller and more important than he was: he looked like a toy man dressed in adult clothes and playing at being a grown-up. Perhaps it was this sense of being a runt that made him take up with such relish the 'shabby vices' that reek of manhood – alcohol and tobacco. By his late twenties Baker had already acquired a persistent 'smoker's cough' – he was forever clearing his throat and hawking up sputum – and his unlaundered office clothes bore the whiff of mince and cold lard, like a butcher's smock.

One Alton resident described Baker as 'really only half a man' – a reference not only to his miniature (homunculus) form but a jibe at his virility. We do not know if Baker suffered from any kind of urological or genital defect, or

---

140 Richard von Krafft-Ebing, *Psychopathia Sexualis: A Medico-Legal Study*, 7th ed, trans. Charles G. Chaddock (London: F.J. Rebman, 1894), p. 63.

if he was impotent or sterile like a hybrid farm animal; and we cannot say if his ferocious appetite for uncooked meat and raw eggs was all part of the same depraved obsession with *freshness* that made him seek out small children for sexual comfort. This subject is complicated by the fact that in the mid-nineteenth century pre-pubescent girls were considered mature agents capable of consenting to sexual relations,[141] so that men whose erotic desires inclined towards young girls and the 'white roses of virginity' (to use Ernest Dowson's phrase) were not necessarily regarded as monsters in the same way they might be today.

The decision of the prosecution to frame Baker's crime as a child rape turned murder illustrates the extent to which the Crown authorities were desperate to establish a motive for the 'senseless' and 'mindless' act. Yet everything we know about Baker tells us that up until that Saturday afternoon his sexual interest in children had functioned largely on a fantasy level or had been limited to touching and petting – molestations, undoubtedly, but not the gross violation imputed by Montague Bere. How, then, can we account for the catastrophic escalation in violence which may have resulted in child rape as well as murder?

Even if we accept Baker's statement that there was no rape or attempted rape, he clearly acted indecently towards Fanny while carrying her into the hop garden.[142] In the past, Baker had taken flight whenever confronted with accusations of child sexual abuse. After the Guildford chalk pit incident, he had disappeared for 15 months while extra-legal negotiations took place between his father and the family of the little girl he had molested. It's possible Baker considered the same course of action here – after all, he was already planning on handing in his notice at Clements and leaving Alton in two days time to seek alternative employment 'up north'. After molesting Fanny he could have let her go and returned to the office and brazened it out: if Fanny complained to her parents and the police were brought in, there were a range of tried and tested 'excuses' available to a professional gentleman in his predicament – he was tipsy and momentarily forgot himself, the hot sunshine had a debilitating effect on his morals, he was a religious man demonstrating Christian affection towards a child. Besides, hadn't Fanny been behaving 'provocatively' down

141 In 1867 the age of consent for girls was set at 12; unlawful sexual intercourse with a girl aged 10 or 11 was only regarded as a misdemeanour carrying a maximum punishment of two years' imprisonment (Offences Against the Person Act 1828), while unlawful intercourse with a child under 10 was punishable by death until 1841, and thereafter by life imprisonment (4 & 5 Vict., c.56). The age of consent was raised to 13 in 1875 (Offences Against the Person Act 1875) and to 16 in 1885 (Criminal Law Amendment Act 1885).

142 While sexual offences against children can range from murder with rape through to less serious acts such as indecent exposure and solicitations for sex, crime statistics suggest that fewer than 8% of sex offences against females under 10 years involve rape or attempted rape. See Dennis Howitt, *Paedophiles and Sexual Offences Against Children* (John Wiley & Sons, 1995), pp. 77–78.

Introduction.

by the river, shamelessly exposing her red petticoats? In the end, it was her word against his. Statute law stated that defendants could not be convicted on the unsupported testimony of a child, with the consequence that many cases involving the sexual abuse of very young children never reached the criminal courts through lack of evidence.[143]

But Fanny screamed, and according to Baker's prison confession he was panicked into murder. Yet the fact he had brought two knives with him on that lunchtime country walk suggests some degree of criminal planning, and there were bramble scratches on his thighs implying that Baker's trousers had been down that afternoon while he was in the Hollow. There can be no doubt he knew exactly what he was doing when he cut Fanny's throat, and there can be no doubt he knew his actions were wrong, otherwise why would he make efforts afterwards to conceal the crime and divert the police investigation? The one thing we cannot say with certainty is whether he raped Fanny before he murdered her, although the integral role of alcohol as a precursor to sadistic sex offences against children is well understood.[144]

Of course, it was the abuse of the body in the wake of the murder – the colossal butchery – that sets the case apart from most other crimes of the period. It was savagery on an almost unimaginable scale, and an atrocity of the very worst kind. There is nothing in Baker's confession that even begins to explain his behaviour: he admitted to being 'bewildered' by his actions, and he set about his gruesome work 'without considering why he did so'. He could not say why he returned to the scene hours later to enact a second round of mutilations.

At one time he may have been an habitué of the meat markets and tripe dressers in Guildford; as a young man he may have found himself obscurely excited at the sight of animal carcasses dripping on hooks in the cattle stalls. There was a major outbreak of rinderpest (cattle plague) in Britain in 1865–66, when tens of thousand of cattle sickened and died, or were slaughtered to contain the epidemic.[145] Rural counties like Hampshire, Cheshire and Surrey were especially devastated, and for ghouls like Baker, who found pleasure in loitering around accident spots and scenes of tragedy, the wholesale culling of livestock will have had a particular attraction.

But all this is speculation. The criminal dismemberment of a corpse is such a rare event there is hardly any scientific research on the subject. Most cases appear to be unplanned and disorganized affairs, committed by a male known to the victim, and perpetrated while under the influence of alcohol.[146] Beyond

---

143 Louise A. Jackson, *Child Sexual Abuse in Victorian England* (London: Routledge, 2000), p. 93.
144 Howitt *op cit*, p. 209.
145 Sherwin A. Hall, 'The Cattle Plague of 1865', *Med Hist* 1962, Jan; Vol 6(1), pp. 45–58.

this, almost nothing is known about the psychiatric and personality correlates of criminal mutilators. It is far easier to fall back on superstitious notions of Baker as a werewolf or a brute possessed by some ravenous, demon fury. Yet this perception of Baker as a wild animal was belied by the fact that he led a mostly unremarkable and quotidian life in a solicitor's office, and that in his own fashion he actually seemed to like children and enjoyed their company. This paradox lies at the heart of the Baker case, and we are no nearer understanding the man and his crime today than we were 150 years ago.

*

Mr and Mrs Adams eventually moved away from Alton. They couldn't bear to be constantly reminded of the murder of their daughter. By 1881 they had settled in Beckenham in Kent with their daughters Lillie and Minnie. In old age and widowed, George Adams was living in Farnham in Surrey; his daughter, Lizzie, who had been with Fanny on that awful day in August 1867, was able to take care of her father during his final years.[147]

*

Broadmoor Criminal Lunatic Asylum opened in 1863. If Frederick Baker had been found not guilty but insane, he would probably have ended up there. At the trial in Winchester, Samuel Carter spoke of asylums as 'living tombs'. Being committed for murderous madness, he said, was 'a shutting out from all hopes and pleasures'.

Baker may have sobbed in court at the intolerable prospect of spending the rest of his life in an asylum, yet the indications are that he might have adapted quite readily to the regimen at Broadmoor, falling back once more into the role of semi-invalid and finding solace in the familiar routines of the sick-room. At Broadmoor patients were encouraged to spend their days gardening and playing croquet and strolling round the meadows and parterres of the 53-acre estate in the Berkshire moors. There was a cricket club, a billiards room, and a well-stocked library. For lunch the patients were offered beef, mutton, roast pork, and crispy rashers of bacon, and they were allowed to smoke and drink beer in moderation.[148] Just outside the asylum grounds, beyond a low stone wall, there

---

146 Ann H. Ross and Eugénia Cunha (eds), *Dismemberments: Perspectives in Forensic Anthropology and Legal Medicine* (London: Academic Press, 2018), pp. 184–5.

147 'Alton Tragedy Recalled', *Alton Papers* No. 21 (2017), pp. 45–6. George Adams died in Farnham Union Workhouse in 1908.

148 BRO: D/H14/A2/1/1/1 Superintendent John Meyer's report for 1866, in *Annual Reports of the Superintendent and Chaplain of Broadmoor Criminal Lunatic Asylum.*

Introduction.

was a cottage school for the use of staff children: the little girls' voices will have carried across the grubbed fields to where the patients rested on the terraces.

Frederick Baker might have felt very much at home there.

Leading Dates in the Frederick Baker Case.

1838	Birth of Frederick Baker in Guildford
1854–5	Baker suffers severe attack of typhoid fever
1855-65	Baker employed as attorney's clerk in Guildford
1859	Birth of Fanny Adams in Alton
1865–66	Baker disappears for 15 months
1866	Baker moves to Alton
1866–67	Baker employed as attorney's clerk in Alton
1867	
24 August	Murder of Fanny Adams
	Arrest of Baker
25 August	Post mortem on Fanny Adams
27 August	Inquest on body of Fanny Adams
29 August	Committal hearing
5 December	Trial of Frederick Baker – first day
6 December	Trial of Frederick Baker – second day
	Baker convicted of murder
22 December	Baker confesses
24 December	Execution of Frederick Baker

South Street, Guildford, about 1860.
The keep of Guildford Castle can be seen in the background.

Reproduced by kind permission of the Guildford Institute.

'The Alton Murder. Portrait of Fanny Adams. House in which the parents of the murdered child reside. Tanhouse Lane and Field, where the murderer met his victim.' *Illustrated Police News, 14 September, 1867 © The British Library Board.*

Tanhouse Lane, Alton in the 1840s, looking towards Amery Hill. The home of Fanny Adams and her family was behind the artist.

From the 'History of Alton' by William Curtis (1896).

Flood Meadows looking back towards Tanhouse Lane, around 1895–1905.
St Lawrence's Church is visible at the left-hand edge of the picture.

'Murderer carrying his victim into the hop plantation' and
'Murder and mutilation of the body.'

Cutpond Lane (now Amery Street) viewed from the Market Square. At the bottom, out of sight on the right hand side, is the Leather Bottle public house.

Photograph by W.P. Varney (between 1903 and c1909). Private collection.

Alton High Street. On the right is the Swan Hotel and opposite, just beyond the shop with the white awning and the bay window, is the building formerly occupied by Clements solicitors where Baker worked at the time of the murder.

Old postcard, early 1900s. Private collection.

'The Barbarous Murder at Alton. Finding the Remains of Fanny Adams;
Portrait of the Prisoner; Prisoner Mobbed upon entering Winchester.'

Winchester Great Hall. *Private collection.*

'The Alton Murder. Portrait of Dr. Swaine Taylor.'
Left: The trial, with Baker in the dock. Right: Minnie Warner brought into court.

Illustrated Police News, 14 December, 1867 © The British Library Board.

Left: Mr Justice Mellor c1873. *Private collection.*
Right: Dr William Curtis (1802–1881), Alton, Hampshire, 1864

Left: Dr Henry Sharp Taylor. Painting by Eden Upton Eddis (after 1878).
Reproduced by kind permission of Guildford Borough Council.

Right: John Rand Capron.
Reproduced by kind permission of the Guildford Institute.

'The execution of Frederick Baker for the murder at Alton.'

Illustrated Police News, 28 December, 1867 © The British Library Board.

The Trial, Confession, & Execution

OF F. BAKER,

At Winchester, for the Wilful Murder of Fanny Adams, a little girl, at Alton.

COPY OF VERSES.

Tune—Cottage and Water Mill.

In a lone, gloomy cell, lamenting there lies,
For a cruel murder condemned for to die;
His days and nights passed in sorrow and pain,
In the prime of his life, Frederick Baker his name;
His hours are numbered, and he must prepare,
With blood in his soul before his Maker to appear,
His doom it is fixed, here he cannot stay,
For it is clear that none else Fanny Adams did slay.

And while Fanny's soul it is bless'd upon high,
At Winchester scaffold now Baker must die.

It was in last August, and sad was the day,
That innocent Fanny with her playmates did stray,
From the town of Alton, not dreaming of strife,
That she in full bloom should so soon lose her life,
But the murderer, Baker, did her decoy,
On purpose her innocent life to destroy,
And the angels wept o'er the scene on that day,
When the murderer Baker did poor Fanny slay.

How Baker was taken it is needless to tell,
Or the sad details which to all is known well,
How the mangled remains of poor Fanny was found,
To the pitying gaze they lay scattered around,
How the heart-broken mother with frenzy gone wild,
And in anguish wept for her darling child,
And for vengeance called by night and by day,
On the villain that poor Fanny Adams did slay,

When Baker was committed, and in prison did lie,
All knowledge of this foul deed he did deny,
And now that his victim is in the cold grave,
By falsehood he strove hard his life for to save;
For like most brutal cowards he dreaded his fate,
When he for his crimes did his trial await,
For the spirit of Fanny haunted him night and day,
Saying, villain, it was you who did poor Fanny slay.

When at the bar for the murder was tried,
In the face of them all his guilt he denied,
But it was so clear to all those around,
That his doom it was fixed, and he guilty was found,
The Judge said, Frederick Baker, your sentence now hear
For your fate on the scaffold you must now prepare.
I'd have you to your God for your soul's welfare pray,
For it's plain to the world you poor Fanny did slay.

Now Baker is cast, and the last scene awaits,
And on Winchester scaffold he has met his fate,
That his sentence was just is the country's cry;
He was not fit to live, and unpitied did die;
While tears for poor Fanny bedims every eye,
And Baker for mercy to his offended God did cry,
That he would forgive, and the sinful soul save,
Of the monster who did poor Fanny Adams slay.

And while poor Fanny's soul is with angels on high,
On Winchester scaffold Frederick Baker did die.

Printed for the Vendors.

This morning, the wretched criminal Frederick Baker suffered the extreme penalty of the law at Winchester Gaol, for the atrocious murder of Fanny Adams at Alton, on the 24th of August last. It is satisfactory to state, that since his condemnation, the conduct of the unhappy man underwent a total change for the better, and he began to realise the awful condition in which he was placed, and his callous demeanour was changed into one of deep dejection. The prisoner has been assiduously attended by the chaplain of the prison and to such a state of religious feeling had he been brought, that he fully acknowledged the justice of his sentence. The sheriffs with their usual attendants arrived at an early hour at the prison and immediately proceeded to the condemned cell, and found the prisoner engaged in prayer with the chaplain. After the usual formalities had been gone through of demanding the body of the unfortunate prisoner into their custody, the executioner was then introduced to the prisoner.

Patiently he submitted to be pinioned. During this very trying and painful operation he frequently exclaimed, "May the Lord have mercy on my soul." When the work of pinioning had been completed, the wretched man thanked the chaplain, the governor of the prison and likewise the officials. He expressed great contrition for his crime, and hoped that his fate would be a warning to all those who have been living a careless life.

The procession that was to accompany the wretched man to the gallows was then formed, and slowly betook its way to the scene of the execution, the chaplain of the prison, reading in a very impressive manner, the burial service for the dead. As the prisoner ascended the steps of the gallows, there was a simultaneous movement amongst the great crowd of people that was packed as close as they could be, witnessing the scene. As soon as the prayer was finished, the executioner advanced, and after drawing the cap over the head of Baker, arranged the rope round his neck. Almost in an instant thereafter the bolt was drawn, and the unfortunate man after struggling for a short time soon ceased to exist.

On Thursday, December 5, Frederick Baker, a lawyer's clerk was placed at the bar of the Winchester assizes, on the charge of having horribly murdered and mutilated a little girl named Fanny Adams, in a hop-garden at Alton, on the 24th of August last.

The atrocity of this murder created the most profound sensation against the accused man, not only in the county in which it was committed but throughout England. It will be remembered that on the summer's afternoon in question, a group of young children were at play in a place known as the Hollow, adjoining a hop garden at Alton, and bordered on one side by a high hedge. While thus gambolling about a man suddenly made his appearance among them and spoke to them. First he gave two of them a penny to run a race along the slope; next, he offered them a halfpenny if they would go with him into a contiguous field, where he picked some berries for them. They, in both instances confidingly assented, when he bade the two older return home, and lifting Fanny Adams—eight years and four months old—he carried her away behind the hedge, and there perpetrated the horrible crime.

The prisoner, who has got very stout upon prison-fare, appeared perfectly calm and self-possessed, but spoke in a low tone when he pleaded not guilty.

Mr. Montague Bere and Mr. Bullen prosecuted, and Carter defended the prisoner.

Mr. Montague Bere stated the case for the prosecution. He detailed the circumstances of the murder, and said he would conclusively show that the prisoner was the man who gave the children the halfpence, and who subsequently carried away the unfortunate child into the hop-garden, leaving it to the jury to say whether he was the perpetrator of the horrible crime alluded to.

The first witness called was the young child, Minnie Warner. She said: On Saturday we went to play in the Hollow with Fanny Adams, and her little sister. A young gentleman came and gave us some halfpence and sent me and the little girl home, having first picked some berries for us; he took up Fanny and carried her away.

Jane Gardner said: I am a near neighbour of the deceased. On Saturday, I heard that the child was missing, and went with her mother in search. We met the prisoner near the Hollow, and I asked him what he had done with the child he took away. He said, "I've not seen one." Minnie Warner came up at the moment. I then said to the child, "Did this gentleman give you some halfpence to day?" She said, "Yes, threepence." He said, "No, threehalfpence." I said, "What did he give Lizzie, and what did he give Fanny?" Minnie Warner said, "A halfpenny." I said, "What did he do then?"—"He told me to go home and spend it; and he took Fanny up the Hollow, behind the high hedge in the hop-garden." The prisoner was standing close to my side all the time, and I told Mrs. Adams to give him in charge of the police. He offered to go with us, and said he was to be found at Mr. Clements' the solicitor. I went home and at about eight o'clock I heard some one screaming, "The head is found!" I then went to the hop-gardens and saw the head and trunk of a child laying in a heap on the ground.

Eliza White, a woman who had been cutting wheat, saw in returning home the children playing in the meadow and the prisoner lounging near, smoking. She passed on, and heard one of them call out as if in play.

George Norris, a shepherd, was crossing a field in the neighbourhood, and saw Baker with his hands under his jacket. When Baker saw him he turned back as if to avoid him.

Alfred Vince, a boy eight years of age, deposed to having seen the prisoner come from the direction of the hop-garden, and wash his hands in the bathing-place just previous to his being spoken to by Mrs. Gardner.

Harriet Adams, the mother of the murdered child, deposed that she went with Mrs. Gardner in search of her child, and confirmed the evidence given by Mrs. Gardnar.

Thomas Swain deposed to finding the left foot in a clover field on the opposite side of the Hollow.

Joseph Waters, police-constable deposed to finding an eye near the bridge, over Brood Flood, on the Alton side, at the bottom of the river Wey. Police-constable Masterman found a second eye in the same river.

William Walker deposed to finding the stone produced, covered with blood, hair, and small pieces of flesh.

Maurice Biddle, the prisoner's fellow clerk at Mr. Clements stated that him and the accused had a glass of ale together at the Swan. The boots at the public-house said he was going away on Monday, and Baker said he would go with him. The boots said he could turn his hand to anything, but Baker could not, and Baker replied, "Yes, I could turn butcher!"

Police-constable Watkin who had charge of the prisoner while at Messrs. Clement's office, said that the prisoner asked him whose child it was. Witness told him Mr. Adams's. He replied that he could not see how they could trace it to him any more than giving it a halfpenny. He also said to Biddle that he could not see how he could get off as it seemed so straightforward; but he was innocent.

They have found some blood on my sleeve which I can't account for. The doctor seemed to think it was it; but as for my boots being wet that was nothing, as I am in the habit of walking in the dew; but if the case is gone on with I must defend it, and if I can't get off I must be hanged; and that's all I can say.

George Adams, the father of the child, deposed to the remains being those of his child.

Ann Murrell was called and cross-examined. She spoke to seeing the prisoner on the day in question near the hop-garden a little before three and betwen five and six o'clock

Dr. Taylor stated the result of his analysis of the articles of apparel worn by the prisoner on the day of the murder. He found spots of blood on the coat, on the trousers, and on the vest; also blood on one of the pocket-knives. The thighs of the trousers, too, were greatly stained by bloody water. He detected, however, an extremely small quantity of blood, and in cross-examination said it was possible that the stains found on the coat might have been produced by a bleeding of the nose

Dr. Leslie deposed to the state in which he found the remains of the child, and this closed the case for the prosecution.

Mr. Carter rose to address the jury on behalf of the prisoner, and argued that the prosecution had not made out their case strong enough to show that the prisoner was the man who had committed this horrible deed. He then contended that no motive whatever had been shown, and that if it was the prisoner who committed the crime he must be mad; endeavouring to support this part of his theory from the total abstinence of any attempt on the part of the murderer to conceal the remains of his victim. He asked, who on earth could suppose the prisoner to be in a sound state of mind? The prisoner's father only four years ago was so attacked, and would but for opportune prevention inflicted injury on those nearest and dearest to him. And again a cousin of the prisoner's was similarly afflicted but all this he would show in the evidence.

Frederick Baker (the father of the prisoner) was called. He said—The prisoner from his birth was always very sickly and was constantly under the hands of the doctor. He was always nervous, and complained of pains in the head. He left me in April, 1865. Before he left me I used to watch him to his office as I was afraid he would make away with himself. I saw him in May last, and his manner and demeanour struck him with horror,

Mary Ann Baker, the sister of the prisoner said he was a always a delicate child, and suffered very much after he had had typhus fever. Witness remembered the match with his sweetheart being broken off, after which the prisoner was very desponding, and threatened to destroy himself.

Alfred Johnson, a bricklayer, had known the prisoner 16 years. In November, 1864, he had a conversation with witness, and he then thought him out of his mind.

John Davis said he had known the prisoner many years and always considered him of unsound mind, from his extreme peculiarities.

Mr. Wm. Curtis, a surgeon at Alton deposed to the insanity of certain relations of the prisoners.

Mr. H. S. Taylor, surgeon, had attended the family for 25 years. The prisoner was always very delicate. His father had an attack of acute mania five years ago. Witness always looked upon the prisoner as weak-minded.

Mr. Carter then summed up the evidence he had called, concluding by expressing his confidence that the jury would see fit to acquit the prisoner.

Mr. Bere replied, contending that the case for the prosecution had been substantially proved, and that every fact pointed directly and unmistakeably to the prisoner as the murderer, and that the second defence set up of insanity had in no way been supported.

The Judge summed up, and the Jury returned a verdict of Guilty. Judge then passed Sentence of Death

Minnie Warner and Lizzie Adams
beside the gravestone of Fanny Adams. Carte de visite.

Private collection.

HAMPSHIRE ASSIZES, WINCHESTER CASTLE

Thursday 5 December to Friday 6 December 1867

Before Mr Justice Mellor

Frederick Baker
Indicted for the Wilful Murder
of
Fanny Adams.

Mr Montague Bere
and
Mr Bullen
appeared for the prosecution.

Mr Samuel Carter
appeared for the defence.

First Day –
Thursday 5 December 1867.[149]

No trial within the memory of living man has excited such interest as that of Frederick Baker for the murder of Fanny Adams at Alton on the 24th of August last. From an early hour the approaches to the Court were besieged by individuals anxious to obtain admission.

Never was the unsuitability of the Crown Court for the administration of justice more fully demonstrated than on this occasion. Throughout the trial the Court was most inconveniently crowded. During the early part of the morning it was evident from the noise outside that there was great dissatisfaction on the part of the excluded, who kept up such a clatter that the learned Judge directed the Under-Sheriff to send out a body of police to apprehend any one who should continue the disturbance and he would commit them to prison. This had the desired effect, and silence was established.

The learned Judge took his seat on the bench at half-past nine precisely, and the prisoner was at once arraigned. He answered the charge in a firm tone of voice with a plea of 'not guilty.' He seemed to be in good health, although somewhat agitated and very pale; but during the day he was by no means nervous, taking notes of the evidence, handing written suggestions to his attorney, and looking round the Court, occasionally appearing to derive gratification from the large number of people congregated on this solemn occasion. More than once he was seen laughing. Having pleaded to the indictment, the prisoner was allowed a chair, and he remained seated during the day.

Mr Montague Bere, Recorder of Southampton, conducted the case for the prosecution, assisted by Mr Bullen; and Mr Carter defended the prisoner. The counsel for the prosecution were instructed by Mr Coxwell; for the defence by Mr Sparkes of Guildford.[150]

Opening Speech for the Prosecution.

Mr Bere opened the case for the prosecution by observing that, if this were **Mr Bere**

---

149 Transcript of the day's proceedings amalgamated from the *Hampshire Advertiser*, Saturday 7 December 1867; *Hampshire Telegraph*, Saturday 7 December 1867; *Hampshire Chronicle*, Saturday 7 December 1867; *Hampshire Independent*, Saturday 7 December 1867; *Western Gazette and Flying Post*, Friday 13 December 1867; *Police News Edition of the Trial and Condemnation of Frederick Baker* (1867); Home Office files TNA HO 12/176/79865.

150 Richard Sparkes, a graduate of Marlborough College, in partnership with J. Rand Capron.

Baker.

Mr Bere

a usual case of murder, he should abstain from making some remarks which he considered it his duty to address to them on this occasion. But inasmuch as this case, from the innocent age of the victim, from some of the brutal circumstances connected with the dismemberment of the body, and from certain peculiarities of conduct on the part of the person charged, had created such great, such universal attention, he should not be expressing a mere matter of form if he asked them to dismiss from their minds anything they might have heard or read about this case, either as regarded the circumstances of the murder itself or the conduct of the prisoner. He called upon them earnestly and sincerely to allow themselves to be guided in their deliberations and their verdict solely and simply by the evidence that would be placed before them.

The learned counsel then proceeded with a minute detail of the evidence he was about to produce. The principal facts were as follows. Fanny Adams, the deceased, was the daughter of George and Harriet Adams, who lived in the town of Alton. At about one o'clock on the afternoon of Saturday, the 24th of August, she, with her younger sister, Lizzie, and another child named Minnie Warner, left her father's house and went out to play in a field called 'Lower Flood Meadow'. In the immediate neighbourhood of this field was a lane called Hollow, on one side of which was a hop field and on the other a clover field, a high hedge and a ditch being on the side of the former so that persons in the ground could not be seen, while the hedge on the clover field side was low.

The last time that Fanny was seen alive was about half-past one when the prisoner approached the children and after some conversation gave them some money. Fanny Adams was taken away by the prisoner up the lane leading to the hop field, where her body was afterwards found. He should prove this not merely by the evidence of the child Minnie Warner, whose accuracy they might perhaps be inclined to doubt, but he should put this matter beyond all doubt by the evidence of a woman who saw him with the three children, and going away with one of them. Furthermore, this evidence would be corroborated by a statement of the prisoner himself, who admitted that he was the man who gave the children some half-pence – a fact which he believed his learned friend for the defence would not dispute. Therefore, he thought the jury would have no doubt that the prisoner was the man last seen in the company of the little girl while alive.

About five o'clock on the Saturday afternoon, some enquiries were made as to the reason for Fanny Adams not returning home. The prisoner himself was asked what had become of the child, the answers to which would be detailed to them. It was not until between eight and nine

78

First Day – Thursday 5 December 1867.

o'clock in the evening that suspicions were aroused. A search was then made in the field where she was last seen with the prisoner, and where in different parts of it portions of her body were found. He said 'portions' because it had been dismembered in every possible way – head, legs, arm, lungs, and indeed everything. Almost all the parts, except the breast bone and one other portion, had been recovered. That the child was murdered, therefore, he thought there could not be the least doubt. The real question for them to determine was whether the prisoner at the bar was the man who committed the murder.

Now, there were no eyewitnesses to the deed, and, therefore, no direct evidence could be placed before them. But the prosecution sought to make out the charge by what was known as circumstantial evidence, by which he meant that there were a number of circumstances and facts, all of which, perhaps, if each were taken by itself, would not be conclusive, but, when joined together, made a chain linked so firm as to render it impossible for the person around whom it was formed to escape. And in some respects this was a more reliable species of evidence even than direct testimony, because a man or a woman looking on might be mistaken, but when a number of independent witnesses testified to a number of facts, each showing the accused to be the guilty person, the probability of a mistake was by no means so great.

A woman who had seen the prisoner with the child, and who would be called, heard a cry soon afterwards, though she said it was not one of pain or anguish but rather that of a child who had been detained from its parents and wished to rejoin them. The prisoner was not seen again until two o'clock, when he was spotted leaning over a gate looking into the field. At that time the murder must have been completed. The prisoner was next seen in Alton between two and three o'clock, but it did not appear that there was anything material in what then took place, so unless his learned friend desired to examine the witnesses, he (Mr Bere) did not propose to call then.

About four o'clock in the afternoon the prisoner went to the house of Mr Clement, his master, where he had a conversation with the cook, who gave him a letter to post. At that time he exhibited no peculiar signs of terror or excitement, or anything that might be supposed to indicate his having committed a murder.

Between half-past five and six o'clock the prisoner was again seen in the vicinity of the hop-ground. A witness, on seeing him leaning over a gate near the hop field, thought it her duty to go to the house of the mother of Fanny Adams. A little boy named Alfred Vince would tell them that while near the lower gate of Flood Meadows he saw the prisoner doing something to his hands and the wristbands of his shirts, at a point where

Baker.

Mr Bere the water in that meadow could be approached. Other witnesses would be called, who would prove him near the Basingstoke Road.

Mrs Adams would tell them that she saw the prisoner coming out of the gate opening from the Hollow. She asked him what had become of her little girl; he denied all knowledge of her but said he had given her a half-penny. He refused to divulge his name but gave Mrs Adams his address and told her where he was to be found. There was nothing then suspicious or improper in his conduct. However, at this time his hands were in his pockets, and therefore, supposing that they bore any traces of blood or washing, they would not be able to be seen. When he walked away he crossed a bridge at a spot near where the two eyes of the child were subsequently found. It would also be proved that when he left, and turned into the turnpike road towards Alton, he did something to his trousers.

He returned to his master's office about 6 o'clock, where a fellow clerk, Maurice Biddle, would relate a conversation that took place between them. They went out together and did not return till eight o'clock. The prisoner was then very much excited, and said he had been accused of taking away a child, but he knew nothing about it.

About eight o'clock that evening, the murder was discovered, and suspicion fell upon the prisoner. He was questioned about it when he made various statements, neither confessing his guilt nor strongly denying it. Shortly afterwards, the prisoner was taken into custody, and, on being examined, the bottom of his trousers were found to be wet, and two knives were discovered on him, such as the medical men would say might have been the instruments with which the dismemberment was effected. Subsequently in his office was found a diary containing this extraordinary entry in his own handwriting: – 'Saturday. Killed a young girl. It was fine and hot.'

These, he believed, were all the circumstances with which he should detain them, and after submitting them he should ask them as reasonable and sensible men whether the case was not made out against the prisoner as the murderer. He should show him as the last person seen with the child alive, he should show him as having been in the field where the child was killed, he should show him near every place in which parts of the body were found, he should show him to have had blood upon his clothes, he should show that he had been possessed of instruments with which he might have dismembered the body, he should show him to have made such remarks as might indicate his guilt, and then produce the extraordinary entry in the diary, which, if they believed it, was an absolute confession of his guilt. The eminent Professor Taylor would be called before them to speak as to the blood found on the prisoner's clothes. It was not within the power of human science to say, even when blood was fresh, whether it belonged to a human being or some other mammalian. But it was within the power of science to say that the blood found on the prisoner's clothes was that of a mammal, and it was for them to take into consideration whether this was likely to have come from contact with an animal, or whether it was not the result of a murder. When the prisoner's attention was called to this blood, he gave no account of it; on the contrary, looking at his hands, he said that he could not see any.

The jury would probably ask what the prosecution believed to have been the motive of the prisoner. He would tell them plainly. Minnie Warner would tell them a story about the conduct of the prisoner in the previous week, and if they believed this they could have no doubt at all that the prisoner took the child to the hop field for a certain purpose, and that in trying to effect that purpose he killed her. A stone would be produced, found near where parts of the body were discovered, and covered with blood, which the medical men had no doubt was the instrument used to cause death by fracturing the skull.

Death having been thus caused, they believed the prisoner returned to Mr Clement's – where he worked – and allowed a considerable interval to elapse between the time of the murder and cutting up the body. This was an important fact in the case, because he had no doubt his learned friend might have insisted that if the dismemberment had taken place directly after the murder a much larger quantity of blood would have been found upon the dress of him who cut it up than was discovered upon the prisoner's clothes. But in the interval – as the Crown put it to them – the blood became congealed, and hence there would be but a very small escape from the body as it was cut up.

That dismemberment, they suggested, took place for a double purpose – perhaps in order the more easily to conceal the body but expressly for the purpose of concealing the original offence, for the body was so dismembered, especially in its lower parts, that it was utterly impossible for surgical skill to trace any offence of the kind he had suggested.

He believed these were the main facts that he had to lay before them, and if he proved them he should ask the jury for a verdict of guilty; and though his friend called witnesses to convince them that the prisoner did not know the difference between right and wrong at the time he committed the murder and was not responsible for his actions, he should still ask them to say by their verdict that he committed the murder, although they might excuse him on the grounds of insanity. As he should have another opportunity of addressing them before the case was concluded, he should now place the case for the prosecution before

Baker.

Mr Bere

them. He then proceeded to call witnesses as follows: -

Thomas Stopher

THOMAS STOPHER, sworn and examined by Mr BULLEN.

I am a county surveyor living in Winchester. I have been employed to prepare plans. I produce one prepared from an actual survey of the spot. I placed certain figures and letters on it to indicate the various places of importance pointed out to me principally by Superintendent Cheyney, assisted by other constables. The scale is a quarter inch to a chain.

Cross-examined by Mr CARTER.

The distance from Mr Clement's house to the corner of the hop garden in the most direct way is about 780 yards.

Minnie Warner

MINNIE WARNER, sworn and examined by Mr BERE.

[*Before being examined, the witness was asked a few questions by his Lordship. She confirmed she went to the National School in Alton and to church on Sundays, and understood that if she told a story she would be punished. She told the judge she had taken an oath before, meaning at the inquest hearing.*]

My name is Minnie Warner. I am eight years old next birthday. My father's name is Mr Warner; my mother's name is Mrs Warner. I live in Tanhouse Lane in Alton.

Did you know Fanny Adams? — Yes, sir. I went for a walk with her on Saturday, August 24th. It was after dinner, about one o'clock. Lizzie Adams was with us. Fanny Adams is eight or nine years old; Lizzie is younger. We went to Flood Meadows and a young gentleman came down the meadow behind our backs and spoke to us.

Is he here? — Yes, sir, up there, sir [*pointing to the dock*], the man sitting down.

What did he say to you? — He said – 'Hello my little tulips, here you are again.' He played with us in the meadow and then he said he would give me a penny ha'penny to run into the Hollow with Fanny. We did that. He gave Fanny a half-pence and Lizzie a half-pence. He picked some blackberries for us. He went down with all of us into the Hollow and picked some berries and gave some to each of us. He then told Lizzie and me to go home and spend our half-pence.

He told Fanny to come along with him and he would give her two pence more. I saw him open the gate. He lifted Fanny up in his arms and carried her away, up the Hollow and into the hop ground. Fanny cried out, saying her mother would be calling her and she wanted to go home. I and Lizzie went straight home and spoke to my mother.

Later in the afternoon, when I was with Mrs Gardener, I saw the man

First Day – Thursday 5 December 1867.

who had given us the half-pence. That is the man there [*pointing again to the dock*]. I had seen the man before that – the Saturday before, playing about the meadow with Ellen White and Annie Kemp.[151] Fanny Adams was not there then. He had some talk with us that Saturday.

Minnie
Warner

[*Mr BERE said he proposed to ask the witness what the prisoner's conduct was towards these girls on the previous Saturday, which did not appear on the depositions. He had given his learned friend notice of it.*

Mr CARTER said he did not complain of his learned friend, but it was serious to admit such evidence now.

Mr JUSTICE MELLOR said it could not be excluded, as the prisoner's whole conduct was in question.]

By Mr BERE — He told us to go down the Hollow, and afterwards he told us to go home. We went home and went to bed. He did not give us any half-pence then. I have told all he did that Saturday before.

Cross-examined by Mr CARTER.

We picked berries in the Hollow. They were small red berries, the size of a currant. They have little stones in the middle and are soft in the mouth. We call them hedge haws.[152] He was not smoking when he gave us the half-pence. He did not pick the berries whilst carrying Fanny. Some of Mr Chalcraft's men were about in the fields. A working man passed right by us as we were at play. I did not know him. We played in the meadow from two till four when we went home to spend the half-pence. I knew it was four because I heard the church clock strike. It struck four as the man was carrying Fanny Adams up the Hollow.[153]

I was pleased at having the half pennies given to me, and the berries picked for us. I was not at all frightened. We sat on the grass and played. He pulled down the branch for us so that we could reach it to pick off the pretty red berries. I didn't cry, but Lizzie did. She had something in her eyes. Fanny cried when he was taking her up the Hollow. I heard crying in the night. I did not go to bed so early that night because I waited up till Fanny was found. I heard Mrs Adams crying.

Re-examined by Mr BERE.

It was nearly five o'clock when I got home. My mother had had her

---

151 The *Hampshire Telegraph* gives their names as Ellen Kemp and Lizzie Adams; the *Western Gazette* has just Emma White; the *Hampshire Advertiser* and the *Chronicle* give Harriet White and Annie Kemp. In fact, Minnie's playmates were Ellen White, aged 5, of Amery Hill, and Annie Kemp, aged 7, of Tanhouse Lane. Annie and her family later moved to Spitalfields Road; their next door neighbour was Thomas Gates.

152 They were hawthorn berries.

153 Of course, these times are wildly inaccurate, a point later picked up by Baker's defence counsel.

Baker.

Minnie Warner

tea. We had been to Knight's to spend our money on mixed sweets.[154] I spent all the money except a farthing. Lizzie gave her half-penny to her mother, and I gave some of my sweets to Lizzie. Next day my mother told me to throw the farthing away.

Eliza White

ELIZA WHITE, sworn and examined by Mr BULLEN.

I am the wife of Joseph White, who is a sawyer living at Alton. A little before two o'clock on Saturday August 24th I was coming home from work, and as I was passing along the footpath in Harris's field[155] at the top of the hop garden I saw a man at the bottom corner of the field near the Hollow. There were three children with him, two in front of him and one behind. I knew the children perfectly well – they were Minnie Warner and Elizabeth and Fanny Adams. I never saw the man before, but I know now that he is Frederick Baker.

Mr JUSTICE MELLOR: Do you see him now? — He is sitting there with his head leaning back [*pointing to the prisoner in the dock*].

Witness continued: It was about two o'clock when I saw the man and the children. I was waiting for my little girl, and I remained there watching them for about ten to fifteen minutes. One of the children was picking berries from the hedge, while the others seemed to be picking flowers from the bank. The man was loitering about with both hands in his pockets. He was smoking something dark, but I could not see whether it was a pipe or a cigar. He was dressed in a black coat, light trousers and waistcoat, and a tall hat. I kept my eye on them. When the children turned and ran into the Hollow, the man went after them.[156] I saw no more of him then. I afterwards crossed over the stile into the meadow, and about a quarter of the way across the field I heard a child cry out from across the hop garden on the farthest side. It did not seem to be a cry of pain, but as if in play. I then went home.

Cross-examined by Mr CARTER.

I had been cutting wheat at the bottom of White Hill. There are many harvest fields about there, and many persons at work – some men were gathering peas in a field adjoining the upper hop garden. Three other women were with me. I was about 100 yards from the man when I saw

---

154 Knight is a very common surname in Alton. There is no obvious candidate for Minnie's sweet shop, but at the inquest Emma Smith stated she was living with her widowed uncle, Richard Knight, at the end house in Tanhouse Lane, five doors down from Fanny's home. This is almost certainly the 'sweet shop' Minnie is referring to – perhaps Mr Knight doubled up as a 'corner shop' selling general provisions and confectionery.

155 The *Hampshire Telegraph* gives Wallis's field, while the trial deposition identifies it as Horace's field. In fact, tithe maps list it as Harris's field.

156 The *Hampshire Telegraph* has 'the man looked at me and then went after them'.

him. My eyes are perfectly good; I never use glasses in reading. He was a little way from the bottom of the field, where there is no footpath. He seemed to be perfectly at his ease. I am sure I saw him take something out of his mouth and put it back in again. The children did not appear to be in any fear. I was going through Chandler's Field when I heard the cry: it was a sound such as a child would raise when caught hold of in play, and not when in pain. I knew nothing about the child being missing till about 7 o'clock, when my little girl told me that Fanny Adams was lost. I said, 'Nonsense, she is not lost, she knows her way for miles round.' My child said a man had given her some money and taken her away. It then struck me that I had seen the children with a man. I cannot swear that I did not pass the same way on the 17th of August. Flood Meadows is resorted to by children for play. The berries the children were picking are called 'hedge haws.' It was exactly ten minutes past two o'clock by the church when I got home. My house is scarcely so far as half a mile from the Hollow.[157]

Eliza
White

WILLIAM ALLWORK, sworn and examined by Mr BERE.

William
Allwork

I am a cricket bat maker and I live in Alton High Street. I remember Saturday, August 24th. I left home that day at ten minutes past twelve, and went to Lasham, arriving there at one o'clock. I got back to Alton about two o'clock. I came back the same way I went by crossing through Flood Meadows by Chalcraft's farm. As I was returning I saw the man I believe to be the prisoner leaning on the gate in the Hollow. He was alone. I was twenty yards from the gate when I saw him.

Cross-examined by Mr CARTER.

I knew the man by sight, having seen him several times in Alton over the past six or seven months, but I did not know his name. He was leaning against the Hollow gate when I passed. The man faced me as I walked along. I did not see him smoking – if he was, I should have noticed it. I saw three children playing by themselves about midway between the Flood Meadows gate and the Hollow gate. I did not take particular notice of them. I heard one child say to the other, 'I'll tell your mother Minnie'. Being a familiar name, I recollect it. I did not hear anyone cry. Two fields off I saw some people harvesting: they were at dinner when I went by.

I don't remember saying anything before the magistrates about seeing any children, but I can swear this incident occurred on the 24th August, and not on the 17th. I remember the day well because I was sent with a telegraphic message to Lasham.

---

157   The *Hampshire Advertiser* has 'half a mile from the middle of Alton'.

Baker.

William Allwork

Re-examined by Mr BERE.

I live in the High Street, about a quarter of a mile from where I saw the children. It was a quarter past two when I got home.

Elizabeth Warner

ELIZABETH WARNER, sworn and examined by Mr BULLEN.

I am the sister of Minnie Warner and I live in the same house as her. On Saturday, the 24th of August, I remember she went out to play with Fanny and Lizzie Adams about one o'clock after dinner. I remember her coming home alone around half-past two, bringing some half-pence with her. She went out again and remained away till four o'clock. On coming back the second time she brought a farthing with her, which her mother told her to throw away.

Cross-examined by Mr CARTER.

I did not give evidence before the magistrates. My sister went out with Fanny and Lizzie Adams the first time. She came back about half-past two, telling me that a gentleman had given them some half-pence. When I asked her who he was, she said she did not know but it was the same gentleman they had met the Saturday before in the meadow. The second time she went out she was alone and joined Lizzie Adams and her mother. She returned at four o'clock and brought home some sweets.

I did not see Fanny Adams at all that day.

George Noyce

GEORGE NOYCE, sworn and examined by Mr BERE.

I am under-shepherd to Mr Chalcraft. On the 24th of August I was in Twelve Acres Field. At two minutes past three o'clock by my watch I saw a man coming towards the hop garden from the old road.[158] I did not see him in the road, but he was coming along the hedge beside the footway by the Kiln Piece. As soon as he saw me, he put his hand under the skirts of his jacket and walked back. I had not known him before.

Mr JUSTICE MELLOR: Do you see him to-day? — I see him there sitting down [*pointing out the prisoner in the dock*].

Witness continued: After he saw me he walked back, then came forward again, and followed me over the stile into Chauntry Piece which leads towards the Hollow. He was dressed in light trousers and a black jacket.[159] I did notice if he was wearing a waistcoat. I saw him between Chauntry Piece and the pea-field.

---

158 Unusually, George Noyce was carrying a watch, hence the precise timing of his encounter with Baker. Agricultural workers generally relied on the chimes from St Lawrence's to tell them the time.

159 Some press reports quote Noyce as saying the man was wearing a high hat or a round hat.

First Day – Thursday 5 December 1867.

Cross-examined by Mr CARTER.

The man was coming from the old road when I saw him. He was not smoking and I did not see him with a pipe at all. He put his hands under the tails of his coat and walked back. I don't remember saying before the magistrates that when he saw me he went up to the stile and got over it. I got over the stile first. I never saw him before that day. I admit that before the magistrates I did say that the prisoner looked like the man, but he had not the same dress on. He came within fifteen or sixteen yards of me, but we went in different directions.

SARAH NORRIS, sworn and examined by Mr BULLEN.

I am cook to Mr Clement, solicitor, of Alton. The prisoner was employed there as a clerk. Shortly before four in the afternoon[160] on the day of the murder I went into the office and gave the prisoner a letter to post. He was sitting down by the window. I remember the time because they were at tea at four o'clock. I left him in the office and did not see him again till half-past six, when I found him in the office again.

Cross-examined by Mr CARTER.

There are three other clerks who work in the office, but I didn't see anybody else there at that time apart from Mr Biddle. Mr Clement was generally at home in the afternoon. When he [Baker] took the letter he appeared quite calm. I don't know that he spoke to me when he took the letter. I saw no marks of blood on his hands. There was nothing excited or unusual in his manner. He left for dinner about the middle of the day, leaving someone in the office while he was away. The clerks leave at different times, so that one is always there. He might have been in the office a considerable time when I saw him at half-past six. I cannot say how long.

ALFRED VINCE, sworn and examined by Mr BERE.

[Before being examined, the witness, a child of about seven years of age, was interrogated by the judge in the usual way to test his capacity for giving evidence. The boy said he did not know how old he was and his father's name was George Vince. He told the Judge: 'I go to church and school. I am come here to tell what is true. I have heard of God; He loves good people, and punishes bad people. I know I am to tell the truth.']

I remember the day when Fanny Adams was killed. About five o'clock I was standing at the new gate in Tanhouse Lane next to the tan yard. I saw a man come out of the Hollow into Flood Meadow. He went to the

George Noyce

Sarah Norris

Alfred Vince

---

160   The *Hampshire Chronicle* times it precisely at two minutes to four o'clock.

Baker.

Alfred Vince

place where the boys bathe and I saw him wash his hands. He had his coat sleeves turned back. I was looking at him and he held up his fist at me. He had on a black coat, grey trousers and waistcoat, and a high hat. After he had washed his hands he wiped them dry with a pocket handkerchief. Before he washed his hands he had red on them. I saw his hands were red but they were white afterwards. He ran towards me about half way to the gate, and I ran away. He did not say anything to me. Afterwards I met Mrs Gardener, Emma Smith, and a few others coming down the lane, so I went back with them to the Meadow. They called the man back and both spoke to him. After they had spoken to him, he went down Turville's Meadow. Mrs Gardener and those with her then went home. I went home and told my mother.

The same evening I went into the hop garden and saw the head and leg part of a child.

Cross-examined by Mr CARTER.

The man was quite a stranger to me. I remember being taken up to the great house on the hill at Winchester[161] last month and being shown a number of men. There was one with a high hat on. He was standing several feet from the others. When my mother and I passed him she gave me a nudge, and I then stopped and looked at him, and said 'That is the man'.

Emma Smith

EMMA SMITH, sworn and examined by Mr BERE.

I am a single woman living with my uncle in Tanhouse Lane, Alton. It is the last house in the Lane, five doors down from the Adams's. The gate at the end of Tanhouse Lane is about ten yards off our house. I remember the 24th of August last. I was standing outside my house between a quarter-past and half-past five when I saw a man coming down the Hollow out of the hop garden. He crossed the lane, looked over a gate for a short time, and then came down the lane towards Flood Meadow. I later heard it was Mr Frederick Baker, but I did not know him at the time, nor do I now. He was dressed in light trousers, a dark coat and a black high hat. I told Mrs Gardener there was a man coming down the Hollow and she and Mrs Adams went to speak to him.

Cross-examined by Mr CARTER.

I can't say how far off he was when I first saw him. The Meadow was between us. I couldn't see anyone in the hop garden at that distance. I had been standing in my garden for half an hour before seeing the prisoner. I had seen nobody in Flood Meadows before that – nobody

161   Winchester Gaol.

First Day – Thursday 5 December 1867.

washing his hands at the bathing place, nor any little boy like Albert Vince loitering about. I wasn't able to distinguish the man's features and I could not say if he was smoking.

Alton is sufficiently populous to account for a number of persons walking about the fields in the middle of the day. There were several people in the lane besides Mrs Gardener and Mrs Adams.

Re-examined by Mr BERE.

Mrs Gardener and Mrs Adams were talking to the man for about five minutes, and then he went away in the direction of the toll-house on Basingstoke Road.

HARRIET ADAMS, sworn and examined by Mr BERE.

I am the wife of George Adams, and I live in Tanhouse Lane, Alton. I had a daughter named Fanny, who was 8 years and 4 months old. I remember her leaving home about half-past one in the afternoon on Saturday the 24th of August. She went out to play in Flood Meadows with her sister Elizabeth and Minnie Warner, a neighbour's child. She did not come home again.

Lizzie came back just before two[162] and told me Fanny had gone with a gentleman into the Hollow. She told me the man had given her a half penny and had given Fanny one and Minnie one. Lizzie then went out again. She came back a second time between three and four, but I did not see her join anyone outside, nor did I see anyone with her. Finding that Fanny had still not come back I enquired of the neighbours if any of them had seen her. I spoke to Mrs Gardener about it, but she could give me no information. I then went indoors, and about half an hour afterwards I was standing at my door when Mrs Gardener asked me if I had found her, and I said no. I saw Emma Smith speaking to Mrs Gardener at the door, whence they came and told me that there was a man in the Hollow, and it was the same man who had taken Fanny away.

I went into Flood Meadows with Mrs Gardener. Minnie Warner came with us, following behind. I did not notice Alfred Vince, but there were several other people in the Meadows besides Minnie Warner. I saw a man come out of the Hollow and head towards Basingstoke Road by the bridge. He was dressed in a tall hat, light waistcoat and trousers, and a black coat. It was then about half-past five.

Mrs Gardener called to the man twice. On the second time he stopped and came over. Mrs Gardener spoke to him. She asked – 'What have you done with the child you took away?' He replied that he had not taken

Emma
Smith

Harriet
Adams

---

162   Under cross-examination by Mr Carter, Mrs Adams later corrected this timing to three o'clock.

89

Baker.

Harriet Adams

any child away. Mrs Gardener then said – 'Did you not give the children some half-pence?' and he said 'Yes'. Mrs Gardener then said – 'Here comes Minnie Warner.' Minnie came up, and Mrs Gardener asked her if this was the gentleman who gave her some money. She replied – 'Yes.' Mrs Gardener asked how much he gave her, and she answered –'Three pennies.' The man corrected her, saying 'No, three half-pence.' Mrs Gardener then asked him his name. He replied – 'Never mind my name, you will find me at Mr Clement's office if you want me.'[163] After that Mrs Gardener begged his pardon, and we all left, the man going towards the Basingstoke Road by a path through Turville's Meadow. In order to get to the road he would have to cross a bridge in the meadow. The path comes out by the toll-house, which was then kept by Mrs Porter. I didn't see the prisoner again that day after he left us.

Some stays and a red petticoat and a brown velvet hat were shown me by Superintendent Cheyney at the police station. I recognized them as having been worn by my daughter, Fanny, when she left home.

Cross-examined by Mr CARTER.

I don't think my memory has failed me about the time. It was nearly three o'clock when my daughter Lizzie came back the first time; she was crying because her brother Walter had taken the half-penny which the gentleman had given her. My statement earlier that she came back about two o'clock was a mistake.

The man was quite a stranger to me, and so far as I know he had no ill-feeling towards me or my children. There was nothing unusual about him when he spoke to us. He was not smoking. He stood with his hands in his pocket. Mrs Gardener spoke rather crossly to him, but he gave his address so readily she begged his pardon. She wanted me to give him in charge of the police, but he answered so openly and unconcernedly that I declined to do so.

Flood Meadows is a favourite resort for children. It is hilly ground up to the hop garden. The Hollow rises at both ends, and there is a thick hedge on each side. The child's father was playing cricket that day, and we made enquiry if Fanny had been to him.

Mary Ann Porter

MARY ANN PORTER, sworn and examined by Mr. BERE.

I am the wife of William Porter, a gardener at Alton. In August last

---

163 The law firm of W. & J.W. Clement and Son were located at 42 High Street, opposite the Swan Hotel and close to Baker's lodgings. Much of their work involved conveyancing; Frederick's job was to prepare title deeds and other property transfer documents, and there are some surviving in his hand where he acted as a witness to transactions. A few yards further up the High Street there was a shortcut leading to Amery Hill and the hop plantations. Today the premises are occupied by Barclays Bank.

First Day – Thursday 5 December 1867.

I was living at the old toll-house at the bottom of Turville's Meadow, adjoining the Basingstoke Road. At about six o'clock on the evening of the 24th of August I was sitting at the door of my house when I saw the prisoner coming from Turville's Meadow towards the Basingstoke Road. I had seen him come the same way earlier that afternoon. On both occasions he came out of the gate and passed in front of my cottage, heading towards Alton. The second time he stooped down several times and moved his arms about as if doing something to his trousers or feet.

Mary Ann Porter

Cross-examined by Mr CARTER.

The first time I saw him it was before my husband had his tea at four o'clock. I might have seen about a dozen persons pass my house that afternoon, without my noticing them in particular. It is dusty sometimes in the hot month of August, and persons will take out a handkerchief and dust their feet before entering the town – it is possible the man was dusting the lower parts of his trousers when he stooped down but I did not see a handkerchief in his hands. The second time he passed the house he looked hard at me – that was the reason I noticed him, because he looked me full in the face. He turned his head round as he passed, to see whether I watched him.

Mr CARTER: Not as if he wished to hide his face, then? — No.

Re-examined by Mr BERE.

I did not rise from my seat to look at him. He was not smoking when he went past me. I did not observe any marks on his clothes. I merely noticed the way in which he was dressed. [*Witness described his dress in the same terms as the other witnesses.*]

JANE GARDENER, sworn and examined by Mr BERE.

Jane Gardener

I am the wife of John Gardener and I live in Tanhouse Lane, Alton, three doors from Mrs Adams. I remember hearing from Emma Smith that Fanny Adams was missing. At about half-past five in the afternoon, when I was doing my household work, Mrs Adams came to my home and told me of it. I accompanied her in search of the man, and within five minutes of my leaving home I saw a man crossing the top of the meadow. At the Flood Meadows gate, I called out, 'Hoi, stop!', and he came towards us. I asked him what he had done with the child he had taken away at half-past one. He was speechless almost, and stammered, 'I have not seen a child.' I then said to him, 'Did you not give some children some half-pence today?' and he said he did. In the meantime Minnie Warner came running towards me, and I said to her, 'Minnie, is this the gentleman who gave you some money today?' She said, 'Yes.'

Baker.

Jane
Gardener

I then said, 'How much?' and she replied 'Threepence,' to which the man said, 'No, it was three half-pence.' I asked Minnie how much he gave Lizzie and Fanny, and she replied a half penny each. I then asked, 'What did he then do?' She answered, 'He told me to go home and spend the money, and then he took Fanny in his arms up into the hop garden behind the high hedge.'

I said to Mrs Adams, 'Why don't you give this fellow in charge of the police?' He said, 'I am quite willing to go with you to the police,' and he walked with us several steps. Thinking from his manner that I had done wrong, I said, 'Sir, the reason for my speaking to you in this way is because an old gentleman has been passing this way, giving children half-pence for no good purpose, and if I have ill-judged you, or done wrong in speaking to you, I humbly beg your pardon'. He bowed to me, and I curtsied to him. He then turned around and as the man was going away I called out, 'We will have your name,' but he replied 'I am to be found at Mr Clement's office.'

Cross-examined-by Mr CARTER.

I can't remember when I first heard the man's name was Baker. I don't think I knew his name before I went in search of him. He came straight to us when I called him to stop, there was nothing like running away. He was walking in a leisurely manner. I spoke sharply to him, being rather cross. When I spoke to him about the child he appeared speechless, but as soon as he recovered breath he answered me that he had not seen any child. He was very calm after that. He did not deny, however, giving the children half-pence. I did not know his address until he told me. I did not notice anything particular about his dress. He wore light trousers but I did not see any dirt upon them, nor did I see stains of blood on his clothes or hands, although he never took his hands out of his pockets. He had his hands in his pockets when I first ran up to him. He was not smoking. I saw no wetness about his clothing except his boots which appeared to have been first wet and then covered over with dust which appeared cracked or scratched as if he had been in a wood or something of that sort. When we parted, the man bowed and I curtsied. He was very polite when I begged his pardon.

Mr CARTER: What made you have such a feeling of repentance all at once as to beg his pardon? — What mother wouldn't fly to assist her child?

Witness continued: I can't say how many women were in the lane when the prisoner and I parted. There were a good many children and others standing round when I spoke to him, but I didn't notice anyone in particular. I know Mr Clement quite well.

First Day – Thursday 5 December 1867.

By Mr JUSTICE MELLOR — It was near the bathing place that I met the prisoner.

Jane Gardener

MAURICE BIDDLE, sworn and examined by Mr BERE.

Maurice Biddle

For two years I have been in the employ of Mr. Clement of Alton as a junior clerk. Frederick Baker was an engrossing clerk in the same office. I sat in the same room as him. He had been there for just over twelve months. On Saturday, the 24th of August, I was in the office with the prisoner. He seemed as if he had been drinking, and later he confessed he had been drinking gin and beer when he came in about ten o'clock that morning. He left the office about eleven, and came back after a quarter of an hour;[164] about an hour later he went out again, returning shortly before one. I left the office at one o'clock for dinner, leaving Baker there, I believe, with another clerk.[165] I came back about three. The other clerk, Mr French, was there when I returned. I don't think Baker came in till about twenty-five minutes afterwards, but I can't swear positively to it. He left the office again about half-past four. I went to tea at five, returning at six, about the same time as the prisoner.[166] We remained until just before seven, when Baker and I went out together to the Swan Tap for a glass of ale, which is just across the road. The prisoner at this time seemed as if he had been drinking. Whilst on his way to the Swan, and also whilst there, he said he had been accused by some women in Flood Meadows of taking a child away, but I can't remember his exact words. He added that all he knew about it was that he had given some children a few half-pence. He said if the child was murdered or anything it would be awkward for him and he supposed he should be blamed for it. He said he was going away to the north on Monday, and asked me if

---

164   Baker nipped over to the Swan Tap for a drink. According to several sources, he made a clumsy pass at the barmaid: 'It appears that Baker called at a public house he had been in the habit of using on the morning of the murder, he had some refreshment and flirted with the barmaid for some little time, and endeavoured to snatch a kiss from her. The landlady of the house in questions expressed her surprise that he should begin the day in such an unseemly manner, whereupon Baker replied "Oh never mind, you will not see me again" but little notice was taken of this observation at the time, but afterwards the words seemed to possess an awful significance: the question was very naturally asked, did he at that time while toying with the barmaid contemplate the consummation of a tragedy that took place later in the day?' *Police News Edition of the Life and Examination of Frederick Baker* (1867), p. 2.

165   According to the *Hampshire Telegraph*, Biddle testified that 'I left at one for dinner, leaving Baker alone in the office.' Biddle's trial deposition states 'I left the office about 1 o'clock on the Saturday afternoon and whether he [Baker] was there or not I do not know.'

166   The *Hampshire Chronicle* has Biddle arriving back at the office around a quarter past six, and Baker about five minutes later.

Baker.

**Maurice
Biddle**

I would go with him. He meant that he intended leaving and not coming back again. He also said there had been a similar case of a child being lost at Guildford, but the girl turned up in that case.[167]

When the boots[168] came in, the subject of going away was again brought up. The boots said he was going away on Monday and Baker replied, 'We may as well go away together.' Boots said, 'You would not do to go with me, for I can put my hand to anything, but you can't.' Baker said he could turn his hands to butchering. We stayed there till a little before eight, and left together. We went to a grocer's shop, where Baker ordered some provisions, and afterwards to a chemist's, where I left him at the door.[169]

I returned to the office. Having heard something at the office about a murder, I went back to the chemist's shop where I found Baker. I said to him, 'Baker, they say you have murdered a child.' He said, 'Never, Maury; it is a bad job for me, then.' I said, 'Well, let's go to the office and see if there's any truth in it.' We then went to the office. When there, a person called Doggrell[170] came in and asked 'Where's Baker; they say he has been and murdered a child,' or some such words. I told Doggrell that Baker was in the office, and Baker stepped forward. I don't remember the exact words he used but said he was innocent and it was a bad job for him.

I left the office for two minutes for the purpose of ascertaining if the report of the murder was true, but meeting Superintendent Cheyney in the street I came back with him. Mr. Trimming, the senior clerk, was with Baker when I returned. Baker was leaning against a desk – not his desk but another one further away – and smoking a cigar. Shortly afterwards Superintendent Cheyney took him into custody.

I was aware that the prisoner kept a diary, and I know his handwriting. [*The diary was handed to him.*] The last entry, dated 24th August, is in his handwriting.

Cross-examined by Mr CARTER.

I have often seen the prisoner make entries in his diary, which he keeps in the office, locked in his desk, but I did not see him make an entry

---

167   A reference to the case of Jane Sax, murdered by James Longhurst in 1866. See Appendix H.

168   George Gatehouse was employed as a servant at the Swan. His duties included cleaning and polishing shoes and boots, and other menial jobs.

169   Baker popped into the chemist shop to buy some scent. Perhaps the stink of butchery was oppressing him. The chemist shop at 49 High Street was called Trimming (no relation to William Trimming, the senior clerk at Clement & Son).

170   William Doggrell, twenty-three, worked in his father's bakery shop at 2 Market Square, Alton.

that day. There are four clerks at the office – Mr Trimming, Mr French, the prisoner, and me. Our desks are not side by side. One of the Messrs Clements was there as well. I remember it was twenty-five minutes past three when Baker came back from dinner because I looked at my watch. I don't recollect the prisoner telling me at half-past four that I might go to tea then. I left at five, and I think Baker went out at half-past four. The clerk French was in the office when I went to tea.

Maurice
Biddle

When Baker spoke about the women accusing him of taking the child away, he appeared rather excited.[171] I have known the prisoner for twelve months, and in all that time he has never complained of violent pains in the head, nor of bleeding from the nose occasionally. On the afternoon in question I did not notice anything particular about his dress; I did not see any blood about him.

Mr CARTER: Was he not a restless sort of man? Fond of walking? — He was fond of walking about in his leisure hours.

Witness continued: When reference was made to what the women had said he remarked that he supposed if anything happened to the child he should be blamed for it, but the word murder was used also. The first I heard of the child being murdered was a little after eight, from Mr Trimming, and afterwards from Doggrell. When I told him that he was accused of murder, he said 'Never, Maury.' I did not notice him doing anything at his desk all that day. The prisoner went to the chemist's for some scent.

By Mr JUSTICE MELLOR — I have seen him before when he has been drinking. He appeared excited then, but not at other times.

[*The entry in the diary referred to above was then read out in court by the Clerk of Assize. It said, '24th of August, Saturday.— Killed a young girl. It was fine and hot.'*]

WILLIAM TRIMMING, sworn and examined by Mr BERE.

William
Trimming

I am senior clerk to Messrs Clements, solicitors, of Alton, where I have been employed thirty or forty years. I remember Saturday, August 24th last. I went to the office at ten o'clock that morning. Probably I was the first there. The prisoner was there between ten and eleven o'clock. As I went out, at about a quarter to one, I saw the prisoner coming back from the Swan Tap. I did not return to the office till a quarter-past six. When I came back, the prisoner and the other clerks were there. He was there until shortly before seven, when he left with Biddle. A few minutes afterwards Mrs Adams came to the office and made an enquiry. I only saw her the once that evening. About half an hour later, on hearing of the murder, and on Biddle coming back, I directed Biddle to go fetch Baker.

---

171   The *Western Gazette* has 'rather annoyed'.

Baker.

William
Trimming
That was about eight o'clock.

When the prisoner came into the office he said, 'You never accuse me of doing such a thing?' I replied, 'I don't accuse you, but Mrs Callender[172] says you have murdered a girl and cut her head off, and that the police are after you.' Baker said, 'It is a serious thing to be accused of. What had I better do?' I said, 'If I were you, I would call upon the child's friends and see what it all means.' Biddle said, 'Come on, I'll go with you,' and just then Doggrell came rushing in and said, 'Have you heard of this dreadful murder? They say a fellow in your office has done it, and is gone off by train, and the police are after him.'

Biddle said, 'Baker is here,' at which point Baker stepped forward and said, 'Yes, here he is; but he is innocent.'

Some other conversation took place, during which Baker said several times that it was a serious thing to be accused of. I advised him to go to the police, but Baker replied he should not do that; if the police wanted him they would be sure to come after him. He remained in the office for perhaps ten minutes until Cheyney arrived.

He was dressed both morning and evening in the same dark coat and light waistcoat and trousers, and a high hat.

[A letter addressed to Sir W. Bovill, dated the 24th August, and declared to be in the prisoner's handwriting, was here put in evidence. It read as follows:–]

Alton, 21st August 1867

Sir William, – Hoping you will excuse the great liberty I take in addressing these few lines to you, thinking you might interest yourself in my behalf, is my only object. I am a son of Frederick Baker, of South Street, Guildford, tailor, who, on the various occasions on which you were a candidate for the representation of that town, gave his vote and interest in your behalf; and I believe you once said if I wanted a situation, or I wished to better my position in life, you would use your interest in my behalf. I am now anxious to do so, and this is the reason for making this appeal. I was for five years and upwards in the employ of Messrs W. H. and M. Smallpiece, and can produce a good testimonial from them. I was a member of both institutions for twelve years and more, and for some time a member of the committee of the Working Men's Institution, secretary to the Debating and Elocution Society, a working director of the Penny Savings' Bank, for ten years and upwards was a Sunday teacher in Holy Trinity and St Mary's National School, and

---

172   Almost certainly Charlotte Callender, a widow, of Anstey Road, beyond Eggar's School. In 1871 she moved to Normandy Street with her son Francis.

am now employed by Messrs Clements and Son, of Alton, solicitors, where I have been for one year and upwards, and can obtain a good testimonial from them. My chief duties have been magisterial, tax, and poor-law business, drawing deeds under the supervision of the principal and engrossing. My objective for leaving is only on account of seeing no chance of progress or advance of salary. My age is 29. Should you feel kindly disposed to use your interest in procuring a situation for me, or improving my position, I shall be truly grateful.

William Trimming

Humbly apologizing for this intrusion,
I remain, Sir William,
Your most obedient Servant,
Frederick Baker

PS. Any communication can be made to the following address – F. Baker, Mrs Kingston's, High Street, Alton.

Cross-examined by Mr CARTER.

I was in the office all the time from seven o'clock till he was taken into custody, and I am confident he could not have made the entry during that time. I believe he made the entry between twenty minutes past six and before he left at a quarter to seven, but I cannot say he did. I noticed nothing unusual in his dress that day, nor in himself, except that he had been drinking from early in the morning. He appeared excited all evening. I considered that he was muddled with drink. When the conversation took place about the murder, his manner was not such as to cause suspicion. I did not think there was any foundation for the charge at first. He made no objection to going to the child's friends. He might have been going there with Biddle when Doggrell came in.

I have looked at the diary since this affair. There appears to be an entry on every day, or nearly so. There are entries of marriages and deaths, and other small things, and of work he had not done, and how he employed himself on Sundays. I don't know that there is any record in the diary of a man hanging himself at Headley.[173]

[*Mr Carter read an entry in the diary on the 27th May: 'A child drowned in King's Pond—it was fine and hot.' Mr Carter also pointed out that the expression 'fine and hot' was of frequent occurrence in the diary.*]

I knew nothing of his application to Sir W. Bovill.

173 On 3 February 1867, Edward Hill, 73, of Headley, committed suicide by hanging himself from a beam in the washhouse attached to his cottage. See *Hampshire Advertiser*, 9 February 1867.

Baker.

William Trimming

I was not called before the magistrates, being then engaged in taking depositions.

Thomas Gates

THOMAS GATES, sworn and examined.

I am a labourer in Mr Chalcraft's employ at Alton. I look after the hop garden. On Saturday the 24th August I heard that a child had been murdered just above Lower Flood Meadow; I went there about twenty minutes before eight. The first thing I found was a piece of a child's dress in the hop garden, covered in blood. Walking on a little further, towards the top of the garden, I came across the head of a child lying on two hop poles on the ground. It was dirty. I took it up by the long hair, and laid it on my arm. I then went a few yards further found a leg and thigh separated from the body, which I also picked up and placed on my arm. Coming down towards Flood Meadows I found the trunk of the body about fifteen or sixteen yards from the hedge which separated the hop ground from the meadow. The body had been cut open like a sheep that had been killed; I looked inside and found it was all cleaned out – the bowels were gone. I laid the head, leg, and other part down by the trunk. I was frightened and greatly shocked by what I saw. I remained there till the police came. Charles White took away what I had found.

Cross-examined by Mr CARTER.

I was induced to go into the field by what Mrs White told me. The hop ground is five minutes' walk from my house. It was getting on nearly dark when I arrived there. I was shocked and overcome with what I found.

Charles White

CHARLES WHITE, sworn and examined.

I am an engine driver living in Alton. I went into the hop field with Constable Thomas Light in search of the body and saw Thomas Gates there. Under instruction of the policeman, I picked up the portions of the child, wrapped them in a cloth and apron, and carried them to the Leather Bottle public house on Amery Street. Afterwards, Constable Light came and took them to the Station.

The following day I and several others again went into the hop field in search of the missing portions of the body. I was present when the intestines were found. A man named Henry Allen found the lungs. I also found a child's hat in the middle of a hedge, not far from the spot of blood where I thought the murder had been committed. I tied them all together in a handkerchief and took them to Superintendent Cheyney at the police station.

First Day – Thursday 5 December 1867.

Cross-examined by Mr CARTER.

The murder spot was about 20 yards from the gate. Standing there, I could see down the hill to Tanhouse Lane. I looked about but I did not find a knife, or axe, or hatchet, or anything of that sort. The ground was in a state of cultivation.

HARRY ALLEN, sworn and examined.

I am a coach painter living in Alton. On Saturday night, shortly before nine o'clock, I went into the hop garden with Charles White. At first I did not find anything, but I went home and got a lantern and returned to the garden. I then found a heart, which I gave to Constable Light at the police station. Next morning, at daylight, I renewed the search in a stubble field adjoining the hop garden. There I found an arm under the hedge covered with some hedge clippings. Later, I also found the lungs. Charles White took the lungs and the arm to the police station.

Cross-examined by Mr CARTER.

The arm was the only part of the child which seemed to have been covered over. I saw Gates with the parts he found.

THOMAS SWAYNE, sworn and examined.

I am a shoemaker residing at Alton. On Sunday morning, about half-past six, I found the left foot of a child in a clover field on the left hand side of a lane called the Hollow, next to Mr Chalcraft's hop garden. It was about eight yards from the hedge. I took it to the police station.

JOSEPH WATERS, sworn and examined.

I am a Constable in the Hampshire Constabulary stationed at Bentley in the Alton Division. On Sunday, the 25th August, I went with other constables to the hop garden, but could find nothing. I searched next day with a similar result. But on Tuesday, around three o'clock, after searching in the river Wey for two hours, I found an eye in the middle of the stream, on the lower side of the bridge towards Alton. There were ten inches of water.

PC Masterman who was aiding in the search, found a second eye about a yard off, below the bridge. I took both of the eyes to the place where the coroner was holding an inquest, and gave them to Dr. Leslie.

Cross-examined by Mr CARTER.

The bridge is about 700 yards from the hop garden, about a quarter of a mile.

Charles White

Harry Allen

Thomas Swayne

Joseph Waters

Baker.

Thomas Light

THOMAS LIGHT, sworn and examined.

I am a Constable in the Hampshire Constabulary stationed at Alton. On Saturday the 24th August I went with the last witness to Mr Chalcraft's hop garden and there found half the body of a child. I had it removed first to the Leather Bottle, and then I took it to the police station. I put the remains in a cart shed, which was locked up. Other parts were afterwards brought to the station, which I put in the same place.

William Henry Walker

WILLIAM HENRY WALKER, sworn and examined.

I am painter living at Alton. On Sunday, August 25th, I searched the hop garden and found a stone close to the spot where the head was found. [*The stone was produced by Superintendent Cheyney.*] It was covered with blood, some long hair, and three small pieces of flesh. I noticed two hop poles were lying nearby. I took the stone to my father's house and left it in the front room till it was produced at the coroner's inquest. It was called for by Mr Cheyney when I was out.

Cross-examined by Mr CARTER.

I put the stone in the open window of the front room. I don't know what kind of a stone it is, but it seems to be a sort of flint. Of course, there were other stones lying about the hop garden; some were larger and some smaller. [*The witness delivered his evidence in so unsatisfactory a manner – he appeared to be trifling with the answers he gave – that his Lordship told him that he was not there to show his quickness of repartee, but to give evidence. This was a very solemn matter.*]

William James Walker

WILLIAM JAMES WALKER, sworn and examined.

I am the father of the last witness, who lives with me. I remember my son bringing home the stone on Sunday morning the 25th of August. On the Monday I gave it to Police Constable Watkins for Superintendent Cheyney.

William Cheyney

WILLIAM CHEYNEY, sworn and examined.

I am a Superintendent in the Hampshire Constabulary stationed at Alton. At about eight o'clock on Saturday night, the 24th of August, information was brought to me at the station that a child had been murdered in the Chalcrafts' hop garden. I went towards the place and met Charles White who was carrying a bundle which contained some of the remains of a child. He took the bundle to the Leather Bottle, where I examined it.

The bundle contained the head of a female child which had been severed from the trunk. The eyes were missing, having been scooped

First Day – Thursday 5 December 1867.

out. The right ear was cut off and missing. There was also a leg and a thigh, apparently of a young child, with a boot and stocking on. The stocking was tied above the knee. The trunk had been opened and the insides removed. The right leg had been torn off from the trunk and the left forearm cut off at the elbow. The left foot had been cut off and was missing. The lungs and intestines were also missing. Some clothes of a female child had been found which were torn to pieces. There was a dress which appeared to have been cut up the front. The clothes were shown to Mrs. Adams, who identified them as having been worn by the deceased.

William Cheyney

I had the parts removed to the police station, and sent for Dr Leslie. I then proceeded to make enquiries.

Finding that Frederick Baker was suspected, I went to the office of Messrs. Clement between eight and nine o'clock, and saw the prisoner there. He was standing in the office with his hands in his pockets and his hat on. I said, 'Have you heard that a child has been murdered?' He answered, 'Yes; they say it's me, don't they?' I replied – 'Yes, you are suspected.' He said, 'I am innocent, and I am willing to go where you like.' I said, 'What knives have you about you?' He produced two [*produced in court*] – a white handled one having three blades, and another with a buck horn handle having two blades. The largest blade of the latter is a little blunt at the top, and there is a slight smear near the edge, apparently caused by blood – at least, looking more like blood than anything else.

I said to him, 'I can't lose sight of you. I must leave a constable with you while I make further enquiries.' I left Constable Watkins with him. At this time I did not observe anything unusual about his clothes, but I did not take particular notice of them then.

I went and saw Minnie Warner and other witnesses, and from what they told me I returned to the office and told the prisoner I should take him into custody on suspicion of having killed Fanny Adams in Chalcraft's hop ground. He said he was innocent. I told Baker there were witnesses who would prove that he had given the deceased a half penny and the others three half-pence. He said 'That proves nothing because I am in the habit of giving children half-pence when I am out for a walk.'

I then took him with me to the police station, where I searched him. In his pockets I found a bunch of keys, the letter which has been just read, a cigar, a pocket comb, a piece of soap, and the sum of £1 6s 1½d in money. I told him to take off his clothes, and when he had done so I found that his left boot and stocking were quite wet, also the left leg of his trousers. I asked him how he accounted for these being wet, and he said that proved nothing for he was in the habit of stepping into the

Baker.

William
Cheyney

water when out for a walk. The other leg of the trousers was damp, although drier than the other. The trouser legs looked as if they had been recently washed, but there appeared to be spots of blood on them. I then told him to take off his shirt. The left wrist band appeared to have been washed. I found faint stains of blood on the wristband. I asked him how he accounted for the blood on his shirt sleeve, but he offered no explanation.

The following day some other parts of the body were brought to the police station, such as the intestines and legs. The ear which had been cut off was also brought in, I think, by the witness Allen. I put all the parts together ready for Dr. Leslie's autopsy examination. Afterwards they were locked up.

The following day, on Monday 26th, I went to the office of Messrs. Clement with the keys I had taken from the prisoner. Superintendent Everitt accompanied me. I unlocked the desk drawer which was pointed out to be Baker's. I found a diary, which I now produce. Under the date of Saturday, 24th August there is an entry which reads 'Killed a young girl. It was fine and hot.' I was afterwards present when that entry was shown to Baker in his cell by Superintendent Everitt, who asked the prisoner if it was his handwriting. He admitted it was, saying 'Yes, I wrote it after I saw the women, but I did not mean to enter it like that. I was intoxicated at the time.'

He was extremely excited when I took him into custody, but whether from drink or not I cannot say.

I took the prisoner's clothes to Dr Taylor on Saturday the 31st of August, also the stone, knives, and socks. I received them back from him on the 19th of October. They have been in my custody ever since, and I now produce them.

Cross-examined by Mr CARTER.

It was Superintendent Everitt who asked the prisoner if the entry in his diary was in his writing. I think I made a slight mistake before the magistrates in repeating to them his statement.[174] If he had said 'No' his answer would be taken.

Mr. CARTER: But you know that if he had said so, witnesses would be called to contradict him.

[*His Lordship censured the practice of the police putting questions to*

---

174 It is not clear what 'mistake' Superintendent Cheyney is referring to here. Press reports of his evidence at the committal hearing and at the trial are substantively similar, although the *Hampshire Telegraph's* account of the trial has Cheyney (rather than Everitt) questioning Baker about the diary handwriting.

First Day – Thursday 5 December 1867.

William
Cheyney

prisoners in custody. Answers not taken down at the time are very liable to be misunderstood, and a very serious injury might be done to a man. If a prisoner volunteers to make a statement, a question, in order to ascertain exactly what he meant, might be put; but policemen ought to refrain from putting questions for the purposes of entrapping prisoners into statements.]

Witness continued: There were several gaslights burning when I saw the prisoner in the office, but I did not take particular notice of his clothes at that time. I merely looked at them. I was not aware that his trousers were wet till after he had taken them off. I don't think one leg could have been out of the water more than two or three hours. If the prisoner had walked up the river Wey coming to the station, his left stocking, boot, and trouser could not have been more wet, and I believe he might have wrung water out of it.

A small, very rusty penknife [*produced*] had been found in one of the gardens, but it was even smaller than the knives found on the prisoner.

The water of the river Wey was not many inches deep and it was clear, so that a tolerably good search could be made of it.

I had not seen the prisoner about town that day.

GEORGE WATKINS, sworn and examined.

George
Watkins

I am a Constable in the Hampshire Constabulary stationed at Alton. I took charge of the prisoner at the office of Messrs. Clement on the evening of the 24th August when the Superintendent left. The prisoner asked me whose child it was, and I told him that I thought it was George Adams's. He said he did not see how they could trace it to him any more than he had given the child a half-penny, and that he had often done before. Biddle then came in and made some remark to the prisoner, who replied, 'I don't see how I'm to get off; it seems all so straightforward, but I am innocent.' I think he added, 'I suppose I must consider myself your prisoner.'

I had him again in custody at the police station. When his clothes were taken off, he said, 'They have found some blood on my sleeve, which I cannot account for. The doctor seems to think it was me because my boots were wet, but that proves nothing as I am in the habit of walking in the dew and washing my boots even before going to the office in the morning.' He also said, 'If the case goes on I shall be defended, and if I don't get off I suppose I shall be hanged. That is all I have to say, and that is all I intend to say.'

I wrote down this conversation, and I produce the paper.

A foot was given to me by Mr Swayne at the police station.

Baker.

George Watkins

Cross-examined by Mr CARTER.

I wrote down the conversation when I was relieved from duty, and within twenty-four hours of its taking place. I read it over last Sunday. I had the paper with me when before the magistrates.

Mr CARTER: Then why did you state then that his boots were 'dirty' instead of 'wet?

Mr JUSTICE MELLOR: In my experience magistrates' clerks write down the substance of what was said in evidence rather than the exact words made use of.

Witness continued: I didn't take particular notice whether his boots were dirty or clean. I did not observe whilst in the office that his clothes were dripping with water, nor did I notice that the legs of the trousers were wet or damp.

George Adams

GEORGE ADAMS, sworn and examined.

I am the father of Fanny Adams. On Sunday morning, the 25th of August, I was shown the remains of the body of my daughter at the police station by Superintendent Cheyney, and I identified them as those of my lost daughter.

*

It now being nearly six o'clock, his Lordship intimated that he was fatigued, and that he would proceed no further that night. There were two important witnesses, including Professor Taylor, to be examined on the part of the prosecution; and really he felt quite exhausted. There was not even a place for his arm to rest whilst taking down the evidence. Addressing the jury, he told them they would be properly cared for, and he implored them to refrain from discussing the case, much less attempting to come to a conclusion until they had heard the whole of the evidence.

The Court then adjourned, the jury being conducted to their lodgings in the charge of a bailiff.

Second Day – Friday 6 December 1867.[175]

The trial was resumed at half-past nine this morning. The excitement on the part of the public was even greater than on the previous day, and the court was again densely crowded. The prisoner, however, appeared as calm and collected as on Thursday. The arrangements of the police were excellent, and every effort was made by Colonel Forrest[176] and the authorities to accommodate the representatives of the press, within the circumscribed and angular spaces of the horridly inconvenient court. The first witness called was

ANN MURRANT, sworn and cross-examined by Mr CARTER.

Ann Murrant

[*Witness, who gave evidence before the magistrates, was called by the prosecution for the purpose of enabling Mr CARTER to cross-examine her.*]

I live at the Friends' Meeting House, which is near the church.[177] On August 24th, at ten or fifteen minutes to three, I was going up Amery Hill which leads to the church, when I saw a man come out of the alley, and we both met at the churchyard gate. He was then coming from the hop garden. He opened the church gate for me. He was a perfect stranger to me then, but I am positive he is the prisoner [*pointing at Baker*]. I looked at him, but nothing about the man or his appearance struck me as peculiar, save his civility in holding the gate open for me.

I saw him again between five and six o'clock on the same day. I could not tell the time more particularly. He went up the old road a little way. He came through the churchyard and he went into a footpath that leads into Kiln Piece and towards the hop field and the Hollow. I only noticed him that second time because he stared so hard at me and my little girl.[178] His eyes are somewhat large and expressive [*prisoner here smiled*]. I

---

175   Transcript of the day's proceedings amalgamated from the *Hampshire Advertiser*, Saturday 7 December 1867; *Hampshire Telegraph*, Saturday 7 December 1867; *Hampshire Chronicle*, Saturday 7 December 1867; *Hampshire Independent*, Saturday 7 December 1867; *Western Gazette and Flying Post*, Friday 13 December 1867; *Portsmouth Times*, Saturday 28 December 1867; *The Police News Edition of the Trial and Condemnation of Frederick Baker* (1867); the Home Office files at TNA HO 12/176/79865.
176   Captain John Forrest, the long-serving Chief Constable of Hampshire.
177   Still in use today at 39 Church Street. Alton has a strong tradition of Quakerism. Mrs Murrant moved to Butts Road in Alton sometime before 1871.
178   This was Louisa Murrant, aged four.

Baker.

did not speak to him. He appeared to be taking a gentle walk and was walking perfectly quietly.

FREDERICK FRENCH, sworn and examined.

[*Witness was called by the prosecution at the request of Mr CARTER*].

I am a clerk in Mr Clement's office. I have been employed there since 1838.[179] I remember the day of the murder. I arrived at the office at about half-past ten. Baker was already at the office, as was Biddle. Baker left to go to dinner about ten past one, returning around three twenty-five, at which time I went to dinner. When I returned at around five, Baker was not there. I saw him again at ten minutes to six, when he entered the office alone. He said he wanted to see the master and I told him to go to him at once. Biddle arrived five to ten minutes later. I left the office about half-past six to go home and get something, and I returned almost immediately, or after a lapse of about ten minutes or quarter of an hour.

Cross-examined by Mr CARTER.

Mr Clements goes to dinner about six. Just before then Baker went to the front office to see him. I did not observe anything particular about Baker's dress. There were no signs of blood or dripping water from his trousers, or anything of that kind.

I did not see him at ten minutes past five. I cannot recollect that he was there, but I would not swear that he was not. He might have been in the front office, but my belief is that the prisoner was not there. Trimming was certainly not at the office.

The prisoner had not complained to me of headache, but he had complained of being unwell. On one occasion, some time previously, the prisoner suffered a nose bleed and went to the kitchen to get some water. I cannot remember any other occasion when this had occurred.

Baker generally left for dinner at one.

ALFRED SWAINE TAYLOR, sworn and examined by Mr BERE.

On Saturday August 31st, Superintendent Cheyney brought various articles of clothing to me at Guy's Hospital. I conducted various chemical and microscopical experiments on them to ascertain their condition.

On the black cloth frock coat there were a few spots of coagulated blood, all of them small – one on the left side of the collar, others on the right side of the coat in front, on the outside of the right cuff, and on the lower part of the skirt on the right side. There were also superficial stains mixed with blood and dirt inside the cuffs, both right and left. There were many other stains on the coat and on the sleeves, but they were not

179   1830 is given in his deposition, but this is incorrect. French was forty-one in 1867.

Second Day – Friday 6 December 1867.

Alfred Swaine Taylor

blood, being the result of dirt and mud. The spots of blood were all small and all in front, and none behind.

The next article I examined was the pair of woollen trousers. On these I found, in front of both legs in the region of the thighs, a general staining of a reddish colour, which I afterwards found to be blood diluted with water. The thighs of both sides were stained, but the left more than the right. There were some spots of blood or bloody water on the legs of the trousers low down both in front and behind. There was no appearance of blood in the pockets, none around the buttons, where I have often found marks in similar cases, and no blood on the waistband. I produce both coat and trousers, which I have cut for the purpose of testing. The trouser marks are so diluted with bloody water that it is rather difficult to see them by a yellow light like that produced by the gas now burning.

The next article I examined was the waistcoat. There are some superficial smears of blood in front on both sides, and slight indications of diluted blood at the front. The colouring matter has been washed into the woolen, as well as in the trousers, so that blood was found inside as well as out, this being the effect of the application of water.

The next article was the cotton shirt. This was generally free from blood marks, save at the wristbands, which had been folded back. Distinct stains of blood diluted with water had stained the edge of each fold. The holes here made were cut out for the purpose of analysis, which showed this was not what was called blood chemically, but bloody water. There were also some yellowish coloured stains of a mucous nature on the flap of the shirt.

I did not find any marks of intercourse on the clothing.

The socks appeared much stained on the soles and near the toes, but not by blood. There was one superficial smear of blood on the fibre of the cotton near the ankle of one sock.

I also examined the flint stone produced, on which I found coagulated blood, such as might issue from the body of a living person or one recently dead. It had a comparatively fresh appearance, and possessed all the characteristics of venous blood. There is some portion of it still on the stone, and visible to the eye. There was hair on the stone also.

I next examined two pocket knives. I took them both to pieces. I found no blood on the white-handled one – there were only small spots of rust. On the one with the buckhorn handle I found a small quantity of coagulated blood mixed with rust; it was inside, where the brass plate fastened on the horn, and it corresponded with a smear on the outside. There was not a particle of blood in any other part of the knife. I used a microscope to examine the letters of the maker's name, and the indent for the nail, but I found no trace of blood. Despite the rough, textured

Baker.

**Alfred
Swaine
Taylor**

surface of the buckhorn handle being very favourable for the retention of blood, there was none. On the inside of the knife I found a little rust, but it was old rust – there was no sign that either blade had been recently washed. If the knives had been recently washed I should have expected to find new rust.

Mr BERE: Can you say when the bloodstains came on the child's garments? — We can only say as a matter of opinion. I should say that it was within two or three weeks of the time I examined them. They generally had all the characteristics of recent stains. The older the blood the browner it becomes, and the more difficult to dissolve. Human blood, when fresh from the body, can be identified under the microscope, but when it becomes dry on articles of clothing there are no scientific tests by which it can be distinguished from the blood of other mammals. All that can be determined is that it is the blood of a mammal, and not the blood of a fish, reptile, or bird – the cells of the blood in mammalian animals are round, and those of the three other classes oval.

The true sign of death is the stoppage of the heart. Blood ceases to circulate in the arteries at the instant of death, but in the capillary veins it might remain fluid for an hour or so after death. If the body of a child were cut up an hour or so after death, blood would not spurt out because spurting takes place from the arteries in life. Rather, the blood would flow when the veins were cut.

Cross-examined by Mr CARTER.

[*The Professor was cross-examined at some length as to the workings of the human circulatory system, and the grounds of his analysis.*]

The blood ceases to circulate when the animal is dead, at least in the larger vessels; in the capillary vessels it remains for some time after. It was formerly supposed, from the arteries being empty at death, that they were distended by air—hence the derivation of the word.

There were spots of blood on the coat and knife similar to that on the stone. In applying my tests I could determine more recent from older blood. I do not believe that the blood found on the stone was more recent than that on the coat.

If the buckhorn-handled knife had been used to dismember and disembowel a body, I should have expected to have found much more blood on it. The whole of the cavities of the knife ought to have been completely filled with blood. No man could have protected it from the flow of venous blood. I therefore conceive it impossible that this knife was used for this purpose.

Blood such as I have described finding on the buckhorn-handled knife might have been caused by the cutting up of a beef-steak or mutton-

Second Day – Friday 6 December 1867.

chop. A thimbleful of blood would make a great show.

Alfred Swaine Taylor

There were only a few spots of blood on the coat, and generally the quantity of blood on the clothes was exceedingly small. They were so slight that a person might pass the wearer of the clothes and not notice them. Bleeding from the nose might account for the stains on the coat and waistcoat. Bleeding of the nose, when it does not occur from violence, is often very sudden, especially in excitable and irritable persons. Headaches can cause such bleeding, and might save an attack of apoplexy by relieving congestion. An attempt to stop the bleeding by putting up the hand to the nose might account for the marks on the wristbands of the shirt.

Mr CARTER: How long do you think it would take an inexperienced person to cut up the body in this way? — If he had a proper sharp weapon, such as a table knife, I think he might do it in half an hour or less. The breast bone is easily cut from the ribs, but the separation of the pelvis from the trunk, which was not here done, would be the most difficult operation. The main difficulty would probably be about the head, but in a child of this tender age the seven bones would not be very firmly knit together, and, bending the head back, it could be cut off without difficulty. If the deed were done hurriedly the clothes of the operator would become covered in blood, but by tucking up his sleeves and taking other precautions I believe a man might avoid staining himself, except his hands.

You have spoken of stains. Don't you think the use of red ink in a solicitor's office might account for these marks? — Oh, no. No colouring matter but blood could have produced them. I think the blood may have been on the clothes for three weeks. During the last ten years I believe I have had eight or nine cases submitted to me by the Home Secretary in which spots of blood were to be examined in connection with charges of murder.

MR CARTER: In your opinion, is not the enormity of this crime evidence of insanity?[180]

[*Mr BERE objected to this question. His Lordship interposed. He thought that question could scarcely be put to Dr Taylor. He said he utterly repudiated the popular idea that the perpetrators of unusually horrible crimes must necessarily be insane.*]

Witness continued: I am familiar with a disease called homicidal mania. The symptoms are that violence is committed by a person on a sudden impulse, and very often on persons to whom the perpetrator is devotedly attached, typically the mother or some near relative. In these

---

180 The *Hampshire Independent* has: 'Could you attribute an act such as this to any cause of mental or medical disease?'

Baker.

Alfred
Swaine
Taylor

cases there is generally no premeditation, no accomplices, and rarely any attempt to deny the crime or conceal the deed – rather, there is an attempt by the perpetrator to justify or glorify their act under some delusion, or to ascribe it to God. As a rule, persons suffering from this disease are indifferent to punishment or consequences. However, sometimes they display no incapacity of intellect. There are cases on record in which persons suffering from homicidal mania exhibit no gloomy, melancholic, or irritable disposition: the disorder sometimes shows itself in those who have been remarkably kind, of gentle demeanour, and quiet conduct, with no previous manifestation of mental aberration, but in such cases they were labouring under a delusion, as in the case of McNaghten,[181] who shot Drummond by mistake. In the case of Greenacre[182] no intellectual insanity was noticed before the act. A person who had been quiet might be attacked by a sudden paroxysm of this kind.

[*Dr Taylor was asked several questions by learned counsel with reference to particular cases of homicidal mania cited, but his Lordship ruled the witness could not be examined as to cases which had not been brought under his notice. These cases were merely hearsay evidence, and could not therefore be admitted in a criminal court. His Lordship said that Mr Carter might, if he liked, ask Dr Taylor if he thought, after hearing this case, there were symptoms of homicidal mania in the prisoner, but his Lordship thought that would be an irregular question, and if asked to pass an opinion on it he should say it was an extremely dangerous question. Mr Carter bowed to the hint and declined to put this question to the witness.*]

Witness continued: I agree that insanity is liable to be transferred by hereditary descent, especially on the side of the mother. Where a person's relatives on both his father's and mother's side have shown traces of homicidal mania, the presumption is that the person would be subject to these paroxysms in the same way, but I should fall back on the whole of the circumstances under which an act of violence had been committed in order to form an opinion as to insanity. Homicidal mania is generally characterised by no attempt to conceal an act, and I should look with suspicion on any case where this was not a symptom.

Louis
Leslie

LOUIS LESLIE, sworn and examined by Mr BERE.

I am a surgeon practicing at Alton. I am a doctor of medicine and a member of the Royal College of Surgeons. I am Divisional Surgeon to this Police Force. Between nine and ten at night[183] on the 24th of August

181 Daniel McNaghten (1813–1865).
182 James Greenacre (1785–1837), the Edgware Road Murderer.
183 Some newspaper reports indicate between eleven and midnight.

Second Day – Friday 6 December 1867.

I was called to the police station to see the body of a child. The following morning I again went to the station and made a full examination.

Louis Leslie

I found the remains of a female child of seven or eight years of age. There was the trunk, and separated from it the head, both legs, one arm, and part of the other arm. One arm had been separated at the elbow joint, and one leg had been separated at the ankle joint.

The head was partly decomposed and infested with vermin. At the junction of the two parietal bones with the occipital bone I found a contused wound completely fracturing the skull. There was also a bruise on the right side of the head and another on the left causing extravasation of blood under the scalp but not extending to the brain itself. There was a cut, a very deep one, extending from the forehead above the nose to the end of the lower jaw, and dividing the vessels and muscles. The right ear was severed from the head and both eyes were cut out. On the left side was a cut extending from above the ear to the end of the lower jaw, entering the cheek and dividing the muscles of the face as far as the angle of the mouth.

On removing the skull cap I found a wound separating the periosteum from the bone. The *dura mater* was much congested, and there was coagulated blood on the brain corresponding with the injury to the skull. The blow on the head might have been inflicted by the stone produced – such a blow would cause immediate insensibility and probably death might follow though not immediately. When I first saw the stone before the coroner there was blood and hair upon it.

I found three incisions on the left side of the chest between the ribs, the longest being 3 inches in length, the second two inches, the third one. I also found a deep cut in the armpit of the left arm, dividing the muscles, but not separating the arm from the trunk. The forearm on the left side was cut off at the elbow. The left leg was nearly cut off at the hip joint – it was still hanging to the pelvis – and in the front there was a deep cut dividing the muscles and vessels of the thigh. The left foot was separated at the ankle joint.

There was a deep incision entering the chest between the fourth and fifth ribs on the right side, and a cut on the right side beneath the armpit which did not divide the muscles. The right leg was torn from the body after attempts to divide it from the trunk. There was a deep cut on both sides, dividing the femoral vessels.

There was a dislocation of the spine between the dorsal and lumbar vertebrae. The sternum or breast bone was missing, and the whole of the contents of the pelvis and chest were removed. There were five incisions in the liver, three in the lungs, the spleen separated, and the heart was cut out. The vagina was missing and has not been found. In my opinion the

Baker.

dismemberment took place after death.

I saw the prisoner at the police station about ten in the evening on the 24th August. I examined his trousers and found them to be wet and apparently stained with washed-off blood. The right trouser leg and the boot and sock were quite saturated with water. The right leg trouser was much wetter than the left. I said to the prisoner, 'Your trousers are wet,' and his reply was, 'Yes, unfortunately for me they are wet, but that proves nothing for I am constantly in the habit of getting into the water.'

His shirt was removed, and I said to Superintendent Cheyney in the prisoner's hearing that there were marks of blood on the shirt. The superintendent said to the prisoner, 'How do you account for that?' He said, looking at his person, 'I can't account for it; and I see no scratches or cuts that would explain it.' The prisoner was about to say something to me, and I said I have nothing to do with it. I have been through the hop garden, but not since the murder.

Cross-examined by Mr CARTER.

On Saturday I saw a crowd round the office and I saw Baker arrested.

I examined the remains on Sunday. I was occupied for about two and a half hours. I went at three and left at half-past five. I stated before the coroner that in my view it was possible – but not probable – that the knives produced might have dismembered a child's body in this way. I still retain that position. I believe a larger knife must have been used. I think a person having undisturbed possession of the hop garden might do the dismemberment in an hour or three-quarters of an hour without his hands being covered in blood, but there was fear of interruption because the murder scene was a very public place close to the town and surrounded by persons engaged in harvesting, etc. It would not require any great skill in a person to separate the head from the trunk of a child of that age – it might be done in ten minutes. The separation of the back bones is a difficult operation, but if you bend the back it is easily done. The thigh was torn from the body; there had been some previous attempt to cut it, but it was not entirely separated by the cutting.

In my opinion death was instantaneous, and the poor child suffered no torture. Dismemberment took place after death, and not long after it; within half an hour or so, perhaps. I speak as confidently as I can. A person need not be covered with blood if he pulled up his sleeves and stood out of the way. Very likely he would have stains on him, but they would be small and barely noticeable, and a practiced eye would not see them without a minute examination.

Having heard the analysis of Dr Taylor regarding the knives, I think it is possible one might have been used, but not probable. The shorter the knife the more the vessels would be torn. The cuts on the thigh were numerous and short.

There was a small piece of earth on the skull, but I saw no earth on the stone. The prisoner was excited that night when I saw him. He was not intoxicated then, but it appeared to me he had been drinking during the day.

Re-examined by Mr BERE.

The greatest effusion of blood would be caused by taking out the heart and emptying the pelvis. It would not necessarily take a long time. The skin was drawn back from the edge of the cuts, indicating that the dismemberment took place shortly after death while the body was still warm.

[*This closed the case for the prosecution.*]

Opening Speech for the Defence.

Mr CARTER then addressed the jury on behalf of the prisoner. He began by saying there was no one outside his profession that could form an adequate idea of the difficulties of the position in which he found himself as the advocate for the prisoner. The circumstances of this case were so peculiar, so different from anything that he had met with in the course of upwards of 20 years' experience, that he approached it with painful feelings of responsibility – feelings that overrode him, he might say, in the night, and partially paralysed his powers when he thought of the terrible consequences of a mistake. The duties of his learned friends were comparatively light when compared with the fact that he was the only advocate for the prisoner, whose means and those of his friends did not enable them to call in additional or stronger means of defence, and probably he might say that he was indebted to the charity of individuals for being able to make this appearance and to call witnesses. He must say that his learned friends had conducted the case for the prosecution with a propriety and calmness that befitted the occasion.

He said his defence would necessarily present a double aspect, though he admitted that from that very circumstance it was unfavourably affected. First of all he would argue that the prosecution had not sufficiently made out that the prisoner's was the hand that committed this dreadful murder; and secondly, that even if members of the jury came to the conclusion that the prisoner was the murderer, he should produce evidence before them showing that he could not be held responsible for his actions and should therefore be acquitted on the ground of insanity. If he succeeded in rendering the case for the prosecution doubtful with the first line of defence, he need not press the other. It would be less difficult

Louis Leslie

Mr Carter

Baker.

Mr Carter   and embarrassing to him could he confine himself to one line of defence.

He asked them in this case of life or death to give their full attention to his statements. He felt himself impelled to do everything in his power to spare the unfortunate prisoner from the terrible penalties of this offence should he be found guilty, and to save the public from the dread spectacle and example of the gallows.

The case for the prosecution, he asserted, had failed in several very important particulars. The evidence was contradictory and unsatisfactory. Witnesses had been called to-day who were not examined before the magistrates – that of the little boy Vince being an example – and their evidence had altogether broken down. The facts showed Baker in so many places at very nearly the same time that he could not have been where the murder was committed unless he possessed that wonderful faculty of being in two or three places at one time. At all events they occupied so much time that it seemed to him they left no time to execute that which had been done, much less to accomplish that which must eventually have been executed. In fact, after this testimony, the most innocent man in the world who might happen to have been in the neighbourhood might just as likely have been charged with this terrible crime as the prisoner. Prejudice weighed heavily against a suspected person, and every additional witness called rendered the case more complicated. He ventured to say that upon a calm review of this case, the evidence that really told against Baker came from only one or two witnesses, the chief of which was the little girl Minnie Warner.

The offence was so unaccountable, so inexplicable, that he believed no person could hear or read the details of this case without exclaiming instinctively, 'The man must be mad.' Was there any adequate motive in this case, any premeditation or malice which distinguished 99 out of every 100 murders that were committed? No, there was an entire absence of anything of the sort, albeit a theory had been set up that this murder arose from the gratification of lust, and that the mutilation was committed in order to destroy the identity of the body and conceal the existence of the minor crime. But this theory failed because an analytical examination proved the non-existence of intercourse. If the person desired only the concealment of another offence, why would he cut out the eyes and broadcast the deed by scattering the limbs and organs about the fields on either side of the lane? Might he not have dug a hole and buried the body in much less time than was required to cut up the body in this horrible manner? No, the jury must look for some sign of object and motive. People did not, if sane, commit such extraordinary offences as this without some constraining motive on their part.

Look at the supposed instrument with which the dismemberment

Second Day – Friday 6 December 1867.

was committed. Was it probable that he could have perpetrated it with such a small knife? And was his demeanour before and after the crime consistent with guilt? He went to and from the office, and on no occasion did he indicate, either in person or in dress, that he had committed such a terrible offence. If he had cut up this body he must surely have been covered with blood, yet his clothes failed to show anything like those traces that would naturally be expected after such extraordinary and unparalleled mutilation. He ventured to suggest that the most skilful person who ever entered a dissecting room could not have done it without being smeared with blood.

The theory of the prosecution was that the body was cut up on the prisoner's second visit to the field, after he had gone back to the office to get a suitable knife. If this was not so, where was the need of the witnesses as to the prisoner's comings and goings at the office? But if that was the argument then it clearly proved there could not have been any premeditation to commit the act. Any person fond of country walks and having a bleeding nose, fixed upon by presumption, would be liable to be placed in jeopardy.

The prosecution had failed to show that the prisoner had any weapons other than the two knives, which, after listening to Dr Taylor's evidence, the jury would not venture to believe were the instruments used. If they did it would be very rash, and might cause them perhaps to deplore their belief hereafter. The two knives were produced to show the prisoner's guilt, but it had not been a successful production. The prisoner never had another knife but these two. The proof of the weapon, as of the motive, in his judgment therefore failed. He did not say that it was impossible for the prisoner to have got rid of such a weapon, but none of his fellow clerks or any other person had said they had ever seen him possess others.

Dealing with the statements of the prisoner, the learned counsel argued that the prisoner had always denied the charge. He said, 'Never, Maury, it is a bad job for me,' and he also asserted his innocence in other words and to other persons. He never confessed that he was the murderer, and he never admitted to any complicity.

The prosecution asserted that the diary contained an absolute confession of guilt. He did not complain of his learned friend having called it a confession of guilt. When he first saw it, he (Mr. Carter) thought it was a marvelous entry for a man to make if he was in a sane state of mind. What was it? – 'Killed a young girl; it was fine and hot.' It read more like the words of a madman or the chronicling of an idiot, as if the horrible employment itself was fine and hot. But the words did not necessarily mean that the prisoner killed her. If it were intended to

Baker.

be a confession he might as well have gone and confessed it to the first person that spoke to him on the subject. Suppose it had been 'A young girl killed; it was fine and hot.' The inversion would alter the meaning materially. Might not the sentence mean that?

Singularly enough, there was an entry on May 7th which read 'A child drowned in King's Pond.'[184] Suppose it had been 'Drowned a child in King's Pond' – according to the construction put on this by the prosecution, the prisoner might have been charged with killing that child, whatever the evidence given at the inquest. It was inconsistent with sanity, it was inconsistent with guilt. Had Baker committed the act, nobody could conceive his going home and entering such a sentence.

Now, to illustrate how often the prisoner chronicled fine weather he might mention that out of the 236 days between 1st of January and the 24th of August 162 days were stated to be 'fine', which, if true, left only 74 for uncomfortable weather – a state of climate which would take half England to the neighbourhood of Alton. On January 28th the personal pronoun *I* was introduced, but in reference to the entry last August it was omitted. February 2nd contained an entry as to Sir. R. Tichborne's return[185] and there were other items of a miscellaneous nature. There was not a particle of evidence in them to show a disposition of guilt.

It was very seldom that a man stepped at once from innocence to a terrible crime of this kind, except where the mind was affected by the taint of insanity. Yet this was the theory suggested by the prosecution, that the prisoner did so step at once, and that, too, without motive or indication of it beforehand. Crime was the result of a process of step by step, but not of the Colossus-like stride of innocence to a murder of the most horrid description. Were there any traces of this prisoner having shown any signs of this relapse beforehand? In the absence of revenge, or motive of any kind, the prosecution fell back on the supposed assault on the poor child by the prisoner, yet the linen taken from him and examined by Dr. Taylor showed no traces of intercourse.

Mr Carter said there was nothing in the diary to point to such a catastrophe; on the contrary, it was evident from the entries in other parts of the of the diary that the prisoner had continually attended

184 A reference to the death of Arthur Fowler, aged nearly five, who drowned while playing in a culvert beneath the railway embankment near King's Pond, Alton. A verdict of 'accidentally drowned' was returned at the inquest at the Royal Oak Inn, Alton on 9 May 1867. See *Hampshire Advertiser*, 11 May 1867.

185 Roger Tichborne, presumed drowned off the coast of Brazil in 1854, who supposedly returned to England in December 1866 to claim the family inheritance. The 'Tichborne Claimant' is an infamous legal *cause célèbre* of the Victorian period. Sir John Mellor, who presided at the trial of Frederick Baker, was one of the three judges at the lengthy criminal trial in 1873 of Arthur Orton, the Tichborne Claimant.

Second Day – Friday 6 December 1867.

church, often twice every Sunday in Alton and other villages, and his observations thereon, including remarks on the sermon, also appeared. It was clear he did not go there to learn murder. But the last entry, which has been distorted into a confession for murder, became in consequence incomprehensible, and would be met by the jury individually with the exclamation, 'Good God!, what could possess the man; he must have indeed been mad.'

But again, was it possible, whatever his state of mind, to believe that the prisoner's hand accomplished this act? No human eye saw it committed and the only witness placing the prisoner in the neighbourhood of the hop garden at the time of the murder was the little girl Minnie Warner.

[*The learned counsel then proceeded to criticise her testimony and contended that she was mistaken.*]

She had told the court that she played with the prisoner from two till four o'clock, yet the testimony of Elizabeth Warner, her sister, showed that Minnie had returned home around half-past two, while the clerk Biddle had testified that Baker was in the office at twenty-five minutes past three. If Minnie was mistaken – although he accepted that the mistake might have arisen from an imaginative turn of mind and not from an intention to deceive – what became of her other statements? If she was mistaken as to points of time, might she not be mistaken upon other points of her testimony? There was exaggeration in her testimony which was as difficult to encounter as prejudice.

William Allwork saw the prisoner at two o'clock leaning on a gate in Flood Meadow. At that time there were some children playing about, and the deceased was alive and well. However, contradicting this, Eliza White, an intelligent witness, swore that a little before two o'clock she was in the pea field and the prisoner at the bar was at another gate smoking. If she was mistaken what reliance was there on human testimony? She saw him take his cigar from his mouth and spit. No other witness spoke of his smoking. She did not recollect anything about what happened in the previous week, but her memory was fresh on this point, although her child, Ellen, was with prisoner on August 17th.

One of the witnesses had spoken of the prisoner having had his hands in his pockets. That indicated listlessness and calmness, and it was said that smoking itself acted as a sedative; therefore the prisoner smoking and having his hands in his pockets, and having children playing near him, did not show signs of passion. He ran after the children, playfully caught the deceased, who cried out in play, and after that she was not seen alive.

When was death inflicted? And here time becomes a dreadful essential for their contemplation.

Baker.

Mr Carter

Ann Murrant's evidence was most important. She said she saw the prisoner enter the churchyard. He opened the gate for her at about a quarter before three. This was when the murder must have been committed. In that brief time he must have committed the horrid murder and dismemberment, and yet here he was face to face with a woman, after effecting all this, without stains of blood, without agitation or passion. Was it possible to believe this theory? He for one could not, and he trusted they did not either. The woman remarked nothing peculiar about him. Macbeth says – 'There's murder in thy face.' The murderer says – ''Tis Banquo's, then. It has spurted in his face.'[186] But Baker had no stains of blood on him, even though the blood of this tragedy must have gushed out in streams from the child's body.

At two minutes past three, George Noyce met the prisoner on the footway heading towards the hop garden from the old road, but this was inconsistent with the prisoner being in his master's office at half-past three. Between five and six o'clock Ann Murrant saw the prisoner a second time, this time going back towards the hop garden, and if so there must have been some wonderful fascination for the prisoner in thus flitting backwards and forwards.

He left the office at half-past four and returned about six o'clock. Between a quarter and half-past five Emma Smith saw him coming towards Flood Meadows from the hop garden. He was met by Mrs. Adams and Mrs. Gardener. The latter said she ran to meet the man and cried, 'Hoi, stop.' The prisoner turned and faced her. The crime must have been committed by this point. What was there, then, in the prisoner's demeanour to suggest guilt? Nothing. He answered so readily and seemed so fair and free from blame that Mrs. Gardener apologised to him for suspecting him. He bowed to her, and she curtsied.

He hoped he had not been tedious. If any mistake was made by himself or the jury it could not be rectified hereafter. Although the prosecution had made out a great case of suspicion, he submitted that the Crown had shown the prisoner to be so often in Alton that he could not possibly be guilty of the crime; their theory had left the prisoner no time wherein to commit this murder. At the furthest he was not away from the office for two hours, for no longer than any other person there, and it was physically impossible for him to have perpetrated the crime.

The jury had been warned against prejudice. The death and horrid dismemberment of a young child would naturally create prejudice and

---

186 *Macbeth*, Act III, Scene IV. Either Mr Carter has misremembered his Shakespeare, or the *Hampshire Advertiser* has badly garbled the quotation. It should read: Macbeth: 'There's blood on thy face.' First Murderer: 'Tis Banquo's then… My lord, his throat is cut.'

Second Day – Friday 6 December 1867.

horror, and no doubt a mob would murder the prisoner if they had a chance, in their ideas of mercy and pity.

The learned counsel then opened the second part of his case. He stated that it was the opinion of some scientific men that there were acts which in themselves were evidence of insanity. He hoped to have been able to elicit from Professor Taylor more than he was able to ascertain on this occasion with respect to the opinions generally entertained by medical jurists on the insanity of persons, and how far they might be tainted with hereditary affliction. He alluded to Dr Taylor's evidence in relation to mania of a homicidal character, and read an extract or two from his great work on medical jurisprudence to show that many motiveless murderers were insane. Dr Taylor admitted in his work that persons subject to attacks of homicidal mania might be seized with them, although there had been no premonitory symptoms of excitement or irritation, and that a person might be insane although he knew that he was doing wrong and knew the consequences; and if that were so, he (the learned counsel) contended, whatever the judge might say, that a man in such a state was not responsible for his acts. He apologised for the length of time he had occupied.

The learned Judge said he must say that Mr Carter was perfectly justified in using as much time as he pleased, and to make such observations as he thought to be in favour of his client, and he must say he did not think he had wasted any time. He had kept most closely to his points. Speculations of medical men it might be as well to omit, but the convenience of no one should be thought of.

Mr Carter then thanked the learned Judge for his observation. He continued his defence by stating that if a man was insane, no matter what science or law might assert or lay down, he should be relegated to an asylum. Was such a relegation an escape? Yes, but it was an escape from the gallows only to gain the silence, solitude, and condemnation of a living grave. It was placing a person in a living tomb, cut off from all hopes and pleasure, and from the sympathy of friends and neighbours. No more pleasant walks in the countryside. He hardly knew whether death was not preferable. The defence of insanity was certainly not an encouragement to the commission of any offence.

[*At this point the prisoner exhibited the only emotion he had displayed during the trial by crying for a few minutes. He wept at the thought of the agony he would endure if shut up in a lunatic asylum for life.*]

He proposed to call witnesses to show that the prisoner was a sufferer from hereditary insanity. He would show that many members of the prisoner's family had been insane, and that the prisoner himself had been frequently in a state of mind fitting him only for a lunatic asylum. The

Baker.

Mr Carter   prisoner's father had suffered from a precisely similar mania, and four years ago had shown a propensity to assault, even to destruction, his own son and daughter. Only the intervention of family friends had prevented it. His cousin also was insane, and had twice been in Bethlehem and twice in other asylums. His sister, and others of his family, had died of brain fever. The prisoner himself, he should show, was a weakly, puny and excitable character. A few years ago, he was disappointed in love, which resulted almost in suicide at Guildford by drowning, from which he was only saved by the timely assistance of a witness who would be called before them. Had he done so, would not the verdict of a jury then have been temporary insanity? He trusted, however, that after listening to the facts of the case the jury would come to the conclusion that the prisoner was not guilty.

Mr. Carter's address, which lasted two hours, exhibited close reasoning and much eloquence, and obtained deserved eulogium from the learned Judge in the course of one or two breaks in the speech.

The following witnesses were then examined on behalf of the prisoner

Frederick Baker Sr   FREDERICK BAKER, sworn and examined by Mr CARTER.

I am a tailor residing in South Street, Guildford. The prisoner at the bar is my son. As a child my son's health was always indifferent. He was always a very backward child. He was much under the hands of the doctor. His nervous system was always bad, and he complained of pains in the head, which were frequent and continuous, and always attended by nausea. From his birth he was subject to frequent bleeding at the nose. Owing to his state of health, I did not send him to school till he was 12. He then went for three-and-a-half years. He was sent to school very weakly, and remained there for three years. When he was sixteen he had a violent attack of typhus fever, and remained ill for a long time; indeed, I sat up with him fifteen nights. He always complained thereafter of pains in his head.

We put him into the office of Mr. Smallpiece, solicitor, where he remained for five and a half years.[187] After that, he was at Mr. Lovett's.[188] He often came home and complained that his duties were more than his head was able to bear. At dinner time he would often burst out crying. He was under my roof till he was twenty-six and in the whole of that time I never knew him drink any intoxicating liquors.

In 1864 my son kept company with a young woman, which continued

---

187   The well-known firm of Guildford solicitors at 138 High Street. The partners were William Haydon and Mark Smallpiece. In 1861 they were entrusted with the prosecution of Johann Karl Franz (alias Auguste Saltzman), one of the defendants in the Kingswood Rectory murder case.

188   Philip W. Lovett, solicitor, of 53 High Street, Guildford.

Second Day – Friday 6 December 1867.

till the beginning of 1865 when she broke off the engagement. In the Christmas of 1864 some of the family paid a visit to Alton to see my sister, who had married Richard Row, who is now in an asylum.[189] Frederick did not come with us but joined us later. He came on Monday evening and returned with me to Guildford the next day. He was very desponding, had nothing to say, and marched about the road.

In January, 1865, my son came home in a state of great excitement. He appeared quite out of his mind. Before Christmas he had told me his young woman had quite given him up. He told me he could not get over it, and but for a friend he should not have been alive. I told my son if he had come home to me I would be a friend to him as a father. He said he had no friend save the one he had named. He was very excited. There was no quarrel between us – I have never in my life quarreled with my son. He went to bed and sobbed for two hours at least. I heard him rise up many times in the night. He was the same after breakfast, and if it had not been for many prayers he should not have been alive.

He desired to get lodgings elsewhere. From that day he often came home in a very excited state, and this continued till April, 1865 when he disappeared for a year or fifteen months. I saw him again in July, 1866. I watched him secretly, fearing he would make away with himself. His bearing and manner alarmed me. On one occasion he stopped out all night; next day I went to the office at Guildford to remonstrate with him. He had never stopped out before. I said 'How came you to stop out all night, without letting me know?' He replied he did not want to tell me because he knew I would have made an objection. He then said he would go and drown himself that moment, and tried to rush past me, but I caught hold of him and pacified him. I remonstrated with him on several occasions when he said he would leave the town. He was in the habit of crying every night, and his mind was very bad.

In Alton he entered Mr Clement's service. I received letters from him, and they were of a desponding character. [*They were not produced, and their contents could not be spoken of*]. I saw him last May in Alton. His appearance and manners struck me with horror. He was restless and excited. During a visit to London the previous February, before he left Guildford, we went on a boat trip from London Bridge to Pimlico, and I was afraid he would jump overboard.

Cross-examined by Mr BERE.

I know my son was a member of a literary institute for twelve years.

---

189 The press reports have slightly scrambled Mr Baker Sr's testimony. His sister, Mary Ann, married William Trimmer Row in 1835 in Shalford in Surrey, and it was William's younger brother, Richard, who was incarcerated in an asylum. The Row family lived at 61 High Street, where they ran a watch and clock making business.

Frederick Baker Sr

Baker.

Frederick Baker Sr

He was secretary to a debating society and a member of an elocution society. I have heard he was a director of a Penny Savings' Bank, and for ten years he was a Sunday school teacher.

Was it some alleged misconduct that caused him to leave Guildford in April 1865? — Not any, that I am aware.

Mr Carter objected to this line of examination as affecting the character of a man on his trial.

His Lordship said that, as his absence had been attributed to eccentricity, the question was admissible.

WITNESS: I am not aware that some alleged misconduct was the cause of my son leaving Guildford. He has not been charged with any misconduct. I last saw him on May 27th, the last Monday in the month.

Mr BERE: That is so; there is an entry in the diary for that day – 'Father came to Alton; it was fine and mild.'

Mary Ann Baker

MARY ANN BAKER, sworn and examined by Mr CARTER.

I am the prisoner's sister. I am three years older than him. I have always lived with him at my father's home. Growing up, my brother was always very weak. I remember the time he suffered very much from typhus fever. I knew all about his engagement with a young woman, which was broken off by her. It had a bad effect on him, making him very unhappy and depressed. Several times he spoke to me threatening to destroy himself. Once he said he had attempted to do so, but a young man had saved him. His depression was much greater some days than at others.

Just before he went away in April, 1865, he was particularly unhappy, inasmuch as he had seen the woman with another man.

Alfred Johnson

ALFRED JOHNSON, sworn and examined by Mr CARTER.

I am a bricklayer residing in Guildford. I have known the prisoner for fifteen or sixteen years. In 1864, when I was working at the National School, I remember the prisoner came over and entered into a conversation with me for a quarter of an hour. He appeared queer and like an insane person in his face and talk. I noticed it, as did the men who were working with me. I saw him next day in the churchyard. I noticed the look he had, and spoke of it to my wife. I often observed a similar look on his face. I know the prisoner's father had been out of his mind.

Cross-examined by Mr BERE.

I had a second conversation with the prisoner the following day, and he appeared not so odd on that occasion. It did not strike me to go tell the father.

Second Day – Friday 6 December 1867.

JOHN DAVIS, sworn and examined by Mr CARTER.

John Davis

At present I am working as a bricklayer, but formerly I was acting sergeant in the Guildford Borough Police for 11 years.[190] I know the prisoner well and saw him frequently while he was at Mr Lovett's. Sometimes he would accompany me for an hour or two on my beat. I frequently observed his peculiar manner. While engaged in serious topics, he would make grim faces or suddenly start laughing or break off the conversation most abruptly and leave without saying anything. I know he had an engagement with a young woman, which was broken off. He often became excited, and would walk about most hurriedly. Save these things he was inoffensive. Once, in 1864, I suspected him of attempting suicide. I saw him making for the river Wey. I stopped him on the bridge, and asked him what he was going to do. He said he would do something that would be talked about and made a rush as if to drown himself, but I caught him by the collar. I believe the prisoner would have jumped into the river if he had not been stopped. On another occasion I saw him with a dagger and a pistol, with which he threatened to shoot himself. His manner was so alarming that night that I took him home and told the family they must look after him.[191] The father was also looked after by a man named Serle. The prisoner's excitable manner continued till I lost contact with him in December 1864.

Cross-examined by Mr BERE.

I do not consider anyone insane who comes in as he did from the country, at one or two o'clock.

SARAH KINGSTON, sworn and examined by Mr CARTER.

Sarah Kingston

The young man Frederick Baker lodged with me till the 24th August this year.[192] I always found him to be very quiet and still. He often remarked to me how low he was in spirits. Sometimes he would rise

---

190 Constable Davis was caught up in the Guildford Guy Riots of 1865. On Boxing Night he and several other officers were assaulted outside the White Lion Hotel in Guildford High Street by a gang of between fifteen and twenty men armed with bludgeons and wearing masks and bizarre costumes. He was struck on the head and felled to the ground. Arrests were made, but by the time the case came before the Spring Assizes on 31 March 1866, Davis had already left the Borough Police to become a bricklayer. McCloskey (2016) speculates that Baker may have been involved in the Guy Riots.

191 The pistol and dagger incident is reported only in the *Hampshire Advertiser* and the *Hampshire Independent*. Davis's trial statement makes no mention of it (TNA HO 12/176/79865).

192 Sarah Kingston's lodging house at 69 High Street was four doors up from where Frederick's aunt and uncle, Mary Ann and William Trimmer Row, lived and ran their watch and clock repair business. In 1867 Sarah Kingston was fifty-six. Her husband, George, was a fruiterer. She became widowed in 1870.

Sarah Kingston

from his seat, and go out in the garden and lie down and smoke his pipe on the seat. He was generally a well-conducted young man. He used to look very wild about the eyes. My husband remarked to me on the 24th of August that he looked bad yesterday, and I said he looks worse this morning.

Cross-examined by Mr BERE.

The prisoner did not drink to my knowledge. I never saw him tipsy or the worse for liquor except once, which was some time in the summer. He usually came home early in the evening and generally went to bed around ten. He was in the habit of locking the bedroom door.

William Curtis

WILLIAM CURTIS, affirmed and examined by Mr CARTER.

I am a surgeon living in Alton. I have practised here for forty-two years. I am a member of the Society of Friends. I attend professionally the Row family at Alton. Mr William Row and his younger brother Mr Richard Row are first cousins to the prisoner.[193] The older Mr Row and the prisoner's mother were brother and sister. William Row is a nervous man, and is presently suffering from a febrile attack. Richard Row is a patient at Fareham, in the County Lunatic Asylum and is never likely to recover. He had his first attack of mania twenty years ago.[194] He has been in Bethlem Royal Hospital twice, and twice in private asylums. He recovers at intervals, when he joins his brother in the family watch and clock making business. His mania is usually very violent, and he would, if not restrained, be homicidal. The family are always careful to keep things out of his way.

Cross-examined by Mr BERE.

I have seen Richard Row when he required two or three persons to restrain him. He has never been committed to an asylum for any specific act.

Henry Sharp Taylor

HENRY SHARP TAYLOR, affirmed and examined by Mr CARTER.

I am a surgeon living at Guildford. I know the prisoner and his family very well, having attended them for twenty-five years.

As a child the prisoner was very weakly and of delicate health, and a remarkably nervous and sensitive person. If I spoke to him, he would

---

193 Several newspaper reports, and the witness's trial statement, incorrectly state that the brothers were cousins of the prisoner's father.

194 The doctor's gloomy prognostication proved to be correct. Richard Row died in Fareham Lunatic Asylum on 27 March 1895, aged eighty.

blush deeply and his lips would quiver. He had a severe attack of typhoid fever, which left him in weak health and weak mind, as is customary. The prisoner's mother died under my charge from consumption. She was a very nervous woman. Four years ago the prisoner's father had an attack of acute mania. He had delusions, and displayed a tendency to violence. On the day I saw him he had tried to strike his daughter and another woman with a poker. He thought his daughter had attempted to poison him. An attendant was indispensable to take care of him for ten days. His daughter succeeded to take charge of him after that time.

I lost sight of prisoner for a year, but for a year or two before he left Guildford I observed a great change in his health and demeanour. He changed from a meek, inoffensive man, to a swaggering, intemperate person in appearance. I always looked upon him as having a weak mind, which would be increased by the family taint of insanity.

By Mr JUSTICE MELLOR — Homicidal mania is a desire to kill someone without motive. It has different forms – it can be impelled by some indomitable impulse, or it may arise due to some delusion. Both types are connected with a disease of the mind. I did not regard the father as having homicidal mania.

[This closed the case for the defence.]

Henry Sharp Taylor

Closing Speech for the Defence.

Mr Carter then summed up his case, dwelling on the mysterious character of the disease of insanity, and asking the jury whether, after the evidence they had heard, they would doubt that the prisoner was insane. He contended that the hereditary taint of insanity was shown to have existed in this case, and the uncontrollable, irrepressible motive spoken of by Dr. Taylor was the consequence. A violent blow or a trouble would paralyse the brain, and to a young man nothing was more likely to destroy his mind than the affection of a man for a woman. He hoped, however, the jury would believe the first defence set up, that the prisoner was not the person who committed the murder. He concluded by expressing a hope that they would not convict the prisoner unless they were compelled to do so by the force of the most irresistible evidence.

Mr Carter

Closing Speech for the Prosecution.

Mr Bere, in reply, contended that the case he had opened had been sufficiently proved. While admitting that the time he had suggested for the crime had not been fully made out, he argued that in all other respects his main propositions had been conclusively established. Commenting

Mr Bere

Baker.

Mr Bere on the evidence, he said that there were some points which the jury must believe (such, for instance, as his giving the children money), for the prisoner had even admitted them. There was no doubt of the murder, and the prisoner was the last person seen with the girl. He had shown the prisoner to be present at every spot where portions of the remains had been found.

There was no doubt that the little girl Minnie Warner was mistaken as to the time when she first came home. She might have come home at four o'clock, but she had been at home before. It really made no difference. The question was, did they (the jury) believe that she went out to play? that she met that man, who gave her and the others money? and that the last she saw of Fanny Adams was when he was carrying her away? There were some things which must be believed.

But then came the question – was the prisoner the man who committed the offence? His learned friend had strongly put before them that the entry in the diary was not a simple confession of guilt. It was a curious form in which it was put; the verb first – 'Killed a young girl,' but it mattered not. Were the diary entry read as the prisoner's counsel suggested, 'A young girl killed,' he contended that it was still stronger evidence of guilt, because there were but two occasions on which it could have been written, and on both these it must have been made at a time when no other person but himself could have known that the child was murdered, because the hope in the mind of the mother of the child that she had gone to her father was not dispelled, and the search commenced till twenty minutes to eight, before which time the entry must have been made. The jury no doubt remembered the prisoner's statement that he intended to leave Alton, and he put it to the jury that it was an evidence of his knowledge that he had committed an offence which would render it advisable at all event to leave Alton, to say the least.

The learned counsel then summed up the evidence as to the stains of blood, and said that both the facts and the scientific evidence showed that the clothes and the stone connected the prisoner with the crime.

Referring to the second point of the defence, Mr Bere thought his learned friend was under a misfortune to have to deal with such a case which required a double defence, because if the latter were admitted, it proved the untruth of the first. He argued that in the whole history of criminal trials there was never a case in which the evidence was so weak and worthless. It could not be admitted that typhoid fever or anything of that kind led to homicidal mania – two fine words, which meant uncontrollable desire to kill; and then the plea that there was no motive was what the prosecution could not admit – they believed that the child had been outraged, for the part of the body which could not prove it had not been found. In cases in which the defence of insanity was set up they had the prisoner traced day by day, his conduct in the gaol, et cetera, but they had not a single piece of evidence in support of insanity in this case, and the conduct of the prisoner was inconsistent with that of men seized with a homicidal mania, and consistent only with the conduct of a bad man. The jury were asked to sanction the monstrous idea that the prisoner was unaccountable for his actions, but it would be most unsafe for them to arrive at such a conclusion.

According to their answer to these questions, so would be their verdict.

Mr Bere

Summing up by the Judge.

His Lordship commenced summing up about six o'clock.[195]

This is undoubtedly one of the most remarkable cases it has ever been my lot to try. It depends very much, and almost exclusively, upon the evidence of presumption arising from the conduct of the prisoner, from the acts and admissions he is supposed to have made, as well as an entry in his diary, which is in his handwriting. The case has been conducted on both sides with much propriety and with very considerable ability, and whatever the result of this enquiry may be, it is impossible but to say that the learned counsel for the prisoner has discharged his duty with great zeal and with very considerable skill, and he has very successfully shown that there is great reason to doubt whether the theory of the prosecution is the true theory on certain matters.

At the same time, I must guard you against one or two observations by the learned counsel for the defence. In his address, the learned counsel appeared to suggest that the jury has to consider whether or not the scaffold or the gallows is a proper punishment for this country to retain. That is the punishment assigned by the law for the offence of murder, and the question of whether it is right or wrong is not one that you and I have anything to do with. I must, however, be permitted to say that I am by no means prepared to agree with the observations of the learned counsel as to the wisdom or propriety of abolishing the punishment of death in all cases. It has been my long experience that there are certain crimes for which there is no other secondary punishment suitable, and that there is no punishment which has to some minds the same deterring effect as the sentence of death. You must discharge your duty upon your oaths, as I must discharge mine in sight of the public and before the country, and you must do so within the bounds of the law and the limits of the evidence.

Mr Justice Mellor

195 The *Hampshire Advertiser* incorrectly has the judge beginning his summing up at 'twenty minutes past six o'clock'.

Baker.

**Mr Justice
Mellor**

Now, two defences have been set up by the learned counsel in this case. The first disputes that the prisoner murdered the child. The second says that if the jury comes to the conclusion that the prisoner was guilty of killing and dismembering this unfortunate child, the prisoner is entitled to acquittal on the ground of insanity because he was not responsible for his acts. In this situation the jury would return a verdict of not guilty on the ground of insanity. An acquittal in these circumstances does not mean an escape or a sort of compromise, but a confinement in a criminal lunatic asylum during Her Majesty's pleasure. You must exercise the greatest care before you give effect to such a plea as that; it must be clearly proved, otherwise it would be easy to set up such a plea in all extraordinary cases.

It is the prosecution's case that the prisoner took the deceased into the hop ground, and sent the other two children home. It has been suggested he did so for an improper purpose. However, the part of the child's body which could alone prove this theory has not been recovered. On the other hand, it is fair to say that the prisoner's shirt bore no marks of the kind.[196] In fact, this theory of the prosecution as to the motive for the crime is less important than the question – Was the prisoner the person who committed the murder?

There could be no doubt that the prisoner was the last person seen with the deceased. As to the witness Minnie Warner and the discrepancies in her evidence regarding timing, it was a matter of everyday observation that even grown up persons might be misled in this respect. You have seen the manner and conduct of the little child, and could very well judge whether she might not have made a mistake. In questioning children of such tender years as to their sense of responsibility, I rather judge by their general intelligence, making allowance for the fact of their appearing for the first time in a public court, than by any formal answers to the questions put to them. With respect to the evidence given by the child Vince, it appears to me that the child possessed intelligence and sense of responsibility enough to enable him to be a witness, but up to a certain point children's evidence should be watched with care, though their story was less likely to be invented.

It is worth noting that nothing appeared to have been said about 'murder' until the prisoner used the word to his fellow clerk.

After suspicion fell upon him, the prisoner seems to have been willing to answer any questions put to him, and to have acted not only as an innocent person would, but with great readiness and self-possession. He smoked his cigar in the office, and no excitement was seen about him.

---

196   A reference, of course, to the fact that Fanny's vagina was missing and that no semen stains were found on Baker's linen.

Second Day – Friday 6 December 1867.

This demeanour is worthy of consideration when you turn your attention to the question of the prisoner's mental state at the time.

Mr Justice
Mellor

It has been suggested by the learned counsel for the defence that the entry in the diary is merely typical of the type of entry habitually made by the prisoner. [*The Judge read several of them.*] It is a remarkable entry for a murderer to make. It might be of importance, therefore, to show when the entry was made, since this might have some bearing, in you minds, on the second defence. If it were made before any suggestion had been offered that the child was murdered, it indicated that the prisoner knew what no one else had then known; if it were made after the murder was known, the entry loses its importance. Unless, by some foresight, he was induced to suppose from what the women said, or their tone, that the child was killed, one could not understand it.

The evidence shows the prisoner to have been in the company of the little girl, to have taken her into the field, to have gone to the office, and then returned to the spot or near to it. All these facts are said to indicate the prisoner's guilt. Are they so cogent as to fix him, in your opinion, with it? If you have a real and substantial doubt then the prisoner must have its benefit, because no man should have his life forfeited except upon clear and convincing proof.

Supposing, however, you are perfectly convinced of the guilt of the prisoner, then comes the most important part of the enquiry – was he responsible to the law for his actions? No doubt the evidence shows that there was some insanity in the family, and you have also heard the testimony that he himself exhibited certain eccentricities, and there was a good deal made of the early history of his life, which strictly speaking has little bearing on the question. The doctor said his father's was not a case of homicidal mania, but one of delusion – that they were going to poison him. I do not know what you might think, but my own opinion is that if we were to be put down as insane for doing strange acts in our time, few would pass as sane men.

The defence has made it sound as if few men are sane. Men who are disappointed in love might possibly suffer much mental distress, and on a man of weak mind such a thing would have a greater effect than on one of stronger intellect. It had been said that under such feelings the prisoner had desired to put an end to his existence, but how did that show anything like a homicidal mania? I confess l have great difficulty in understanding this form of disease, but if I understand it, the doctors say that a man under some irresponsible impulse, when his reason has absolutely ceased to act, and he cannot tell the effect of the conduct he is pursuing, becomes a mere machine, without any power of reasoning, but is irresistibly impelled to injure persons loved best, and then glory

Baker.

and boast in it. Whatever might be the opinion of medical jurists on this point, to acquit a man of insanity you must have some evidence of the *bona fide* existence of a diseased brain. In order to render a man irresponsible to the law for his actions he must be unable at the time from a disease of the brain to know the actual quality of the action he is committing, and unable to appreciate that it is contrary to law, and is in itself wicked.

I am bound also to tell you that when the defence of insanity is set up it lies with the prisoner's counsel to prove it. You must be given reasonable evidence of it, and it would be dangerous to accept too readily such a plea just because the crime may happen to be more horrible and atrocious than is usually found in cases of this kind. Take the case against the prisoner, and you will find that he had been upwards of twelve months in the same attorney's office, and nobody appeared to be sensible of any strangeness in his manner except when he was under the influence of drink. But excitement of that kind is not insanity: getting drunk can not be used as an excuse for crime, much less of murder, else we should find men becoming drunk only in order to perpetrate the most wicked deeds. Hereditary disease of the brain might certainly exist, but reasonable evidence must be provided that the prisoner was labouring under such a disease. In the present case when did the homicidal mania commence? When the prisoner went out playing with the children did his homicidal mania seize him, and did he thereupon take the deceased into the field for the purpose of murdering her? If that were so, why separate her from the other children?

You now have all the points before you, and I am quite sure, from the attention which you have paid to the case, that you will act with a due sense of responsibility.

The charge against the prisoner is that he wilfully, and of his malice aforethought, murdered Fanny Adams. If the prosecution has failed to prove to your entire satisfaction that the prisoner committed this crime, then your verdict will be 'Not Guilty'. If the prosecution has proved to your satisfaction that the prisoner murdered the child, then your verdict will be 'Guilty' unless you are convinced he was not responsible for his actions, in which case your verdict will be 'Not Guilty on the Ground of Insanity'.

A solemn duty has devolved upon you, and I ask you to discharge it faithfully to your consciences and in the interests of the country.

His Lordship's summing up occupied nearly two hours. The jury retired at five minutes past seven to consider their verdict, taking with them the diary of the prisoner. After an absence of twenty minutes only, they returned amid the excitement of a crowded court. The names of the

Second Day – Friday 6 December 1867.

jury having been called over, the Clerk of Arraigns asked them if they had agreed on their verdict.

The Foreman — We have.

The Clerk of Arraigns — How say you, gentlemen? Do you find the prisoner, Frederick Baker, guilty or not guilty?

The Foreman — Guilty.

The prisoner appeared to be the only person in court who was not affected by the verdict. He never stirred a muscle, except to nervously squeeze his hands together. The verdict was carried into the body of the hall immediately, and no sooner was it given than a loud hum of conversation and the movement of feet reached the court, rendering it difficult to hear the subsequent proceedings.

The Clerk of Assize — Frederick Baker, you have been indicted for having feloniously and of your malice aforethought killed and murdered Fanny Adams, and on this indictment you have pleaded not guilty, and thereby for your trial have put yourself on your country, which country has found you guilty. Have you anything to say why the Court, on the verdict recorded against you, should not give judgment against you?

The prisoner, who appeared perfectly cool, said nothing in reply.

After the usual proclamations for silence, the learned Judge put on the black cap, and in most earnest and solemn tones addressed the prisoner in the following terms.

Frederick Baker, you have been convicted by a jury of your countrymen of this most dreadful crime – a crime committed under circumstances rarely paralleled in criminal history. For some purpose, probably for the gratification of your lust, you carried that unfortunate child away from her companions and into the hop garden, and whether you there effected that purpose or not is known only to yourself and to Him who knows all things; but it does appear that the poor child was brutally murdered, and afterwards dismembered, with the view, probably, of concealing a crime which preceded the crime of murder.

I feel deeply that a man of your age and in your circumstances should be found guilty of such a horrible offence. I feel it is a shame to our common humanity that such a crime should be perpetrated. I beseech you, prepare for eternity. You must appear shortly before the Great Searcher of Hearts, and it is my hope that you may still, if you apply yourself with all diligence and repentance of the sin you have committed, obtain grace. It is impossible that mercy can be extended to you by any earthly tribunal. Make the best use of the time that remains to you; consider the coming judgment and the interest of your immortal soul. I beseech you,

Baker.

ask God to fill your mind with those impressions which ought to have been produced upon you, from the accounts which I have heard of you from your father. Pray deceive yourself not. Your time is short; prepare yourself for your dread account.

The sentence I pass upon you is the sentence which the law assigns for the crime of murder, and it is this—That you be taken hence to the place whence you came, and thence to a place of execution, there to be hanged by the neck till you be dead, and that your body shall be buried within the precincts of the prison wherein you shall have been last confined. May the Lord have mercy upon your soul.

The prisoner gazed intently at the Judge during the passing of the sentence, but was far less visibly affected than his Lordship. He stood erect at the Bar, with his hands hanging down clutched in front of him. As his Lordship withdrew his black cap, the prisoner turned calmly around and walked slowly away from the dock between two warders, quite unconcerned and showing no signs of any emotion.

The crowded court and hall were soon empty.

Appendices.

APPENDIX A

Contemporary Medical, Psychological and Legal Opinion.

A.1 *The Lancet,* 7 September 1867[197]

A frequent occurrence of the gravest crimes has caused just alarm amongst those who hitherto have been loud in their condemnation of capital punishment. Humanity has recently been outraged by the commission of murders so brutal and cruel, in which the inducement for their perpetration was so trivial and the circumstances urged in their extenuation so unimportant, that the public inquire to what cause is due this fearful increase in the number of the worst offences known to the law. Many reasons have been assigned for this departure from what we may consider as the normal standard of English morality. Without entering *seriatim* into the different explanations which have been offered, we may observe that there is now amongst philanthropists far less inclination than formerly to attribute to insanity many terrible outrages equally explicable on the ground of extreme wickedness and reckless depravity. The plea of insanity has never been ignored in this journal. We have more than once boldly stood between the scaffold and the condemned, and, we believe against popular opinion, influenced the course of justice in their behalf. We cannot recall an instance in which the result has not confirmed our predictions, and intense mania, idiocy, or fatal convulsion established beyond question the condition of the brain of the culprit, of which the most prominent indication has been the crime for which he had been tried. In our present comments we have no desire to depart from our previously avowed principles. If insanity be present, it would be equally just to regard the victim of the saddest of all diseases as responsible for his acts as it would be to hold a fever patient responsible for the utterances of delirium. The abuse of the plea is and has been a cause of proper complaint. We are glad that there is a disposition on the part of the medical profession to reject as reasons sufficient to establish insanity those which are deducible from the mere character of the act, unless there be at the same time present other indications of existing cerebral disorder. Crime which is apparently motiveless, especially if it be of more than usual atrocity, is apt to confound our reason. We picture to ourselves imaginary circumstances in connexion with it, and, in a special case, finding no explanation adequate to satisfy our judgment, we too frequently conclude that no explanation other than insanity is possible. In this conclusion the question is begged. The great majority of crimes are accidental in their complications. Cupidity or lust may lead to outrage, and the fear of discovery induce assassination. A trifling sum may be stolen, and murder be the result;

197   *The Lancet,* 7 September 1867, pp. 300–1.

or an indecent assault, through fear of its detection, eventuate in a desperate attempt to silence its only living witness. Revolting murders, for which no apparent motive exists, are thus too frequently to be explained.

How is the recurrence of such crimes to be prevented? We believe that greater restraint is exercised by the certainty, than by the intensity, of punishment. If loss of life is to be the penalty for murder, let that penalty be exacted, unless a jury, with the approval of the judge, thinks otherwise. The Report of the Royal Commission to inquire into the question of Capital Punishment does not recommend the total abolition of this extreme sentence, but suggests that its application should be limited, and that its carrying out should be modified, and be conducted within the precincts of the prison in the presence of the officials and an admitted few. Accepting it as a fact that capital sentences are to be retained, we are led to ask, Do they deter from crime? To this question we must give an affirmative reply. There are some natures so coarse and brutal, so depraved and vicious, that they retain little other than mere animal instincts, and are only influenced by that which appeals to their fears. We believe that fewer murders would be perpetrated if the punishment which the law awards was certainly carried into effect. It is a false humanity to ignore the deterring influence of capital punishment because of any abhorrence of the character of the punishment itself; and therefore it is that we cannot regret that the present Home Secretary has manifested a disposition to reject those petitions for commutation of sentence which have been presented to him on recent occasions.

It is to be feared that a close connexion might be established between the increase of insanity and the increase of crime. No doubt mental disease is mysterious in its operation and manifestation. No doubt weakened mental power and a low standard of moral sense leave mankind an easier prey to violent passions or criminal desires. It is equally true that such natures are more easily controlled and influenced by fear of punishment: not mere confinement where healthy occupation and wholesome food are to be found, and personal liberty is the only loss, and that a doubtful one, sustained; but punishment where physical suffering is an inherent part of the penalty. Few will deny that to the infliction of the lash is due the discontinuance of that garotte system which rendered life and property so insecure. In a similar manner does the certainty of death as the punishment for deliberate murder deter men of savage and cruel natures from its commission. It is argued that the lash is un-English. We admit the rule, and we prove our proposition in the exception. Murder, mutilation, personal violence are all un-English, and to these offences should the infliction of such punishments be restricted.

These reflections are suggested by a consideration of the case of Frederick Baker, charged with the murder of Fanny Adams under peculiarly revolting circumstances. We earnestly hope that in this case the ends of public justice may be fully attained and satisfied, and that the Government will take care that there is conclusive evidence of the accused's present and past mental condition, should he be proved to have committed the act with which he is charged. We venture to impress this on the authorities, inasmuch as medical authors have cited similar cases, in which diversity of medical opinion

Appendix A.

even now is expressed. Esquirol cites many examples in support of his doctrine 'that there exists a species of homicidal madness in which no disorder of the intellect can be discovered.' Isaac Ray mentions the case of William Brown, who strangled a child whom he accidentally met one morning while walking in the country. On the trial, he said he had never seen the child before, had no malice against it, and could assign no motive for the dreadful act. He took up the body and laid it down on some steps, and then told what he had done, and gave himself into custody. His previous character was exemplary, and there was no suspicion of insanity.[198] Dr. Prichard details the example of Antoine Leger, of whose sanity there were doubts, 'who, seeing one day a little girl near the margin of a wood, seized her, murdered her, sucked her blood, and buried her body.'[199] The cases of Fieldman, Joberd, and others are quoted by psychologists as illustrations of doubtful crime. They present a close analogy to that of Baker, whose diary contains the entry, 'killed a child, fine and hot.' In this shocking case we trust that a careful and repeated scrutiny into the mental state of the accused will be instituted. Should he prove to be insane, one crime less will be laid to the account of humanity. Should he be so sane as to be justly responsible for his acts, any human punishment must prove inadequate to his deserts.

A.2 *The Lancet*, 14 December 1867[200]

We shall take it for granted that the murder of the little girl Fanny Adams at Alton was committed by Frederick Baker. It is no part of our duty to criticize the evidence on this point of the case. Conceding this, we have to inquire whether there is anything in the evidence which enables us to regard the prisoner with any other feelings than those of revenge and detestation, and which may suggest to the Home Secretary the propriety of seriously considering all the facts of the case before he sanctions execution. We are never in humour to be nice in regard to the legal punishment of murderers. We are disposed to approve the firmness with which the present Home Secretary has acted recently in refusing to interfere with the course of the law. There are rough coarse crimes abroad which must be repressed by a corresponding treatment. Still, it remains true that some of the most horrible acts of men are to be regarded as the result of uncontrollable impulses, the subjects of which are to be pitied rather than blamed.

198   William Brown, aged 22, was a private in the Royal Artillery stationed at Woolwich Barracks. In April 1812 he strangled seven-year-old Isabella McGuire. In his summing up at the Kent Assizes, Lord Chief Baron stated that 'the mere atrocity of the act itself must not be considered evidence of insanity – otherwise the most guilty criminals would escape; and here was evidence much too slight to infer any derangement of mind.' (*Stamford Mercury*, 14 August 1812). Brown was hanged on Penenden Heath in August 1812. *A Treatise on the Medical Jurisprudence of Insanity* by Isaac Ray (Boston: Little and Brown, 1838), p. 202.

199   See *A Treatise on Insanity and Other Disorders Affecting the Mind* by James Cowles Prichard (Philadelphia: Carey and Hart, 1837, pp. 279–280).

200   *The Lancet*, 14 December 1867, pp. 740–1.

Baker.

There is no difference of opinion among medical men as to this being occasionally true. The only difference which obtains has reference to the frequency of the case, and the application of the doctrine to individual instances. We admit at the very outset the extreme difficulty and responsibility of any attempt to use this fact in behalf of any particular murderer, especially in behalf of one whose deed has shocked a whole country. Still, it is our duty to state this doctrine in all plainness, and to consider its bearings upon cases as they arise. The extremely horrible and unusual character of a murder is rather a reason for considering the question of unsoundness of mind rather than otherwise. The character of the murder, however, would count for little apart from facts in the history of the murderer and of his family. It is these which constitute the strong evidence for or against a plea of insanity, and to the consideration of them we now invite the gravest attention of our readers and of the authorities. We may say that we speak entirely on the strength of the newspaper reports of the case; but these are sufficient to show that the question of unsoundness of mind must be gravely entertained before Frederick Baker can be hanged. Baker himself was certainly, to say the least, peculiar. In early life he showed great nervous susceptibility. According to various witnesses, besides his father and sister, he was at times very unhappy, very desponding, and decidedly suicidal in tendency. One witness deposed to having prevented the prisoner jumping into the river. Mrs. Kingston, with whom he lodged at Alton, said she always observed how low and dull he was in spirits. He would walk about in the middle of the night; and be watched home by a policeman, who feared he would commit suicide. Such are a few particulars of the character of Frederick Baker. By themselves we should not, perhaps, have thought much of them. But in connexion with his crime they cannot be ignored, and they acquire great importance when viewed in the light of his family history. All sensible medical men will ask, What is the history of this man's family? His father, four years ago, had an attack of acute mania. He was violent, and had delusions; and once attacked his son and daughter because he was under the delusion that they were endeavouring to poison him. A cousin of the prisoner's father is now an inmate of a lunatic asylum, with a homicidal tendency. Taking these proofs of family weakness in connexion with those indications of weakness displayed by Baker from his childhood upwards, we say there is a most urgent case made out for consideration. A man may make himself weak-minded by vice, and may only provoke our censure; but a man who inherits insanity and weakmindedness, and the principal part of whose life has been spent soberly and religiously, is an object of pity and commiseration when he commits a crime whose very horribleness surpasses the comprehension of sane men, and coolly records it in his diary of the day.

We do not say that we have made out a case for exempting Baker from capital punishment, but we think we have certainly shown reason enough why Mr. Hardy should make careful and earnest medical inquiry sufficient to satisfy his own mind that Baker is not a man to be restrained and pitied rather than hanged. Of all the legacies bequeathed from father to son unsoundness of mind is the most pitiable. Mr. Hardy may be sure of the support of the public in giving all fair weight to the evidence which goes

Appendix A.

to show that Baker's crime had its origin in hereditary or constitutional aberrations.

[A copy of the above article was sent by Dr. Henry Taylor to the Home Secretary Gathorne Hardy on 19 December 1867, along with an accompanying note:

I take the liberty of calling your attention to an article in the 'Lancet' on the case of the Convict, Frederick Baker, which may be regarded as an independent opinion as well as representing the scientific interests of the medical profession.

My attention was only directed to the article in question this morning and it seemed to me so important to the case as strengthening my view of it, that I think it right to forward you a copy even at this late hour.][201]

A.3 *The Lancet*, 21 December 1867[202]

Attempts are being made to induce the Home Secretary to postpone the execution of Frederick Baker, with a view to a careful enquiry into the facts bearing upon the plea of insanity, which, it must be admitted, were not urged and relied on by the prisoner's counsel as they might have been. We have already expressed an opinion that the case is one calling loudly for special inquiry, and throwing very great responsibility on the Minister whose painful duty it is to determine on execution or the postponement of it. One of our contemporaries, in criticising the plea of insanity, lightly skims over a few of the facts in support of it, omitting the very weightiest – viz., the acute mania of the father of the prisoner four years ago; and gives us further to understand that the 'homicidal mania dodge' is now discredited. So! Is the hereditariness of insanity discredited? Is it an equal advantage to a man to have a maniac for his father, or a wise and sane man? If not, then insanity may have bearings on a man's crimes, and may be a considerable element in any sound judgment of their criminality. With all deference to our Saturday contemporary, there is a use to be made of the element of insanity in criminal cases which is not of the nature of a 'dodge', a use dictated alike by sound science and true humanity.

---

201   TNA: HO 12/176/79865.
202   *The Lancet*, 21 December 1867, p. 780.

Baker.

A.4 *Journal of Mental Science*, January 1868[203]

The Alton murderer certainly did no credit to his art. His crime was conceived without ingenuity, and executed in the coarsest manner; the only remarkable features in it being its simplicity and atrocity. On a fine afternoon a clerk in a solicitor's office takes a walk outside the town; he sees some children playing in a field by the roadside; one of these, a lively little girl, between eight and nine years of age, he persuades to go with him into an adjoining hop-garden, and the others he gets rid of by giving them a few halfpennies to go home. In a little while he is met walking home alone, and he returns to his office, where he makes an entry in his diary. But what has become of the little girl? No one has seen her since she was taken from her playfellows into the hop-field. Her parents became alarmed; they arouse their neighbours, and an anxious search is made for the missing child. It is ascertained that she was last seen on her way to the hop-field, and when the searchers hurriedly proceed there, they find the dismembered fragments of her body scattered here and there. A foot is in one place, a hand in another, the heart and the eyes are picked up after a long search; and some parts of the body cannot be found at all. The poor child has clearly been murdered, and her body cut into pieces; but what she underwent before she was butchered may be suspected but cannot be discovered, because the 'vagina was missing.' Suspicion fell directly upon the prisoner, and he was arrested. In his desk was found a diary, and in the diary the following entry just made: 'Killed a little girl; it was fine and hot.' Such are the main facts, briefly told, of the murder; it is not surprising that they excited horror and disgust in the public mind, and that the prisoner was denounced as a brutal and unnatural scoundrel, for whom, if he were found guilty, hanging was too good.

Emancipating ourselves from the natural feelings of indignation, let us look at the matter, however, from a purely scientific point of view, in order to draw any lesson that may be procurable from it in that light. In the first place, it is a libel on the beasts to call such a crime brutal – brutes do not violate and murder one another in that way; the crime is essentially and exclusively human. Men are very ready to claim their superiority of virtue and intelligence over other animals; let us not ignore our pre-eminence in vice also. In the second place, to call such a crime unnatural is not to take it out of the domain of natural law. That the murderer was a monstrosity may be admitted, but monstrosities are not self-created, they must have their necessary antecedents in the order of events; not casualty but causality governs them, the universe, and their appearance in it. There is but one answer to the question, so strikingly put by the engraver Blake in his little poem addressed to the tiger—

> Did He smile his work to see?
> Did He who made the lamb make thee?

To any one who has really studied the forms and laws of human degeneracy, so far as these are known, the features of the Alton murder could not fail to excite a

---

203   'The Alton Murder', *Journal of Mental Science*, Volume 13, Issue 64, January 1867, pp. 548–9.

Appendix A.

suspicion, if not to beget a conviction, that there was some taint of madness in the blood of the murderer. He was plainly an instinctive criminal: the impulsive character of the crime, the calm ferocity of it, the savage mutilation of the victim, and the placid equanimity of the murderer immediately after he had supped so full of horrors – all these indicate a bad organization, a nature to which horrors were congenial, whose affinities were devilward. 'Killed a little girl; it was fine and hot.' He puts down the fact as indifferently as he might have done if he had just bathed in the river instead of bathing his murderous hands in the little girl's blood. It is not possible, we fear, to call him actually insane, unless we are content to give up all exact notions of what insanity is; but there can be little doubt that, had his life been prolonged, he would have become insane. The evidence at the trial showed that a near relative of his father was in confinement suffering from homicidal mania, and that his father had had an attack of acute mania. Moreover, it was proved in evidence by independent witnesses that he himself had been unlike other people, that he had been prone to weep frequently without evident reason, that he had exhibited singular caprices of conduct, and that it had been necessary to watch him from fear that he might commit suicide. These testimonies of an insane temperament were not sufficient to stay the course of human justice; this falls on the sinner often with indiscriminating force, taking no thought of opportunities and of that worst of all tyrannies, the tyranny of a bad organization. But it is not so above; 'there the action lies in its true nature'; and it may well be that many sorrowing murderers shall come from the east and the west and find entrance into the kingdom of the redeemed, when some who have, with exultant homicidal yell, rejoiced over their fate on earth, are cast out into outer darkness.

A.5 *Medical Times and Gazette*, 14 December 1867[204]

If the case of Baker, the Alton murderer, were weighed against that of Bordier,[205] and the explanation of criminal insanity offered in either, there can be no doubt in which it would be more readily admitted. The man Baker, besides inheriting a strong tint of insanity from his father, who, within the last few years, has been the inmate of an asylum, and whose family history has been marked by instances of homicidal mania, had himself been remarkable for a weak intellect, and had frequently attracted the attention of persons with whom he came in contact by his strange behaviour and gloomy manner. The policeman of the district used to watch him home for fear he should commit suicide, and Baker himself had confessed to suicidal tendencies. Here certainly is a case which, taken together with the extraordinary character of the crime

204 *Medical Times & Gazette*, 14 December 1867, p. 652.
205 Louis Bordier, a French currier, was executed outside Horsemonger Lane gaol on 15 October 1867 for the murder of his lover Mary Snow at a boarding house in the Old Kent Road. For details of the trial see Old Bailey Online reference t18670923-912.

Baker.

and the unparalleled circumstance of the entry in the journal, might *prima facie* suggest doubt, not perhaps sufficient to permit an acquittal on the ground of insanity, but at least enough to suggest the propriety of some further inquiry into the culprit's mental condition. No mere Medical reasoning, apart from an examination of the present condition of the prisoner by a competent Medical commission, should be allowed to have any weight in the matter. The Home Secretary, were he advised after careful examination by a commission consisting of such men, for instance, as Drs. Maudsley, Blandford, and Wood, that Baker was an irresponsible agent, would doubtless be justified in recommending that his life should not be forfeited to the law. But nothing short of a unanimous expression of Professional opinion, founded on careful examinations, and given by several men who have made mental pathology the study of their lives, would satisfy the public or meet the requirements of the case.

A.6 *Medical Times and Gazette*, 28 December 1867[206]

The execution of Baker, the Alton murderer, may perhaps have left a disagreeable suspicion in some minds that a non-responsible person has suffered the last penalty of the law. We confess that we should have willingly seen a commission of inquiry authorized to examine his medical condition. But much of the uneasy feeling created by the suspicion that Baker was irresponsible when he committed the act is dispelled by the culprit's own confession on the scaffold—that he was led to do it through drinking. A man is certainly responsible for crimes which are immediately the result of habitual indulgence in evil courses, even though those courses may have left him no longer master of himself. We are here, of course, expressing no opinion as to the propriety of capital punishment in such a case, but are simply commenting on the question of responsibility.

A.7 *Responsibility in Mental Disease* by Henry Maudsley[207]

As an example of the second class of cases, in which an insane homicidal impulse springs up suddenly without external provocation in the mind of a person who has the insane temperament, I may instance the case of the Alton murderer, who was tried, convicted, and executed a few years ago. He was a clerk in a solicitor's office at Alton, Hampshire. On a fine afternoon he took a walk outside the town, when he met some children playing by the road-side. One of these, a little girl between eight and nine years of age, he persuaded to go with him into an adjoining hop-garden, and the others

---

206 *Medical Times & Gazette*, 28 December 1867, p. 702.
207 Henry Maudsley, *Responsibility in Mental Disease* (New York: Appleton and Company, 1874), pp. 161–3.

142

he got rid of by giving them a few halfpennies to go home. In a little while he was met walking quietly home; he washed his hands in the river on his way, and then returned to his work in the office. As the little girl did not return, search was made in the hop-garden, and the dismembered fragments of her body were found scattered about – a foot in one place, a hand in another, and other parts in different places. Suspicion fell directly upon the prisoner, who was immediately arrested. In his desk was found a diary, and in the diary there was an entry recently made – 'Killed a little girl: it was fine and hot.' He had killed the child and cut her body to pieces without other motive than the gratification of an impulse which suddenly came into his mind. There was no indication of insanity in his conversation or conduct after his arrest, nor was there any evidence of strangeness in him immediately before the murder given at the trial. But it came out at the trial, where only the semblance of a defence was made, that a near relative was in confinement suffering from homicidal mania, and that his father had had an attack of acute mania. Moreover, it was proved in evidence by independent witnesses that he himself had been unlike other people, that he had been prone to weep frequently without apparent reason, that he had exhibited singular caprices of conduct, and that it had been necessary at one time to watch him from the fear that he might commit suicide. He was found guilty, condemned to death, and in due course executed – all the newspapers heartily applauding. Nevertheless the features of the murder in this case were of themselves sufficient to produce a conviction in the minds of those who had studied the forms of human degeneracy that there was a strong taint of madness in the murderer – that the disease was at least in the stage of incubation. He was plainly an instinctive criminal, if he were criminal at all: the impulsive character of the crime, the quiet and determined ferocity of it, the savage mutilation, his equanimity afterwards, and his complete indifference to his fate – all these indicated an insane organization, ill-attempered, a discord in nature, which, had it not issued as it did, would, sooner or later, have ended in suicide or in unequivocal insanity.

A.8 *The Medical Jurisprudence of Insanity* by J.H. Balfour Browne[208]

It seems to us impossible to distinguish in any way between the mental condition of Cuthbert Carr and the man who in the same year was found guilty of a similar offence at Alton, and who was sentenced to death and executed.[209]

---

208   J.H. Balfour Browne, *The Medical Jurisprudence of Insanity* (London: Churchill, 1871), p. 75–7.
209   Cuthbert Carr raped and murdered five-year-old Sarah Melvin in Gateshead in 1866. Carr suffered from gonorrhoea, and believed in the 'virgin cleansing myth' that intercourse with a virgin girl, the younger the better, would rid a man of sexual infection. He was committed to Broadmoor Criminal Lunatic Asylum, where he died in 1888. For a detailed account of the Carr case, see Jane Housham, *The Apprentice of Split Crow Lane* (London: Riverun, 2016). Belief in virgin cleansing as a cure for people who are HIV+ is prevalent today in sub-Saharan Africa but the actual practice is rare.

Baker.

In many respects the crimes committed by these two men resembled each other. The Alton murderer, who was a clerk in a solicitor's office, upon seeing some children playing by a roadside, persuaded one of them, a girl of eight or nine years of age, to go with him into an adjoining hop garden, and got rid of the other children by distributing some half-pence amongst them. Shortly after that time he was met returning to his office, where he made an entry in his diary to the following effect – 'Killed a little girl; it was fine and hot.'

The child had meanwhile been missed, and her parents became alarmed and a search was instituted. It was ascertained that she had last been seen on her way to the hop field, and in that field the dismembered fragments of her body were found scattered here and there. Some parts of the body could not be found at all. The vagina was missing. These are the main facts of this horrible crime, and it is almost impossible, it seems to us, to distinguish in any way between these two criminal acts, except in so far as there seems to have been a miscarriage of justice in the former, while, as the law at present stands, justice seems to have been done in the latter. With the question as to whether the Alton murderer should have been put to death we have, in this place, nothing to do. But that he was not legally responsible for the crime he committed is to be inferred from all the principles which have been stated above.

[*Balfour Browne earlier quotes the opinion of Dr. James Crichton Browne, medical superintendent at the West Riding Asylum, who had studied Carr while he was undergoing psychiatric assessment at Durham Gaol.*] [210]

1st.   That he labours under mental weakness or defect, which displays itself in stolid indifference as to his future destiny, callousness of feeling, unreasonable obstinacy, and outbursts of violence upon real or imaginary occasions.

2nd.   That this weakness or defect was probably congenital, and became more prominently developed as growth proceeded, and that it would be exaggerated by excitement, exhaustion, loss of sleep, intemperance, or great physical suffering.

3rd.   That he is otherwise of fully average intelligence, apprehending everything that is said to him with clearness and precision, and replying with sense and aptitude.

4th.   That he expresses himself with accuracy and facility, and deports himself with patience and placidity when under examination.

5th.   That his powers of calculation and memory are unusually acute, and that his acquirements are respectable for his position in life.

6th.   That he is perfectly capable of distinguishing between right and wrong, and indeed, does this with nice discrimination.

---

210   James Crichton Browne was the older brother of J.H. Balfour Browne. In a clear breach of patient confidentiality, he allowed his case notes on Carr to be accessed and reproduced by his brother in his textbook on medical jurisprudence.

Appendix A.

7th. That he is perfectly capable of foreseeing the consequences of any act which he may commit, and of regulating his conduct, under ordinary circumstances, with rational forethought.

8th. That he believes in the great truths of religion, but is confused as to the doctrine of rewards and punishments.

9th. That he labours under no delusions or hallucinations recognizable as such.

10th. That he exhibits no signs of labouring, ordinarily, under overpowering passions or morbid propensities.

11th. That his general appearance and manners are such as are usually associated with partial mental defect or eccentricity.

A.9 *Principles and Practice of Medical Jurisprudence* by Alfred Swaine Taylor[211]

In *Reg. v. Baker*, a case involving a charge of murder and the mutilation of a little girl (Hants Autumn Assizes, 1867), the trousers of the prisoner sent for examination had been stained with blood in front. An attempt had been made to remove these stains by soaking them in water. This had carried the red colouring matter into the calico lining, and had given to some patches a strong and to others a pale reddish tint. The direct application of the guaiacum and peroxide indicated blood over a square foot of the calico lining, and beyond this, these liquids produced no change. The degree of the diffusion of the blood, as it had been washed from the front of the trousers into the lining, was thus clearly defined.

211 Alfred Swaine Taylor, *Principles and Practice of Medical Jurisprudence* (Philadelphia: Henry C. Lea, 1873), Vol. 1, 2nd edition, pp. 532.

APPENDIX B

An Open Letter to the *Morning Star*.[212]

_____

Charles Neate (1806–1879) was Liberal Member of Parliament for the city of Oxford (1863–67). Previously he had been a barrister (Lincoln's Inn) and Professor of political economy at Oxford (1857–62). He was the author of 'Considerations on the Punishment of Death' and an abolitionist voice on the Royal Commission on Capital Punishment (1864–66).

In December 1867 he wrote an open letter to the Morning Star *newspaper, reproduced below, in which he argued that Baker had not received a fair trial and that the prisoner's defence was insufficient and inadequate. A copy of this letter was sent by Neate to the Home Secretary dated 14 December 1867.*

'THE CASE OF FREDERICK BAKER'

Sir, — If there is such a thing as homicidal mania which may in any case exempt from criminal responsibility those who act under its impulse, then certainly there was a question which arose in the case of the convict Baker, and which was not fairly tried. The existence of such a mania in his instance was neither sufficiently urged by his counsel, nor sufficiently supported by evidence, nor sufficiently discussed by the judge, and therefore, as we may fairly conclude, not sufficiently considered by the jury.

The counsel, indeed, threw away the case by attempting to cast doubt on the evidence of the act itself, in doing which he tried to explain away that which was one of the chief points of the defence, namely, the entry in the diary – 'Killed a little girl; it was fine and hot.' As to the question of insanity, there was indeed the evidence of the prisoner's father and his medical attendant and others, as to the prisoner's previous mental state, but as to the way in which such facts as were stated would have been viewed by scientific men there was only the evidence on cross-examination of Dr. Taylor, who was called as a witness for the prosecution in his character of an analytical chemist. In that capacity Dr. Taylor, and those who have cultivated, as he has done, the mechanical department of science, have often done great service to the cause of justice; but I am not aware that Dr. Taylor is entitled to be considered an authority upon the very difficult question of what constitutes what is called moral insanity. His evidence certainly in this instance

212   'The Case of Frederick Baker', *Morning Star*, 13 December 1867. Copy dated 14 December 1867 in TNA HO 12/176/79865.

does not convey a high idea either of his scholarship or his research. His etymology of a Greek word, which he unnecessarily introduced, would have provoked the laughter of a schoolboy;[213] and his statement of professional opinion on the subject of homicidal mania was greatly at variance with the fact.

Dr. Taylor gives it, not as his own opinion, but as a conclusion agreed upon by the learned, that in cases of homicidal mania 'the perpetrator is perfectly indifferent to punishment, and never denies the act.' It is very true that in Dr. Beck's 'Treatise on Medical Jurisprudence', which is a very valuable repertory of cases and authorities, the opinion given by Dr. Taylor as the received doctrine is quoted as the opinion of Dr. Prichard; but a little further down in the same page is the following quotation from Dr. Ray, who is, I believe, a greater authority than Dr. Prichard – 'The most of them (homicidal maniacs) have gratified their propensity to kill, voluntarily confess the act, and quietly give themselves up to the proper authorities; a very few only – and those to an intelligent mind show the strongest indications of insanity – fly and persist in denying the act.'

It is very clear that Dr. Taylor's evidence on this point was not correct as to the matter of fact, and as the error was important and was not corrected either by judge or counsel, it is probable that it may have had a material effect upon the verdict; though even in the view taken by Dr. Prichard, and wrongly stated by Dr. Taylor as the received opinion, the entry in the diary would have been strong evidence of indifference to conviction. But the counsel for the prisoner had done what he could to deprive his client of the benefit of that argument.

I pass now with some reluctance to the part of the judge in this matter. First, when the counsel for the prisoner asked Dr. Taylor – his only witness on this point, though an adverse one – whether in his opinion the very enormity of the crime did not afford a presumption of insanity, the judge, apparently with some indignation, repudiated the idea of the enormity of the crime being set up as a defence, and an objection having been taken by the counsel for the prosecution to such a question, was either allowed or acquiesced – it is not clear which – but it is quite clear that the question itself, if put into a proper form, was relevant, and ought to have been pressed. The words 'enormity of the crime' used by the counsel and adopted by the judge, are nothing more than a rhetorical misstatement of the question, which answers itself; but if the question had been asked whether the doing of a dreadful deed repugnant to a sane man, without any assignable motive, did not afford some presumption of insanity, that was a question very proper for a scientific witness to answer, very important for a jury to consider, and one which most thoughtful and educated men would answer in the affirmative.

The judge himself seems to have felt the necessity of a motive to rebut the presumption of insanity, for in passing sentence he expressed strongly his belief that the prisoner had got hold of his victim for some obscene and unnatural purpose, and had then killed her

---

213 A reference to Taylor's remark about the origin of the word 'artery': 'It was formerly supposed, from the arteries being empty at death, that they were distended by air—hence the derivation of the word'. Neate's objection is rather petty.

Appendix B.

to destroy the evidence of that crime. This may have been true; and it was so opened by the counsel for the prosecution. But there was no evidence whatever in support of the charge; and what right has a judge to assume a fact of which there is no evidence? The mere fact of the victim being a little girl affords but a very slight presumption in support of such a belief, for children are usually the victims in such cases, whether the perpetrators be male or female, because madmen and madwomen are habitually timid, and shrink from the idea of resistance.

There was in France a few years ago a very similar case to this. A young woman having enticed a very young child away from its mother, took it up to her room and killed it, and when the mother came to the door to ask for it, said, 'Your child is dead,' and threw the head out of the window. This woman was found guilty of homicide without premeditation, and was condemned to perpetual imprisonment, as this wretched maniac ought to be.[214] If he is brought to the scaffold as a guilty man, whose crime is to be expiated by death, and whose punishment is to be a warning to other men, it is an outrage to human nature and a profanation even of the gallows.— I am, Sir, your obedient servant,

CHARLES NEATE.

---

214   A reference to the notorious case of Henriette Cornier, a twenty-seven-year-old Parisian nursemaid and servant, who in 1825 decapitated a neighbour's infant daughter with a kitchen knife, placing her head and body on the window ledge of her first floor apartment. When the mother came looking for her child two hours later, Cornier threw the head into the street, shouting 'She is dead'. The case attracted widespread interest among European psychiatrists and lawyers.

APPENDIX C

Petition for respite on Grounds of Insanity

C.1 A circular to the inhabitants of Guildford[215]

Friends and Fellow Townsmen,

We desire to call your attention to some features in the case of FREDERICK BAKER now painfully agitating all minds. Learning from our esteemed neighbour, H. S. Taylor, Esq., that he, as the medical adviser of the Baker family for many years past, is very strongly of opinion that there is great presumption of Baker's insanity, we have requested him to put his ideas on paper, in order that those who have had no opportunity of judging as to the state of mind of the unfortunate condemned, may be so far guided by his opinion as to join in an appeal to the Home Secretary for such delay in the execution of the sentence as may enable further enquiry to be made by qualified practitioners as to the sanity, or otherwise, of the prisoner.

We are, yours respectfully,

JOSH. WEALE,[216]	THOS. GILL,
R. TRIMMER,[217]	E. W. MARTIN,[218]
RICHD. EAGLE,	E. W. BROOKS.[219]

Guildford, December 11 1867

---

215 This circular was sent to every householder in Guildford. It was also printed in several local newspapers (see *Hampshire Chronicle*, 14 December 1867). Mr William Tallack of the Howard Association enclosed a copy of the circular in his correspondence to the Home Secretary, TNA HO 12/176/79865.
216 Joseph Weale, a retired woollen draper and former Chairman of Guildford District Council. In 1863 his shop at 148 High Street was attacked during the Guy Fawkes Riots.
217 The Rev. Robert Trimmer, rector of Holy Trinity and St. Mary's, Guildford (1863–82). The Baker family worshipped at St Mary's every Sunday and Frederick had been a Sunday school teacher at the church.
218 E. Waller Martin, a pharmaceutical chemist and dentist at 68 High Street, Guildford. A prominent local Quaker, at one time he was active in the Guildford Working Men's Institution.
219 Edmund Wright Brooks, engineer and leading Quaker philanthropist, active in the anti-slavery movement.

Baker.

C.2 The Opinion of Dr. Henry Taylor (supporting the petition)

Guildford, December 11, 1867.

My Dear Sir,

As one of the witnesses for the defence of Frederick Baker, and being well acquainted with the medical history of his family, I may venture to express an opinion on the verdict now recorded against him.

It is my firm conviction that the prisoner was insane at the time of the commission of the murder, and my opinion is based on the following facts, observed by myself and others.

Insanity, in its most unmistakeable form, that of acute mania, has shown itself in two of the males of his family — his father and his father's first cousin.

The tendency to insanity thus inherited, must have been materially increased by the intemperate habits in which the prisoner is known to have indulged for many years.

Occasional indications of insanity have been manifested by the prisoner during the last three years. The sudden change in his character and conduct; the very absurdity of his excesses; and an attempt at suicide; shew the then unsettled state of his mind.

But it is on the circumstance of the deed itself that I rely most for the proof of insanity. Its unspeakable atrocity may render it a difficult subject for calm discussion; but when we find that no adequate motive has been discovered for the mutilation of the murdered child, and the theories set up to explain it assume the existence of a state of mind wholly inconsistent with sanity; also that no attempt was made to conceal the traces of the horrible crime, the reasonable inference is that the act was prompted by the blind impulses of a madness which is now fully recognized by medical men as homicidal monomania.

Lastly, the circumstance commented on by the Judge as being a 'most extraordinary' one, namely, the entry of the murder in the prisoner's diary, coupled with a note of the state of the weather, shew that for the time at least the writer was either mad or imbecile.

A careful review of the foregoing facts has convinced me, as I hope it will convince others, that the case of Frederick Baker demands a fuller investigation, and that a memorial should be at once forwarded to the Secretary of State, praying that an inquiry be made into the state of the prisoner's mind, and that the execution of his sentence be deferred for that purpose.

I remain, my dear Sir,
Yours faithfully,
HENRY TAYLOR.

Mr. E. W. Brooks.

———————

Appendix C.

C.3 The Opinion of Mr. J.C. Hudson (opposing the petition)[220]

Epsom Road
Guildford
13 Dec. 1867

The Rt. Hon. Gathorne Hardy M.P

Sir

From a circular letter which has just been left at my house, I learn that an attempt is being made in this town, where the friends of the convict F. Baker reside, to get up a petition for 'granting further time for inquiries' instead of letting the sentence be executed at the time appointed – which means, of course, for sparing his life.

Of the persons making this attempt two are Quakers (who are systematically opposed to all capital punishment) and one is a medical attendant of the family of the criminal. So far as I know (and I have lived here nearly 20 years) the general feeling is in favour of the prompt execution of the sentence: in the interest of society, and especially of the poorer classes whose children are unavoidably exposed to the dangerous assaults of men whose brutal passions have never been made subject to control, and who have, in ordinary, no protector but the Law; I, and many others protest against these subtle refinements of medical men and metaphysicians, who would analyse the motives of murderers, till they would exterminate the atrocities of a Cesare Borgia.

What distinction can be rationally made between the wretch who murdered the girl at Shere, and was recently hanged for it,[221] and the wretch Baker, now under sentence of death?

I take the freedom of writing this, because, if a petition should reach you from those residents here, who are now trying to get one signed, it is but proper for you to know that the feelings of a very large portion of the inhabitants are quite opposed to it, and that the humbler classes especially consider their trust in the efficacy of the Law, to be involved in the question.

I have the honour to be, Sir,
Your most obedient very humble servant
J.C. HUDSON

---

220 J.C. Hudson to Gathorne Hardy, 13 December 1867, TNA HO 12/176/79865. Mr Hudson was a retired civil servant in his seventies.
221 A reference to the execution of James Longhurst for the murder of Jane Sax in Shere, near Guildford, in 1866. See Appendix H.

Baker.

C.4 Deputation Request from Mr. J. Rand Capron[222]

To the Rt Honorable Gathorne Hardy
Her Majesty's Secretary of State for the Home Department

Sir,

The case of Frederick Baker, the criminal now under sentence of death, at Winchester has attracted much attention and comment in the Public Prints, and in this way, must necessarily, already, to some extent, have come under your notice.

The shocking circumstances of the crime have ~~accordingly~~ naturally caused a strong and universal prejudice against the unhappy Prisoner, but now that the trial is over, and some time has allowed of a calmer consideration, of the matter, many of those who, from living in the same town know the criminal, and his family cannot help feeling that the question of the state of the Prisoner's mind, before, at, and after his commission of the crime, ought to have a further inquiry than it has met with at present.

It may perhaps be said, that experts might have been called, at the trial; They would have been so, but that it was utterly out of the power of the Prisoner, and his friends, to meet the heavy expense which would be thereby incurred, and the evidence of Mr. H. T. Taylor [sic] was for this reason the only evidence rendered on the point, on Prisoner's behalf. A Memorial is now being signed in Guildford and in Alton praying that there may be such delay in the execution of the sentence as may enable a further inquiry to be made as to the state of the Prisoner's mind, and it is proposed that one or two of the Memorialists should wait on you with the Memorial. I therefore beg the favour of your informing me, if it will be your pleasure to receive a deputation of the Memorialists, and in that case to honour them with an appointment for that purpose.

I have the honour, to be, Sir,
Your obedient servant,
J. Rand Capron [signature]
Solt. for the Defence.[223]

---

222   J. Rand Capron to Gathorne Hardy. 12 December 1867, TNA HO 12/176/79865.
223   The request was declined by Hardy, 13 December 1867, TNA HO 12/176/79865.

Appendix C.

C.5 Memorial from the Inhabitants of Guildford

Memorial from the Inhabitants of Guildford

To the Right Honourable Gathorne Hardy Her Majesty's Principal Secretary of State for the Home Department.

IN THE MATTER of Frederick Baker who now lies under sentence of Death in the County Gaol of Hants at Winchester.

The Humble Memorial of the Inhabitants of Guildford, Surrey.

STATES

That your Memorialists understand that there is hereditary Insanity in the family of the Prisoner and believe that at the time of the commission of the crime of which he has been convicted he was suffering from feebleness of mind and depression of spirits which have produced a morbid and irresponsible state of mind. The absence of all premeditation and of any sufficient motive and his irrational conduct immediately after the commission of the crime most clearly indicate that the Prisoner at the time of his committing the crime was not in a state of mind to be accountable for his actions.

Your Memorialists therefore pray that taking the above circumstances into consideration together with the evidence produced at the Trial on the Prisoner's behalf you will feel it consistent with your high duty to advise delay in the execution of the sentence of Death which has been passed upon him and the institution of a full inquiry into the state of the condemned person's mind.

And your Memorialists will ever pray.

[*There follows the names and addresses of 330 petitioners.*]

———

Home Office, No. 79865.
Date: 17 December 1867.
Frederick Baker.
Sent by Mr. Capron.
Memorial from inhabitants of Guildford praying mitigation on the ground that the Prisoner was Insane.

APPENDIX D

Trial Notes of Mr Justice Mellor[224]

Taunton

Dec 9 1867

The Right Honourable, Gathorne Hardy MP
Secretary of State.
Sir

I beg herewith to transmit a copy of my notes of the case of Frederick Baker who was tried before me at Winchester & convicted of wilful murder. The trial lasted during two long days & the jury after deliberating only for a quarter of an hour, found him guilty & and he was accordingly sentenced to death.

The fact of the murder depended for proof upon circumstantial evidence but of a remarkably prejudicial character coupled with an entry made by himself in his diary, kept locked up in his desk in which he was in the habit of recording common occurrences & the state of the weather – It appeared to have been made <u>before</u> any suggestion had been made that the child had been killed & when it was supposed to be <u>lost</u> only – there was no precise evidence to shew when it was made but strong negative and evidence to shew that it was <u>not</u> made <u>after</u> a charge of murder had been made and characterised in the presence of the prisoner.

The counsel for the Prisoner in addition to any defence acting on the facts set up the additional defence of homicidal mania & and it appeared that in the prisoner's family there had been 3 instances of insanity, one being the case of his father who had been under restraint for a month or two.

The prisoner however had been in an attorney's office for 12 months without exhibiting any sign of insanity or mania of any kind, & both before and after the offence was committed acted in a manner which excited no observation having that tendency, and it appeared to me that the only evidence connected in the horrible nature of the crime itself.

I told the jury that it was not enough to prove a case of mania or insanity which rendered a man responsible for his acts to shew that the crime itself was unusually horrible but that if connected with other circumstances it might satisfy them that such was the case – It appeared to me that the defence of insanity wholly failed.

I am, Sir,
Your very obedient servant
John Mellor

---

224   TNA HO 12/176/79865

APPENDIX E

Correspondence to Home Secretary[225]

E.1 Letter from A Clergyman's Wife

To the Right Hon Gaythorne Hardy [*sic*]

With utmost respect –

I feel convinced that Frederick Baker was deranged – can no exception be made in the highest quarter that his sentence be commuted to confinement for life? The evidences of his aberration of mind at the time of the murder, and previously, are so clear – the protracted manner in which the foul deed was prosecuted and that it was done at all without a motive, either of anger, or jealousy or other passion; and that any other child could therefore have sufficed the purpose equally, show the evidence of Mania at the time – and as to previously deranged mind, he once having attempted to throw himself into the river and meet death for the purpose of 'being talked about'.

Then the testimony of a Medical practitioner that he had attended Baker's father in 'Senile Mania' – and the statement that a cousin was also deranged ; and after all this what greater corroboration of madness can be heeded, that, as soon as the diabolical deed was concluded he wrote down in his diary "Killed a girl"?

Surely a gracious precedent will bias the minds of those in high office to reconsider this case.

I am
Your humble servant –
A Clergyman's wife

Date stamped 11 December 1867

E.2 The Views of Dr William Curtis Jnr

Memorials will probably be presented to the Home Secretary praying him to advise the commutation of the sentence of death passed on Fredk Baker, on the ground of insanity.

I believe this will not meet with the sympathy of the public, and yet there is much to

---

225   TNA HO 12/176/79865/2.

be adduced to support that plea. I have heard much relative to the prisoner's conduct and peculiarities from those who know him well, and was present at the trial, and I have no hesitation in saying that from the insight thus gained into his character, I am perfectly satisfied that he was a man of a very ill-balanced mind – sometimes influenced by sudden and powerful impulse, sometimes depressed, desponding and almost imbecile – easily influenced and possessing a <u>very feeble moral</u> control over his actions.

I must say that I thought the evidence for the defence was not made the most of – the proofs of insanity in other members of the family, and the prisoner's own temporary aberration of mind – the total absence of premeditation, and the apparent want of sufficient motive – the insane measures adopted after the commission of the crime, for instance the fascination which kept him hovering about the spot, and which led to his speedy identification – <u>a thing he might easily have avoided</u> – the evidently useless mutilation, the making <u>no attempt to escape</u> – all tend to give a strong presumptive suspicion, if not a positive proof, of insanity at the time.

If insanity in the ordinary sense of the term cannot be positively proved, I do believe that the influence to which a weak nervous morbid mind may be subjected might induce a temporary irresponsibility in action. I am aware that it is urged, and probably with truth, that he knew right from wrong at the time –and yet if he did it is possible that that knowledge might have little influence over a weak and morbid intellect.

Whether much or little to the purpose everything that can be said on this deed may be, I believe it possible that, although responsible at the beginning, a period of irresponsibility supervened.

After expressing these views I must be allowed to add that I cannot class this wretched criminal with the perpetration of many of the premeditated, coldly-calculated murders which have occurred of late years – but the law condemns him to the same indiscriminating punishment.

Alton Dec; 12th 1867

Esteemed Friend
        Mr Tallack

Upon further reflecting on the case of Baker, views have occurred to me which induce me to write again.

A memorial is being set in fact both in Guildford and Alton and it is a serious question with many whether they can sign it or not. A change appears (tho' I cannot at present see to what extent) to be coming over the feelings of people here. They were horrified at first by the revolting circumstances accompanying rather than constituting the crime, but now pity on the part of many, and desire to save the life of the criminal appear to be prevailing over the sentiments first excited, and I should not be surprised if the memorial gets many signatures. I may be deceived in this.

I do not think the evidence for the defence was made the most of, an opinion participated in by others and under this impression I have written a paper drawing

Appendix E.

attention to some of the facts elicited, and opinions expressed thereon. I enclose this for your perusal and if it can be made useful either in its present shape or in any modified form such as this experience may suggest I shall be glad.

I do not wish it to appear in any shape in public journals in my name. It is the first time a case of murder ever came before me in a professional capacity, and I did not know till just before the trial that I should be called upon in any way – I therefore feel scarcely competent to offer a decided opinion publicly, or willing to admit more than appears in the enclosed paper.

       Your sincere friend

           Wlm [William] Curtis

I now find some who have always spoken very strongly against the prisoner, confess themselves <u>puzzled</u> and say he could not have been in his <u>right</u> mind.

Handwritten note: *The Chief Constable of Surrey brought this paper & stated that most of the more respectable part of the community in the neighbourhood not inclined to sign the appeal referred to.*

E.3 The views of Dr. Henry Taylor

The Humble Petition and Statement of Henry Sharp Taylor, a Fellow of the Royal College of Surgeons practising in Guildford, Surrey, to the Right Hon. Gathorne Hardy, Her Majesty's Secretary of State for the Home Department touching the case of the convict Frederick Baker now lying under sentence of death in the Hants County Gaol.

I, the undersigned Henry Sharp Taylor, do hereby declare my earnest conviction that the said Frederick Baker was in an insane state of mind at the time of the commission of the murder of Fanny Adams; and that the evidence adduced at his trial, was sufficient to establish the proof of insanity in the opinion of scientific men, whose attention has been specially directed to the study of mental diseases.

The evidence to which I refer, went to prove the following points — The existence of insanity in the convict's family; his father, and his father's first cousin having been the subjects of Acute Mania with homicidal tendency.

The convict's intemperate habits, which would conduce to strengthen an hereditary predisposition to insanity.

The total change in the convict's character and conduct which was observed during the last four years, showing a degree of imbecility.

An attempt at self-destruction about three years ago, when the convict tried to drown himself.

The convict's demeanour on the day after the murder and for some time previously.

The unpremeditated character of the act of murder; the absence of any rational motive; the peculiar and unnecessary mutilation of the child's body; the exposure of the remains; and the subsequent conduct of the convict which was remarkable in that he made no attempt to escape and even made in his diary an entry of the murder as his own act, together with a note of the state of the weather always evincing his utter insensibility of the enormity of the crime and his own awful position.

I humbly submit that the foregoing circumstances when reviewed in connection with the convict's personal character and history, afford very strong presumption that the murder was committed by him in obedience to the impulses of a madness now fully recognized by medical men as a distinct form of insanity under the names of Homicidal Monomania and Instinctive Madness.

Also, that the circumstances of the act coincide in a remarkable manner with the character of Homicidal mania as described by the best authorities on ~~medico-legal subjects~~ Criminal Insanity. In support of my opinion I beg to quote the following passage from Dr Guy's *Principles of Forensic Medicine*, page 195.

The criminal acts committed under its influence [the author is speaking of Instinctive Madness] have most or all of the following characters:

They are without discoverable motive, or in opposition to all known motives. A man kills his wife to whom he is tenderly attached, a brother his sister, a mother her infant, or the victim is one whom the madman never saw before in the course of his life, and against whom it is impossible that he can bear any malice.

After the commission of the act he does not seek to escape; he often publishes what he has done;* does not conceal the body from view but openly exposes it; delivers himself up to justice; describes the state of mind which led to the act & either remains stupid & indifferent, or is overwhelmed by remorse. He has no accomplices, has made no preparations, & takes nothing from his victim. Sometimes he has previously spoken of his strong temptation, & begged to be prevented from doing mischief.

These homicidal acts are generally preceded by a striking change of conduct & character, & on enquiry the accused is often found to have an hereditary tendency to insanity, to have attempted suicide, to have expressed a wish for death, or to be executed as a criminal.

In the above extract I have underlined those characters which can be shown to have existed in the convict's case – of which evidence was given at the trial. The absence of some of the above characters may be explained by the natural variations of mental disease as manifested in different individuals.

I beg now to urge upon your serious consideration some points in the conduct of the trial which led in my opinion to the finding of a verdict so directly opposed to the facts and conclusions above stated.

The Plea of Insanity which was raised on the Convict's behalf, was made a secondary point in the Defence & when brought forward at the close of a two days trial, it did not assume the prominence nor command the attention that were due to a question

Appendix E.

involving such important issues.

The want of a skilled witness, or expert, who could have spoken with authority on the various points relating to Insanity – which were raised in the course of the trial, was severely felt by the counsel for the Defence, and this want could not be supplied owing to the limited means of the convict's family.

Hence the inferences to be drawn from the circumstances of the murder ~~which were so conclusive~~ in favour of the convict's insanity were not sustained by a medical opinion and did not weigh with the jury.

On the other hand, the unfounded assumption of the Counsel for the Prosecution, that the extraordinary mutilation of the child's body had been effected for one of two purposes, either to prevent the recognition of the child, or to obliterate the traces of a previous criminal assault, passed unchallenged; although it would have been easy to show that the mutilation was carried much further than was necessary for either of the alleged purposes, which would not have been served by the dismemberment of the body or by the evisceration of its cavities. The fact of the child's clothes being left beside its remains, tended to show that the murderer took no pains to prevent their identification.

The supposition that the body was mutilated in order to conceal the evidence of a minor offence, while no attempt was made to conceal the evidence of the capital crime, is absurd, ~~and as it would~~ unless it was intended to impact irrational or even insane motives for the act. Moreover, it was not supported by any sort of evidence, while the testimony of Dr. Alfred Taylor furnished strong negative evidence against it. The presumption is equally strong that the ~~prisoner~~ murderer who is a person of small size and slight muscular development, selected a young child as being likely to offer only a feeble resistance.

It is presumable also that the mutilation was entirely without aim or purpose & more consonant with the caprice of a madman than with the design of a sane murderer. The whole proceeding so far as it can be gathered from the state of the remains, closely resembles the common mode of slaughtering and cutting up sheep or oxen – & this may have been in the convict's mind when he made the casual remark to one of the witnesses after the murder, to the effect that he could turn butcher!

The importance of combatting this theory of the Prosecution cannot be overestimated. By granting the assumption that the child had been violated before the murder, a stronger feeling was excited against the Convict, at the same time a plausible motive was suggested for both murder & mutilation. By shewing this theory to be untenable, I shall have removed a principal objection to the Plea of Insanity which derives its chief support from the motiveless character of the crime.

I may add that the opinions I have here expressed are strongly endorsed by private letters which I have received on the subject from several distinguished members of my profession whose interest has been awakened by the peculiar and almost unprecedented circumstances of the case.

For the reasons abovementioned I venture to pray that the Memorial signed by myself

Baker.

& 330 others in favour of an inquiry into the state of mind of the condemned may have your earnest consideration.

signed   Henry S. Taylor.

* The entry in the Diary is to some extent an instance of this irrational conduct.

APPENDIX F

The Confession of Frederick Baker

F.1 *The Times*, 24 December 1867

Sir,— I beg to inform you that the father of the child, Fanny Adams, informs me he has this morning received a letter from Frederick Baker, confessing the murder.

I am, Sir, yours obediently,
William Dyer

Alton, Hants, Dec 22.

F.2 The Confession of Frederick Baker[226]

Frederick Baker had made a confession of the crime. The following are the details of his statement:—

While he fully confessed the murder, he denied that he committed any other crime than that on the person of his victim. He said he left the office at half-past 1, and went across Flood Meadows to the first stile at the Hollow. He was followed by the children, and they ran up and down the Hollow for half-pence, which he gave them. Then two of them said they must go home; and they went of their own will, not by his request. He then took Fanny Adams in his arms and went through the gate into the hop ground. There is no doubt he must have done something indecent to her to make her struggle to get out of his arms, and threaten to tell her mother. This was the moment at which Minnie Warner, then on her way home, said she heard a cry. Then it was that 'in an unguarded hour and not with malice aforethought but being enraged at her crying' he killed her—and her death was 'without pain or struggle'. From all we can learn it appears the child in her efforts to get out of his arms was hanging with her head downwards over his right shoulder. While in this attitude he put his left hand into his right waistcoat pocket, and took out his buckhorn penknife, and placing the blade to the thumbnail of his right hand, and while holding the child's limbs with his right arm, he opened the knife, and with his left hand made a stab at her throat, and drew

---

226 Amalgamated from *The Times*, 27 December 1867, *Hampshire Chronicle* 28 December 1867, and *Nottinghamshire Guardian*, 27 December 1867.

the knife upwards. There was a gurgling noise. The blood flowed outwards from him, and he dropped her on the ground. She was dead almost instantly. Bewildered, but not insane, as he himself admitted, he immediately decapitated her, without considering why he did so. He took the eyes out, and partially dismembered the body. He carried the eyes away in his hand. With regard to the time when the deed was done and the period occupied in accomplishing it, it is clear from the evidence that he could scarcely have been occupied more than half an hour altogether at the task. It is plain from the evidence of Minnie Warner's sister and that of Eliza White, that the murder, however perpetrated, could not have been done before 2.10.

He went by the front of Chalcraft's house, and at 2.45, in passing through the churchyard, he opened a gate for Ann Murrant, to which point it would at least have taken him seven or eight minutes to walk from the hop ground. We observe it is stated that at that time he had the eyes in his left hand, and both hands were so bloody he was surprised the woman did not see the blood. From the churchyard he went round by the old road to Odiham, and along between the kiln-piece and the out field, where he almost met Noyce face to face at two minutes past three. He remembered putting his bloody hands behind his back and under his coat. Observing that Noyce went in another direction, he returned into Chauntry Piece field and crossed it, going out at the stile at the south corner of the hop field, into Flood Meadows to the bridge, where he dropped the eyes and washed his hands and shirt sleeves. He then proceeded by the Basingstoke Road to his office, which he entered the back way rather earlier than the witness Biddle states, viz. between 3.10 or 3.15.

He denies most emphatically that he ever used any other knife that the small one he had about him. Three days before, the knife being out of order, he sharpened it for the purpose of making an erasure. After he returned to the office he went to the pump and washed the knife. He took the greatest pains to clean it inside and out, and he oiled it with a feather. He then blunted the knife for the purpose of misleading the police in case suspicion attached to him.

The second visit to the hop field was made about 5.20 or 5.25. He used the stone to batter the head, and it was then that he dismembered the arm and foot. He was not more than ten minutes in doing that. The foot was taken off in two minutes. While he was leaning over the stile in Hollow Lane, with the foot in his hand, he thought he heard some one coming, and he threw it away.

Returning to the office, he made the entry in the diary at the same time he made out his weekly wages' account, which was between seven and eight o'clock. He asserts that he never thought of escaping detection, but yet he appears to have cherished a hope of a reprieve

He has not himself attributed the crime to insanity, but has said he was maddened by drink when he did it.

APPENDIX G

The Case of William Mobbs

G.1 *The Times*, 28 March 1870[227]

An impression had prevailed in consequence of the reprieve of Spinasa[228] and others that the extreme penalty of the law would not be inflicted in the case of the murderer Mobbs, whose execution has been fixed for this morning. The preparations for the execution have, however, been fully made, and on Saturday his grave was dug within the precincts of the gaol. On Friday evening he was visited for the last time by his father, mother, and brother, and the seeming indifference which had hitherto characterized him gave way, and he was at length apparently aroused to a proper sense of the awfulness of the position. He has made a complete confession of the crime, and this entirely negatives what his counsel Mr. O'Malley, jun., advanced in his favour at his trial at the assizes at Aylesbury—viz., that the death of the little boy whom he killed was the result of a sudden quarrel. He had been given to reading much more than is the custom among agricultural labourers in this county, and accounts of murders seem to have been his favourite kind of reading. When apprehended after committing the murder, a *Life of Abel*, translated from the German, was found in his pocket, and this his friends say he was particularly partial to reading in most of his spare time. He says that while he was sitting by the side of the little boy Newbury a sudden thought came into his head that he should like to kill him, and he could not resist the impulse. He asked the poor little fellow, who was not quite ten years of age, what he thought would be done to him if he should kill him. Newbury said that he would be sure to be hanged, and upon that he caught hold of him, pulled his knife out of his pocket, and stabbed him in the throat, afterwards making more gashes in it. Mobbs, who is not quite 20 years of age, is evidently of a very low type of humanity. He has a short, narrow forehead and small head, and great thickness round the base of the skull. His hair is very thick, straight, and stiff, and projects over the forehead, like the thatch of a house, and he has a peculiarity to a remarkable degree which is observed among men of little sensibility of nature – the lobes of the ears particularly large and thick.

---

227 'The Murderer Mobbs', *The Times*, 28 March 1870.
228 In 1870 Jacob Spinasa beat a prostitute, Cecilia Aldridge, to death with a candlestick. Convicted of murder and sentenced to death, he was reprieved by Home Secretary Henry Bruce after the intervention of the Swiss consul-general. See *The Times*, 3 and 4 March 1870; TNA HO 144/26/63070; Hansard, 'Commutation of Sentences – Case of Jacob Spinasa', HC Deb 29 April 1870 vol 200 cc2098–109.

Baker.

G.2 *The Times*, 29 March 1870[229]

Yesterday morning the extreme sentence of the law was inflicted in the Buckinghamshire County Prison at Aylesbury, on William Mobbs, aged 20, for the willful murder of James Newbury, a lad of about 12 years of age. At the time of his trial, Mobbs appeared very indifferent and careless, but since his condemnation he has very much altered in his demeanour. He has been very attentive to the ministrations of the chaplain, the Rev. W. Rawson, who has been most assiduous in his attentions to the culprit. On Thursday last he signed the following confession, which was written at his dictation by the Under-Sheriff, Mr. A. Tindall:–

'I, William Mobbs, declare that when I saw the boy Newbury coming towards me I felt all of a shake and as if I could not help murdering him. I had dreamt of murders, and I had seen a picture of the man Baker murdering the girl in the hop-gardens. It was a very hot day, and we sat down together on the free-board. Newbury laid down, and about ten minutes after we met it was done. I rolled on him, and when on him I pulled out my knife and cut his throat twice. He halloaed out "Oh!" only once. I don't know if he was dead directly. I left him at once. I felt as if I did not know where I was or what I was doing. I went away bird keeping. I left the body where it was. I put my smock where it was found by the police. I had no grudge against the boy, and I never had a quarrel or a struggle with him. When we were sitting on the ground I asked him "What they would say if anybody was to murder him?" and he (Newbury) said, "They would hang him." I replied, "What for murdering varmint?" He said, "Yes." Upon this I immediately attacked Newbury. I had a book about Cain and Abel in my dinner basket. The book was given me by my grandfather, just before he died. It belonged to my uncle Thomas Joyce, my mother's brother.'

He was visited in his cell about half-past six yesterday morning by the chaplain, who was with him until his death. He did not in any way seem afraid, but looked steadily at the drop while his arms were being pinioned by Calcraft. He then walked with firm step to the gallows, and his legs were pinioned. The rope was then adjusted, and after the preliminary arrangements by the hangman the drop fell, the culprit praying earnestly.

The execution was conducted within the prison, no one being present but the representatives of the local Press and the prison authorities, but there were about 100 persons assembled outside the prison. Immediately after the execution a black flag was raised over the gaol gates.

---

229   'Execution', *The Times*, 29 March 1870.

Appendix G.

G.3 *The Times*, 31 March 1870[230]

Sir,—A short time ago you recorded the conviction of several vendors of immoral prints, not on the prosecution of the Government, but of a society whose successful operations have made them insolvent. Today you record the words of Mobbs, the murderer – 'I had seen a picture of the man Baker murdering the girl in the hop-gardens.' Week after week the illustrated records of crime are circulated over the length and breadth of the land. In my country parish the *Illustrated Police News* has a large circulation. Its pictures represent crime in varied phases; its letter-press is explanatory; but its most damaging part is to be found in its advertisements. And yet as the law stands I much question if it can touch this publication. Has no M.P. time to consider first and give notice next of a motion upon this subject?

Surely crime in England should have its share of consideration with crime in Ireland, and it strikes me that it is somewhat important to protect innocence as we spread education; but it unhappily appears that while we are squabbling as to whether religion may be taught in our schools we are permitting vice to be taught everywhere.

Your obedient servant

C.R.

G.4 *The Times*, 4 April 1870[231]

Sir,—I beg the favour of space for a few lines in reply to a letter, signed 'C. R.', printed in *The Times* of Thursday last. In the first place, I deny that police news comes under the category of criminal literature. Its letterpress consists of one or more short articles and an epitome of news which has already appeared in the London and provincial papers. In the second place, with regard to Mobbs's confession, the Alton murder occurred nearly three years ago. At that time there were other illustrated police papers in existence. If a picture representing the Alton tragedy acted as an incentive to the commission of crime, in an equal degree did the book to which the prisoner alludes in the following passage – 'I had a book about Cain and Abel in my dinner-basket. That book was given me by my grandfather just before he died.' Respecting the advertisements to which your correspondent refers, in future all of an objectionable nature will be excluded.

I am, Sir, yours obediently,

G. PURKESS, Publisher

Illustrated Police News, 286, Strand, W.C.

---

230   'Letter to The Editor', *The Times*, 31 March 1870.
231   'Letter to The Editor', *The Times*, 4 April 1870.

APPENDIX H

The Case of James Longhurst

H.1 *The Law Times*, Vol. 43, 7 September 1867, p. 309

A correspondent, whose letter we print elsewhere, refers to a belief which exists in the locality of Alton that the perpetrator of the recent atrocity really committed a murder for which the boy named Longhurst was executed some time since. Longhurst was convicted upon very meager evidence and we agree with our correspondent that steps should be taken to probe the matter to the bottom, and 'if the law should really have so fatally erred, it is due to the memory of the lad who was executed, and to his surviving relations, however humble they may be, to do all which can be done to remedy the error.'

H.2 *The Law Times*, Vol. 43, 7 September 1867, p. 324

AN OLD CRIME. About two years since a youth named Longhurst was tried for a crime somewhat similar to the recent Alton atrocity. He was convicted and executed, protesting his innocence to the last, and fighting for his life upon the scaffold. A weak—a very weak—attempt was made to induce the authorities to spare his life, but the law took its course. Some few people, and amongst them the writer, doubted at the time if the guilt was satisfactorily established, the chief evidence, if not the only evidence, of identity being that of the dying child, who more by signs than words identified the accused. At the present moment a horrible impression has been created in the locality of both these crimes that the lad Longhurst was innocent and that the Alton and Guildford criminal are identical, the party accused at Alton having, it is reported, been resident at Guildford when the offence was committed at that place. Steps should now be taken by those in power to probe this matter to the bottom, and if the law should really have so fatally erred, it is due to the memory of the lad who was executed, and to his surviving relations, however humble they may be, to do all which can be done to remedy the error.

George John Shaw, 8 Furnival's Inn
September 3.

Baker.

H.3 *The Law Times*, Vol. 43, 28 September 1867, p. 369

THE ALTON MURDERER. A highly respectable and responsible solicitor, residing at Alton, wrote to us a letter a short time since giving expression to a popular suspicion that the perpetrator of the recent atrocity also committed a crime for which a boy named Longhurst was hanged. In a short editorial note we referred to this letter, but in no way indorsed its contents. We simply agreed in the hope of our correspondent, that if the law had erred, reparation might be made to the memory of Longhurst. Investigation has shown that the popular suspicion was groundless, whereupon a paragraphist has fathered upon this journal a "random suspicion" and "an unjustifiable assumption." This is scarcely fair. The name and address of our correspondent were both published, and we placed entire reliance upon his knowledge of the facts. Moreover it is perfectly certain, as we learn upon further communication with the writer, that the popular suspicion was very strong in the neighbourhood; and the remarks which we published having served to remove that suspicion, we can scarcely regret that we placed them before the public.

APPENDIX I

Murder and Execution Balladry

I.1 Execution of Frederick Baker (from Charles Hindley's *Curiosities of Street Literature*)[232]

You tender mothers pray give attention
To these few lines I will now relate;
From a dreary cell, now to you I'll mention
A wicked murderer now has met his fate.
This villain's name it is Frederick Baker
His trial is over and his time has come,
On the gallows high he has met his maker
To answer for that cruel deed he'd done.

chorus: Prepare for death, wicked Frederick Baker,
For on the scaffold you will shortly die,
Your victim waits for you to meet your maker;
She dwells with angels and her God on high

On that Saturday little Fanny Adams
Near the hop-garden with her sister played,
With hearts so light, they were filled with gladness,
When that monster, Baker, towards them strayed;
In that heart of stone not a spark of pity
As he those half-pence to the children gave,
But now in gaol in Winchester city
He soon will die and fill a murderer's grave.

He told those children to go and leave him
With little Fanny at the garden gate.
He said, "Come with me," and she, believing
In his arms he lifted her as now I state.
"O do not take me, my mother wants me,
I must go home again please sir," she cried,
But on this earth she never saw them,
For in that hop-garden there, the poor girl died.

---

232   Charles Hindley, *Curiosities of Street Literature* (Reeves and Turner, 1871), p. 205.

Baker.

When the deed was done and that little darling
Her soul to God her Maker it had flown,
She could not return to her mother's bidding
He mutilated her, it is well known.
Her heart-broken parents in anguish weeping
For vengeance on her murderer cried,
Her mother wrings her hands in sorrow
O would for you, Dear Fanny, I had died.

The jury soon found this monster guilty,
The judge on him this awful sentence passed:
Saying, "Prepare yourself, for the cruel murder
You have committed, your die is cast.
And from your cell you will mount the scaffold,
And many thousands will you behold,
You will die the death of a cruel murderer,
And may the Lord have mercy on your soul!

What visions now must haunt his pillow
As in his cell he does lie the while?
She calls to him, "O you wicked murderer
'Tis I your victim calls, that little child!
The hangman comes; hark the bell is tolling
Your time has come, you cannot be saved."
He mounts the scaffold and the drop is falling
And Frederick Baker fills a murderer's grave.

I.2 The Hampshire Tragedy, Being a full and true account of the Cruel Murder!
of Fanny Adams[233]

Kind Friends attend whilst unto you these mournful lines I read,
This tale of horror and of blood will make your heart to bleed;
To think that such a monster on this wide earth should move,
A guilty wretch with heart of stone who scorn'd the Saviour's love.

---

233   William Upcroft, St Simon's, Norwich, August 1867. Copy held at Norfolk Heritage Centre (Broadsides
collection, accession number 13).

Appendix I.

In the quiet Town of Alton, in Hampshire there did dwell,
A lovely Girl not eight years old, whose parents loved so well;
She with her Sister and a Friend , one day did go to play,
In the meadow green so merrily they all did bend their way.

This monster then with evil eye did tempt these Children dear,
And offered them some halfpence so he might lay his snare;
The Sister and companion, he sent them on their way,
Then took his victim to a spot, and there he did her slay.

The lovely cherub he destroyed to feast his eyes with blood!
He cut and hacked her limbs about on the spot whereon he stood;
And took her head and placed it on some hop poles on the ground,
But soon this horrid sight was seen and quickly it was found.

The bloody wretch he ripped up the body as it lay,
And took the heart and threw it in a field not far away;
My pen it cannot half describe the horrid awful scene,
That was witnesses by the neighbours where the murderer he had been.

And Oh! What horror the mother felt, in hysterics she went wild,
When she beheld the bloody head of her lovely darling child!
No mortal never heard of such a cruel horrid crime,
As this that was committed by that wretch not in his prime.

But vengeance will him soon o'ertake, and justice prove his guilt,
He soon will have to suffer then for all the blood he've spilt;
The monster Baker now is safe, in Gaol he is confined,
To take his trial for murder which hangs upon his mind.

Ye Parents who have children dear, now list to what I say,
Watch careful o'er their tender heads and see they do not stray;
For fear that villains should trepan, and innocently beguile,
Who hold to them a murd'ring hand, whilst on their cheeks a smile.

And all young people now I pray let this a lesson be,
To shun the paths of vice and join all good society;
For if that you commit a crime, there is no kind of doubt,
You cannot keep it secret long, your sin will find you out.

Baker.

I.3 The Trial, Confession, & Execution of F. Baker, at Winchester (1867)

In a lone, gloomy cell, lamenting there lies,
For a cruel murder condemned for to die;
His days and nights passed in sorrow and pain,
In the prime of his life, Frederick Baker his name,
His hours are numbered, and he must prepare,
With blood in his soul before his Maker to appear,
His doom it is fixed, here he cannot stay,
For it is clear that none else Fanny Adams did slay.

And while Fanny's soul it is bless'd upon high,
At Winchester scaffold now Baker must die.

It was in last August, and sad was the day,
That innocent Fanny with her playmates did stray,
From the town of Alton, not dreaming of strife,
That she on full bloom should so soon lose her life.
But the murderer Baker, did her decoy,
On purpose her innocent life to destroy,
And the angels wept o'er the scene on that day,
When the murderer Baker did poor Fanny slay.

How Baker was taken it is needless to tell,
Or the sad details which to all is known well,
How the mangled remains of poor Fanny was found,
To the pitying gaze they lay scattered around,
How the heart-broken mother with frenzy gone wild,
And in anguish wept for her darling child,
And for vengeance called by night and by day,
On the villain that poor Fanny Adams did slay.

When Baker was committed, and in prison did lie,
All knowledge of this foul deed he did deny,
And now that his victim is in the cold grave,
By falsehood he strove hard his life for to save;
For like most brutal cowards he dreamed his fate,
When he for his crimes did his trial await,
For the spirit of Fanny haunted him night and day,
Saying, villain, it was you who did poor Fanny slay.

Appendix I.

When at the bar for the murder was tried,
In the face of them all his guilt he denied,
But it was so clear to all those around,
That his doom it was fixed, and he guilty was found,
The Judge said, Frederick Baker, your sentence now hear
For your fate on the scaffold you must now prepare,
I'd have you to your God for your soul's welfare pray,
For it's plain to the world you poor Fanny did slay.

Now Baker is cast, and the last scene awaits,
And on Winchester scaffold he has met his fate,
That his sentence was just is the country's cry;
He was not fit to live, and unpitied did die;
While tears for poor Fanny bedims every eye,
And Baker for mercy to his offended God did cry,
That he would forgive, and the sinful soul save,
Of the monster who did poor Fanny Adams slay.

And while poor Fanny's soul is with angels on high,
On Winchester scaffold Frederick Baker did die.

(To be sung to the tune – 'Cottage and Water Mill')

SELECTED BIBLIOGRAPHY.

Aggrawal, Anil, *Necrophilia: Forensic and Medico-Legal Aspects* (CRC Press, 2011).

Bell, Neil R.A., Trevor N. Bond, Kate Clarke and M.W. Oldridge, *The A–Z of Victorian Crime* (Stroud: Amberley Publishing, 2016).

Browne, J.H. Balfour, *The Medical Jurisprudence of Insanity* (London: Churchill, 1871).

Bucknill, John and Daniel Tuke, *A Manual of Psychological Medicine* (London: Churchill, 1858).

Burney, Ian A., *Bodies of Evidence: Medicine and the Politics of the English Inquest 1830–1926* (Baltimore: John Hopkins University Press, 2000).

Cairns, David J.A., *Advocacy and the Making of the Adversarial Criminal Trial 1800–1865* (Oxford: Clarendon Press, 1999)

Cansfield, Peter, *Sweet FA: The Story of Fanny Adams* (Alton: Peter Cansfield Associates, 2nd edn, 2000).

Carter, Samuel, *Midnight Effusions* (London: Saunders and Otley, 1848).

Chamberlain, Eric Russell, *Guildford: A Biography* (Macmillan, 1970).

Chinn, Samuel, *Among the Hop-Pickers* (London: Shaw, 1887).

Coleridge, John Duke, *Life and Correspondence of John Duke Lord Coleridge: Lord Chief Justice of England* (Heinemann, 1904), Vol. 1.

Goc, Nicola, *Women, Infanticide and the Press, 1822–1922: News Narratives in England and Australia* (Ashgate Publishing, 2013).

Hardy, Gathorne, *Gathorne Hardy, First Earl of Cranbrook: A Memoir* (London: Longman's Green & Co, 1910), Vol. 1.

Hewitt, Martin, *The Dawn of the Cheap Press in Victorian Britain: the End of the 'Taxes on Knowledge', 1849–1869* (Bloomsbury, 2013).

Housham, Jane, *The Apprentice of Split Crow Lane* (London: Riverun, 2016).

Howitt, Dennis, *Paedophiles and Sexual Offences Against Children* (John Wiley & Sons, 1995).

Hughes, Kathryn, *Victorians Undone* (London: 4th Estate, 2017).

Jackson, Louise A., *Child Sexual Abuse in Victorian England* (London: Routledge, 2000).

Krafft-Ebing, Richard von, *Psychopathia Sexualis: A Medico-Legal Study*, 7th ed, trans. Charles G. Chaddock (London: F.J. Rebman, 1894).

Maudsley, Henry, *Responsibility in Mental Disease* (New York: Appleton and Company, 1874).

McCloskey, Keith, *Killed a Young Girl. It was Fine and Hot* (Independently published, 2016).

McConville, Seán, *English Local Prisons, 1860–1900: Next Only to Death* (London: Routledge, 1995).

Osmond, Kevin, *Ghosts and memories: four centuries in the life of a Hampshire market town* (privately published, n.d.).

Oxford Dictionary of National Biography (2004).

Page, W. (ed.), *Victorian history of Hampshire and the Isle of Wight* (London, 1912).

Portal, Melville, *The Great Hall of Winchester* (London: Simpkin & Co, 1899).

Prichard, James Cowles, *A Treatise on Insanity and Other Disorders Affecting the Mind* (Philadelphia: Carey and Hart, 1837).

Ray, Isaac, *A Treatise on the Medical Jurisprudence of Insanity* (Boston: Little and Brown, 1838).

Ross, Ann H. and Eugénia Cunha (eds), *Dismemberments: Perspectives in Forensic Anthropology and Legal Medicine* (London: Academic Press, 2018).

Rowbotham, Judith, Kim Stevenson, and Samantha Pegg, *Crime News in Modern Britain: Press Reporting and Responsibility, 1820–2010* (Basingstoke: Palgrave Macmillan, 2013).

Taylor, Alfred Swaine, *Principles and Practice of Medical Jurisprudence* (Philadelphia: Henry C. Lea, 1873), Vol. 1, 2nd edition.

Watt, Ian A., *A History of The Hampshire and Isle of Wight Constabulary 1839–1966* (Hampshire and Isle of Wight Constabulary, 1967).

ARCHIVAL SOURCES

TNA BRO: D/H14/A2/1/1/
TNA HO 12/176/79865
TNA HRO 284M87/2

ACKNOWLEDGEMENTS

My greatest debt is to Alton historian Jane Hurst who good-humouredly endured and replied to a great many questions on the Fanny Adams case and the history of Alton in general. She also sourced photographs and other documents for me, and gave me a fascinating and invaluable afternoon guided tour around the town and Flood Meadows. She also read the original manuscript in its entirety and made many useful suggestions for improvement.

I am also indebted to Kate Clarke for reading and commenting on a first draft of this book, and for all kinds of help, support and advice.

My thanks are also due to Mark Ripper for providing me with archival source material and for offering much helpful feedback; and to Helena Wojtczak for a thorough reading of the finished book and for assistance with genealogical research.

I am grateful to Bill Citrine for his excellent work designing the two maps that appear in this book, and to Adam Wood for his usual top quality production work.

For permission to reproduce photographs in their possession my thanks are due to the Guildford Institute, Guildford Borough Council, the Hampshire Cultural Trust, Alton Museum, Norfolk Heritage Centre, and the British Library.

INDEX.

Index.

Index.

Index.

Index.

61, 66; argued in Baker's defence, 58, 147, 152, 159–63; rejected by prosecution, 52, 126–7; judge's summary of legal issues, 129–30

hop-picking in Alton, 1–2

Horsemonger Lane Gaol, 33, 141n205

Howard Association, 58, 151n215

Howitt, Dennis, *Paedophiles and Sexual Offences Against Children,* 68n142

Hudson, J.C., 153

Hughes, Kathryn, *Victorians Undone,* 20n36

Illustrated Police News (IPN): founding and tabloid style, 30; circulation figures, 29; artists, 31; coverage of Alton murder case, 5, 30, 31–2, 31n63, 55, 93n164; on Baker's cannibal appetites, 16, 39; on Baker's paedophilia, 17; on Baker's diary entry, 23–4; elevates Baker into 'celebrity criminal', 29–30; denounces *Law Times,* 33; on Baker as criminal mutilator, 45n103, 48; on Baker's execution, 65; blamed for increases in crime, 30, 169; and William Mobbs case, 30, 169

inquest (into death of Fanny Adams), 24–5, 28

insanity defence, 49–51, 53–4, 119, 128, 129–30, 135–6

Jack the Ripper, 40n92

Jefferis tanyard, 3

Jeffreys, Judge, 34

Johnson, Alfred: testifies at trial, 122

Journal of Mental Science, 140–1

Kemp, Annie, 4, 83 & n151

Kent, Constance, 36n83

Kilvert, Francis, 17

King's Pond, Alton, 21, 116 & n184

Kingston, Sarah, 20, 21, 22, 123n192; testifies at trial, 123–4

Kingswood Rectory murder case (1861), 120n187

Kirkham, Gawin, 64

Knelman, Judith, 30

Knight, Edward, 23, 27

Knight, Richard, 84n154

Knight's corner shop, Tanhouse Lane, 6, 84 & n154

knives (murder weapons), 12, 45, 101, 107–8, 112–13, 114–15, 166

Krafft-Ebing, Richard von, *Psychopathia Sexualis,* 16, 17n26, 39–40; describes Baker

case, 66–7

Lambeth Workhouse, 19 & n33

Lancet, The, 58, 60, 62, 135–9

Law Reform Act (1996), 32n67

Law Times, 33 & n69, 171–2

Leather Bottle public house, Alton, 10 & n, 98, 100

Leger, Antoine, 137

Leslie, Dr Louis: examines Baker at police station, 12, 112; conducts post mortem on Fanny Adams, 22, 111–12; testifies at trial, 110–13; as trial witness, 47

Light, PC Thomas, 10, 98, 99; testifies at trial, 100

Lloyd's Weekly, 29

Lombroso, Cesare, 56

London and South Western Railway: special execution excursion, 64

London Evening Standard, 11, 56

London Missionary Society, 42

Longhurst, James, 32–3, 94 & n167, 153 & n221, 171–2

Lovetts (Guildford solicitors), 15–16, 19, 120 & n188, 123

Lunacy Commission, 62 & n, 67

lustmord, 39–40

lycanthropy, 56

Maidstone prison, 57n118

Manchester Martyrs, 60

Manning, George Frederick, 24

Martin, E. Waller, 151n218

Masterman, PC, 99

Maudsley, Henry, *Responsibility in Mental Disease,* 66, 142–3

McCloskey, Keith, *Killed a Young Girl: It was Fine and Hot,* 17n24, 19n33, 123n190

McGuire, Isabella, 137n198

McNaghten, Daniel, 110

McNaghten test for insanity, 50–1, 53

Medical Times and Gazette, 141–2

Mellor, Sir John (Mr Justice): background and qualities as judge, 35; hearing loss, 34; tries Baker case, 77; interventions, 83, 93, 95; rebukes witness, 100; censures Superintendent Cheyney, 42, 102–3; flags at end of first day, 42–3, 104; disallows Carter's line of questioning, 46, 109; rules on hearsay evidence, 110; compliments Carter on handling of defence, 52, 119, 127; summing-

Index.

Index.

Index.

NOTABLE BRITISH TRIALS SERIES.

Notable British Trials Series.

Notable British Trials Series.

* New series.